CRAIG WELDON

Craig Weldon was born in 1974 in Glasgow. He has
been a student, an engineer, a submersible pilot, a
songwriter and studio owner, an itinerant temp
worker, a technical editor, and a public servant –
but the one steady thread has been his love of the
hills and his hill-walking companions.

THE WEEKEND FIX

Craig Weldon

SANDSTONEPRESS
HIGHLAND | SCOTLAND

First published in Great Britain in 2009.
Sandstone Press Ltd
PO Box 5725
One High Street
Dingwall
Ross-shire
IV15 9WJ
Scotland

www.sandstonepress.com

Editor: Moira Forsyth

ISBN-10: 1-905207-26-3
ISBN-13: 978-1-905207-26-8

Cover by Raspberryhmac, Edinburgh.

Typeset in Linotype Sabon by Iolaire Typesetting, Newtonmore.
Printed and bound by Cromwell Press Group, Trowbridge, Wiltshire.

To Katherine

CONTENTS

ACKNOWLEDGEMENTS

This is for all those with whom I have climbed a hill: Brian, Billy, Alasdair, Helen, Ally, Duncan, Jan, various Daves, Andys and Andrews, Matt, Cameron, Simon, Niall, Rebecca, Stuart, Mark, Harry, Pam, Jeremy, Miles, Lynne, Paul, Alan, James and others not mentioned in the book – your companionship is worth more than any amount of hills in the bag. Although everything mentioned in this book happened, there are a couple of places where people have been misplaced, to more easily fit the narrative of the story in the readers' mind. My apologies to those who have found themselves thus renamed.

To those whose work has inspired me to get up the hills – Hamish Brown, Tom Weir, Seton Gordon, WH Murray, John Muir, Muriel Gray, Dave Hewitt, Alastair Borthwick, Ian Mitchell (both of them), Dave Brown, Irvine Butterfield, Jimmie MacGregor, the Ordnance Survey, and the SMC.

To Fiona and Justin for their help in my search for a publisher.

To Sandstone Press for taking a chance on an unproved author and to my editor, Moira Forsyth, for knocking this book into shape – remaining inelegancies are mine alone.

And finally, to Alan Dawson, whose book *The Relative Hills of Britain* was the catalyst for thousands to take up a brand new hill-related pastime, that of Marilyn bagging.

See you on the hill.

LIST OF ILLUSTRATIONS

ABOUT THE STORY TITLES

Each story title has the name of the principal hill covered (which is not always the highest hill mentioned). Let's look at one:

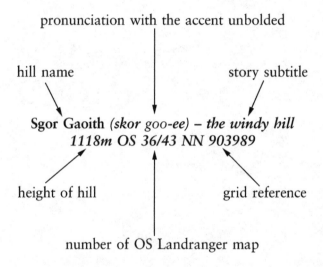

Hill height and name are taken from the appropriate OS Landranger map. Grid references are taken from the appropriate OS Landranger map, or from Dawson's *Relative Hills of Britain* where available. Help was sought with Gaelic pronunciation from Drummond's *Scottish Hill Names*, the Munromagic and Walk Highlands websites, and a Gaelic-speaking colleague. However, any errors or idiosyncracies are my own.

A NOTE ON THE PRONUNCIATION

The pronunciation for Gaelic hill names is intended as a rough guide to English speakers. There are certain sounds in Gaelic that aren't replicated in English, and so correct conveyance of the sounds requires dictionary-standard pronunciation marks. The exact pronunciation also depends upon the speaker's accent, with even native Gaelic speakers saying certain words differently. Thus the pronunciation given should be taken as an approximate guide only. Given these caveats, the English speaker should be fairly close if following the guide.

Notes on the pronunciation:

ch – as in *loch* rather than *pooch*
ay – as in *play*
eh – as in Dundonian *peh*
g – always hard, as in *gimbal* rather than in the spirit *gin*
myal – *m'yal*, not *my'al*

INTRODUCTION

This is a young man's story and one that could be replicated almost endlessly. Any reader will see their younger selves in it, recognise the agony and the ecstasy, the turbulence of finding a place in society, of accepting the unknown challenges of the hills. We are given it straight, from the indulgent early days of a university club to the bitter realities of work (or lack of it), its demands even entailing a spell working in Birmingham (to Craig's credit the douce hills within easy reach of the city came to be taken at their own value). Life wasn't all Munros.

As a Helensburgh lad Craig took himself off to the nearest heights, the Glen Fruin hills, hardly an area any would rank highly, yet, to me, Ben Bowie, is as fine a viewpoint as Ben Nevis. And, hills discovered, there followed a natural progression; early denials, then final accepting of 'the truth, you are a dirty, list-ticking bagger.' There are discovered companions and discovered bases, tents, bivouacs, bothies, bunkhouses, Nancy's, the GUM Club's Clashgour. The Munros influence all.

Nor should Munros be scorned. But being comfortable after the Munros is far harder. I was a wanderer from earliest days and took to the hills as nothing unusual. The Ochils lay above my home after all. (One upon Glen Fruin.) Everything of the outdoors enthralled. I must have climbed about a third of the Munros before I knew what they were. In those days people covered their copies of the tables in brown paper and ticked surreptitiously. I made a desperate raid into Sgurr na Ciche for my last just a few days before going off for my first Atlas winter in 1965, my thinking being that if I got killed out there at least I would have 'knocked the bastards off' (apologies to

Hillary). I'm listed 62 and I know many of those who had completed before. It would still be some years before the big social changes that would see the numbers grow and grow. When I did the Munros in a single walk, out of interest I left questionnaires on remoter summits and these could lie for weeks before the next Munroist arrived. Today there can't be many Munros not giving someone a weekend fix.

Craig obviously relished his student days. I've a feeling student days are a bit less happy now with a variety of constraints and squeezes making necessary demands and sacrifices. The shades fall earlier. As Craig wrote, 'There were a number of things on my mind at that time – job applications, parental and peer pressure, my love life, my future – but they all melted away in the wonderful amnesiac sunshine' of a hill day. As Geoffrey Winthrop Young wrote, 'I lose in them my instant of brief ills./ There is great easing of the heart,/ and cumulance of comfort on high hills.' An example from Craig: 'I woke around 4.00am, the sun already well established in the sky. It was a GLORIOUS morning! Something about this weather awakened vigour in me, and I ran around the hills with my arms outstretched, bathing my limbs in morning sunshine. I attempted to wake the others, only to be told where to go. Waiting until they woke at the sinfully late hour of 8.00am was torture. *C'mon c'mon c'mon!*'

This book covers an incredible amount of mountain days. After all, Munros, Corbetts, Marilyns are merely pegs to hang our adventures on. Without these lists we would not have had such marvellous fun, any of us. We can associate with so much here. See how much of this list you, reader, can tick: losing car keys; climbing the wrong hill; being burned off by someone; burning off someone; drinking away the rickety car's petrol money for homing; being shocked at the attacks of bonxies; losing contact in thick mist; leaving the map at home; table traversing in hut or bothy . . . There are variants of course: Craig bivouacking on the bus roof (-10C), locked out of a bunkhouse, having been off for the Pap of Glencoe at night, or yelling obscenities across a glen only to find the figure a complete stranger. It all 'beats Byres Road on a wet afternoon', bevvies as well as bivvies, highs as well as hardships, monstrous heat as well as over-much wet or the clutch of cold (waking in the car to find the Irn Bru frozen solid) but always the zest, the shocks of the awesome, the moments of glory given.

The writing is deceptively simple but can capture moments or scenes in a few happy words: 'sheared sheep roamed free, shitting on the track and baa-ing at my approach'; 'the snow a beach of a million sparkling diamonds'; 'smooth, sculptured hills rendered soft by their fuzzy surfaces'; 'the glen full of roaring as the stags rut and the hillside seems to be on fire thanks to the changing colour of the moorgrass'. Or in discovered detail: 'a single blade of grass consists of an entire spectrum of colour – white near the root, then spring green, dark green, orange, brown, and black at the very tip.'

One of my favourite quotes goes, 'Experience is the sum of near misses'. Thankfully in today's nanny society the hills are still an area in which young people can test their powers of endurance and learn the skills by their own initiatives rather than being led by the hand. Following a slide show I once did about my continuous round of the Munros I was asked, in shocked tones, 'Do I gather for much of this you went alone?' to which he added, 'In thirty years I've never gone alone'. I think I was more diplomatic than replying, 'You poor sod'. *There are levels, there are levels in which we seek to climb/ There are limits, oh, such limits, in the shortness of time.*

This is a young man's story. Craig had completed his first round of the Munros by the time he was twenty three. That's quite a crash course for gaining experience and by no means unusual for these days. He sometimes made a mess of things, he sometimes had near misses but he gained a richness of experience and an unadulterated satisfaction which my questioner could and would never know. Coping, learning, experiencing can also give those moments of rewarding glow. Nearing the end of this story there are hints of this where Craig takes charge of others when faced with problems, for instance heading unerringly over a plateau in storm and whiteout to hit a remote summit cairn. The feeling then? Wow! 'Better than sex', I once overheard. It is because hillgoers have such a zest for living that they know the preciousness of life.

There is a price to pay. Those weekend fixes don't leave much time for anything else, not even studies, never mind relationships but as an all-consuming demand it avoided so many of the pitfalls of the urban lost. One might stagger back to base at night but on the morrow the heights were there, alluring, encouraging, disciplining. In a critical situation I would feel well placed in the company of mountaineers. Imagine a foe faced by a battalion of Munro Compleatists!

Craig carries us along on a story both personal and universal. John Muir once wrote, 'Few in these hot, dim times are quite sane or free . . . choked with care likes clocks full of dust, laboriously doing so much good, making so much money of so little – no longer good for themselves'. He also wrote, words so echoed in this book, 'Thousands of tired, nerve-shaken, over-civilised people are beginning to find that going to the mountains is going home; that wilderness is a necessity; that mountain parks and reservations are useful not only as fountains of lumber and irrigating rivers, but as fountains of life.' This book is one lad's discovery of that fountain of life.

Hamish M. Brown
Burntisland
Fife

FOREWORD

Imagine a schoolboy, sitting in class in the top floor of his Helensburgh school, looking out to the Glen Fruin hills, daydreaming about what it would be like to visit, but not being allowed to wander them alone. Yet no one else was interested.

That schoolboy was me. One glorious summer day I set off alone on my bike, leaving it at the reservoir. With the frisson of knowing that no one knew where I was if I slipped and broke an ankle, I headed up the green, sunlit ridge of Beinn a' Chaorach, highest of the Glen Fruin hills. At the top, a vista of hills unfurled, wave upon wave of hills, from Ben Lomond that I recognised to those around Arrochar and new, unknown ranges. I had to explore just a little further, see the prospect from those distant summits.

I was hooked. When I left school, the location of the university I chose was more important than the subjects it offered. I went to Glasgow, the nearest in Britain to the hills. It is commutable from Helensburgh, so I lived at home. This did retard my development as a student which occurred, as far as I could ascertain, between the hours of midnight and 6am in nighclubs and halls of residence.

But there was the compensation of weekends with the mountaineering club. My first club friend was Andrew, an owlish but engaging young man who lived in Dumbarton, whom I met on the daily commute. He liked the hills too, and – even better – had a driving licence. Our first few trips together didn't involve the club at all – just the two of us, the green hills of wavy schistose around Crianlarich and Arrochar, and a lot of rain.

We climbed Beinn an Lochain in humid weather from the

Arthurian sword-lake of Loch Restil, a steep climb around small crags to a mist-clad summit, then a narrow ridge in descent, boots sucking in the boggy ground.

We climbed Beinn a' Chroin, an unfashionable Munro south of Crianlarich, in stay-indoors conditions: squelching up the corrie in an inundation, wet hoods flapping against our heads like loose sails as we wandered the summit's several wind-blasted cairns, gripping the edges of the sodden map so it did not fly away, wondering which of the many cairns in the mist was the actual summit, and recalling how enticing the idea of being up here had been in the warm dry sanity of the Glasgow Univerity Library.

We cragged in Glen Croe, where I discovered a leg-quivering fear of rock climbing.

We attended the pub in Glasgow on Tuesday night, listening to the more experienced club members, finally feeling ready to make plans for weekend adventures with them.

And thus my hillwalking career began.

This book will take you through those early days of enthusiasm undaunted by rain, hunger, or poor equipment, to a more relaxed and adult understanding of the world. It's a young man's voyage of awakening up the hills, set in the 1990s and early 2000s. It's more a meandering stravaig than a guidebook, though each chapter is roughly themed, and you'll absorb, or recognise, all kinds of useful examples. Above all it is a paen to the weekend, the baggers' list, and the hills. I'll talk you up all types of hills in all sorts of places and weathers; you'll read a bit about the kind of people you meet up the hills; and you'll see some of the attractions, frustrations, humour and escape that comes from getting away up high, whether for several days or just a couple of hours. I hope you enjoy the stories that follow.

PART ONE

The Club

The roof, the floor, the bothy door of many people's formative hillwalking experiences is their membership of a mountaineering club. Most accounts from Scotland have been of small groups of friends, hardy working class mountaineers and walkers, heading north into the hills with little money but a burning love of the outdoors and a contempt – or possibly envy – of the life of drinking, gambling and womanising lived in the city by their peers.

My club was a university club, the experience more middle class, based round a hardcore of friends with a sharp pride in our self-reliance, a complete dismissal of any landscape south of the Highland Line, and inexplicable difficulties in forming romantic relationships. I felt closer to the accounts of Tom Weir than those from the early days of the stuffy, Victorian Scottish Mountaineering Council, and more distant still from the confident yahoos in the club who could climb well and had girlfriends. Why did I never meet suitable ladies up a mountain in the rain? It was a mystery.

Yet my best, lifelong friendships date from this formative period. Experiencing so many highs and hardships together, seeing so many new and awesome sights, learning to navigate and be self-sufficient, to have confidence in our abilities, and to test the edges of them: this was what university was for, not preparing for some distant job market. I only chose Glasgow, after all, as it was the university offering my course which was closest to the hills.

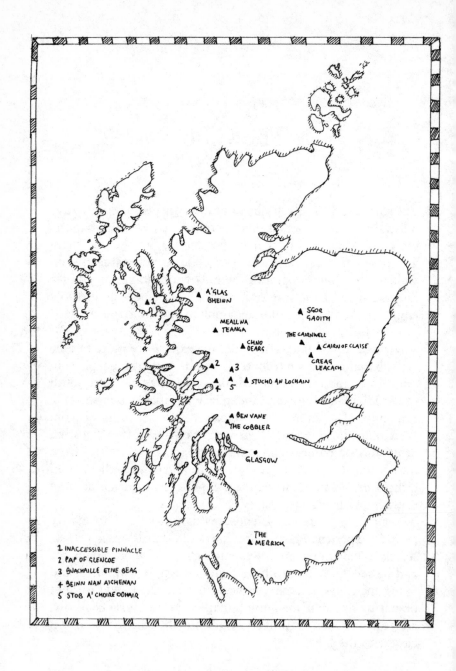

A'GLAS BHEINN

SGOR GAOITH

MEALL NA TEANGA

THE CAIRNWELL

CAIRN OF CLAISE

CHNO DEARG

CREAG LEACACH

2 3

4 5 STUCHD AN LOCHAIN

BEN VANE

THE COBBLER

GLASGOW

THE MERRICK

1 INACCESSIBLE PINNACLE
2 PAP OF GLENCOE
3 BUACHAILLE ETIVE BEAG
4 BEINN NAN AICHENAN
5 STOB A' CHOIRE ODHAIR

Sgor Gaoith *(skor goo-ee)* – *the windy hill*
1118m OS 36/43 NN 903989

The band played hard in the Suie Inn. Drink flowed, chat flew, the entire bar one steaming mass of bonhomie. Locals filled the bar, wisecracking and chatting up the club lasses. Routes were being plotted for next day, as we enjoyed the band and bantered amongst ourselves. After the pub, clubbers tobogganed in kayaks down the steep slope behind the village. A typical Friday night with the club.

A shame about the poor weather next day. But snow lay thick, and it was always good to get out in it. Playing in the white stuff at weekends reduced the depression of winter in dark, dark Glasgow.

A full minibus headed for Sgor Gaoith, depositing us at Auchlean. Soon we were out of the forest, and up the hill on the easy path contouring up the corrie. We entered snow drifts and, at around 750m, played in a corniced hollow, learning safely how to arrest falls with our iceaxes. My dad's axe, boots and compass hadn't been used for ten years due to a knee injury, and so I had inherited them. Onwards for the summit, a bit of compasswork necessary, with nothing to see: below us, according to the map, a 600m drop to Loch Einich. We gingerly made our way up to the frost-blasted cairn, perched right on the edge, and stepped back again onto safer ground.

Nothing much to do except head back downhill, another new Munro and another day spent exercising on the hills. But it beats Byres Road in Glasgow on a wet afternoon any day! It is far better to spend the weekend in the Highlands, the wild Highlands with their fresh snow, sharp air and adventure, than in the grey city of short wet afternoons that is Glasgow in winter.

Buachaille Etive Beag *(booch-al etive bayg)* – *the Wee Buachaille*
958m OS 41 NN 179535

Andrew's pale face hove into view. "Ally took us up the Wee Buachaille," he said. "We nearly died."

Ropeless, they had ascended a distinctly *non*-guidebook route, directly up the northeast face. It was, after all, the shortest route from the road . . . but it had left many tyros on the first club meet of the season in Glencoe, Andrew included, feeling decidedly green that autumn day.

I too, had planned a visit to the Wee Buachaille, and Andrew's description was all I knew of it. So there was little chance I would attempt the northeast face, and approached this hill instead by its easiest route, tagging along with others who had planned a visit to the Big Buachaille. We shared the ascent until halfway up the glen, a wonderful route along a beautifully sculptured river, before parting company and shouting to each other across the Lairig Eilde. I could still hear their roars even across a good couple of miles. They could hear mine too.

It was hard, steep work to reach the lowest point on the Wee Buachaille's long, high ridge where the cloud began; but from there, glasses blurred by droplets of condensation, the summit wasn't too far. I retraced my steps, and decided I might as well expend the small amount of effort necessary to visit the small top above the northeast face, even though, in the mist, nothing could be seen of yesterday's terrifying ascent route.

Then, several years later, the Scottish Mountaineering Club made this top a new Munro – and, unlike many other baggers, I'd already been up it. In your face, SMC!

Stuchd an Lochain *(stucht an lochan)* – *the closet door opens*
960m OS 51 NN 48344

Imagine for a second you are a newly 'out' Munro bagger. You've gone through the early denials of the fact, but have finally accepted the truth – you are a dirty, geeky, list-ticking bagger. This is a key moment in the life of the bagger. There is even a hill when this realisation hits home – and for the West Coast bagger, there is a good chance it will be Stuchd an Lochain. The reason for this is simple: you've climbed all the hills around your home, you've visited the most accessible interesting daytrip hills up the West Coast, and you are standing in the university library skipping lectures and poring over a bunch of maps with a copy of Munro's tables in one hand, and the realisation hits you: the closest Munros aren't up exciting rocky Glencoe any more. They've all been bagged. The closest Munros are in dull old Glen Lyon.

You fall upon the maps with renewed interest, noting with mounting excitement and trepidation the sheer number of previously dismissed dull, rounded lumps that rise well above the magic 3000ft contour.

And you think: *"Aye. Stuchd an Lochain this weekend."*

Matt, Andrew and I arrived at the base of Stuchd an Lochain one misty Saturday in Andrew's car, determined to bag a Munro or two.

We parked by Loch Lyon, heading for the unimpressive summit of Meall Bhuidhe. This rises above Loch an Daimh to the north, a great big pudding bowl, an exercise in navigation, pulling the hood up against the wind, and not much more. Thick, jungly heather clung in sheltered corners of the steep watercourse we followed uphill: the ground peaty and oozing, vegetation covered in globules of rain – a rainbow in each one, huge black slugs slithering about. We pulled ourselves up with handfuls of heather, legs sinking deep into the wet flora and sucking *schhloppp* out of bogs. Higher up, the vegetation changed as the wind returned: thinning, shortening grass, until the stony summit was nearly bald. There was another fellow at the top, and I asked him to take a photo – Matt, Andrew and I posed, our faces half-rubbed-out by the mist, despite the photographer standing barely six feet away. Meall Bhuidhe was an easy enough hill: compass work, and reversing our direction against the constant wind took us down again. It was a shame not to see the panorama over Rannoch Moor, which rewards walkers in good weather.

Back down at the car, we walked the short distance across the dam to the lower slopes of Stuchd an Lochain, our second Munro of the day. It was the first time any of us had descended a hill all the way to the road, only to go up a second hill. We were feverish in our Munro obsession. Thanks to low cloud and mist, we could see nothing of the hill, but we knew that if we reached the end of the dam and headed steeply uphill, we couldn't go wrong. Lochan nan Cat went unseen, as did the northern cliffs of Stuchd an Lochain. This hill was even more of an athletic and navigational exercise than Meall Bhuidhe. Eventually we broke out of the clouds in descent to see grey Loch an Daimh close below.

And so it was true: we were baggers. We headed down past the wooded Allt Conait issuing from the dam, beautiful despite the grey weather, and counted our two precious ticks, a whole galaxy of Breadalbane peaks to come.

Ben Vane *(ben vayn)* – The Principle of Minimum Effort
916m OS 56 NN 278098

First year of university was over, and I had to resit maths. I should have been nervous, as failing the resit would put me back a year. Andrew was certainly nervous. "I'm not convinced you should be here," he said halfway up Ben Vane, worrying. "Don't you think you should be studying?" I had just returned from a Glasgow University Mountaineering Club trip to the French Alps, and yes, probably should have been studying. Andrew's Cassandra-ish concerns were ruining my day on the hill.

It wasn't a great day: low, steamy clouds poured generous bucketloads of rain over our heads. We trudged the mushy path up the hill, threading through innumerable light-grey schistose crags to the cooler, fresher (but just as wet) summit and back down again, where Andrew's borrowed car needed a jump start – he had left the headlights on.

I passed the maths resit and spent the rest of my university career employing PME, the Principle of Minimum Effort: a balancing act of *just enough* studying to allow me to pass exams, thus freeing the rest of my time for hillwalking. I was proud of the PME and, in retrospect, it was an indication of my real priorities.

The Pap of Glencoe – *introducing Brian and Alastair* 742m OS 41 NN 125594

The Clachaig Inn was stowed out, standing room only on a busy Saturday night. Brian was drunk, his breath stinking of stale heavy. A couple sat in the corner enjoying a cosy tête-à-tête, and as the woman rose to visit the toilet, the man sat with a dreamy, distant expression on his face, oblivious as to what was about to hit him. Brian, wild-haired and brimming with barely suppressed energy, saw the empty seat, and made his move.

"Guess where I was last night!" he yelled, thrusting his face at the startled man who recoiled on smelling Brian's breath, desperately looking left and right for his partner. "The Pap of Glencoe!"

The Pap of Glencoe, eh? Well, let me tell you about it.

After closing time at the Clachaig the night before, the club were milling about Glencoe Village Hall, full of high spirits. Brian – goaded by a sober Alastair – talked about going up a hill *now* – it was winter time, dark, well below freezing, and we were drunk, but considered this proposal with some interest. A hill in the dark? Could be fun! Alastair was the tipping point. When he started to pack his substantial rucksack with warm clothes and a sleeping bag, we knew the walk was on.

No one else wanted to join us, so we three potential statistics left the village hall around half-two in the morning, heading east along the backroad for the path up the Pap of Glencoe. I'd never climbed a hill at night before. How would we navigate in the dark? How would we cope with the cold? We left the road and started to ascend the hillside, Brian to the fore walking fast. Suddenly he veered off route and started to bash through chest-high bracken . . . I shouted after him, "Brian, the path!"

But he was deaf to my appeals. Brian had decided to go straight up in a supposed shortcut . . .

'Forget it,' I thought, peching. A drunk Brian could keep up this pace all night, but I had had a skinful too and couldn't. I wanted to take it slowly and carefully, but this wasn't Brian's way. "I'm baling," I told Alastair, then sat on the hillside, taking in the scene. The moon was out on a frosty night, flooding Loch Leven and Garbh Bheinn with silvery light. A sudden darkening and then the moon returned: an owl passing straight overhead. No sound at all. I lay there a bit longer, feeling the cold creep up from the ground and into my stiffening muscles. Stand up and move. Slowly I made my way back downhill to the road, then along it for a kilometre or two to the warm village hall which would avert any nascent hypothermia.

Disaster! It was locked and, at four in the morning, everyone inside was asleep. I couldn't get in, but spotted the minibus parked outside. It had now become very cold indeed, and the roofrack would provide marginally more insulation from the cold than the ground. I climbed up and crawled fully clothed into my sleeping bag, itself inside an orange plastic bivvy bag. As I drifted off, I wondered uneasily if the pre-dawn climbers would get up, half-asleep, and drive off for Ben Nevis without noticing me on their roof rack. Fortunately they didn't.

I crawled out of my bag at dawn. It had been a remarkably comfortable night, despite the cold. An inspection of the bivvy bag revealed the reason: the condensation that normally gathers on the inside of these watertight bags to form an uncomfortable puddle at your foot had frozen, sealing a thin layer of solid sweat all around the inside of the bivvy bag, insulating me. I spotted Andrew who was also bivvying out. He had an expensive down sleeping bag, blow-up thermarest, and state-of-the-art Goretex bivvy bag that had set him back hundreds of pounds. He scornfully eyed my caravan sleeping bag that had cost my parents around a hundredth of the price ten years earlier. "You're mad," he said. It had been -10°C, so goodness knows how cold it was on top of the Pap.

Later, Alastair told me that they had actually reached the

summit and shaken hands on the top. He painted a scene of waking at the cairn at dawn, snug in his Andrew-ish gear, slowly realising that that really *was* Loch Leven down there: then he saw Brian lying in his thin sleeping bag directly on the snow, boots still on, shivering uncontrollably, a pair of ravens circling his pale body.

Brian's beer breath on Saturday night, it seemed, was well deserved.

Meall na Teanga *(myal na chenga) – student clubs and winter gods*
917m OS 34 NN 220925

Autumn. Early darkness. Shivers of anticipation and frost in the air; leaves turning golden, grass brown, rocks black. Coals burning in the bothy hearth; winter adventures and tall tales. Back at uni, the neon-lit, chemically enhanced social round – full of gaiety and high jinks – has begun again. Up on the hills, the gods of winter ride free, chasing summer away down the glens, empty now of tourists and ramblers and trembling in a keen wind.

The club has reconvened, straddling both these worlds. My God, the excitement! Here we come again, winter hills!

One crisp, November day, Billy, Alastair and I decided to visit Invermallie – a new bothy – via Meall na Teanga. We slung a sack of coal for use in Invermallie into the boot, and drove to Mile Dorcha, the Dark Mile, by Loch Arkaig. The trees crowd in on the narrow road, ending at an old stone bridge across the Eas Chia-aig. This bridge featured in the movie *Rob Roy* (where Rob escapes a lynching by jumping off it) and the waterfall above, whilst not large, is one of the most beautiful in the country, with white foam on peat-fed, inky water.

We parked, and wandered up through the trees in Gleann Cia-aig. The trees opened out, the dark glen continuing ahead. Alastair announced that he wasn't, in fact, coming up the hill with us; he had decided to tackle the Corbett opposite. He would be down first, so he took the car key, and we parted.

Billy and I headed steeply up flanks disappearing into mist, with snowy ground higher up, struggling across a couple of tops for Meall na Teanga's summit. Up on the ridge it was icy and very windy. As a result, the ridge between Meall Coire Lochain and the summit was unexpectedly hairy, but we reached Meall na Teanga intact and warier. We descended to the col between this Munro and the next, then yomped upwards in the mist, and the summit came fast. Far too fast in fact.

We consulted the map. *Oh for . . .* I felt stupid. We weren't on the next Munro, Sron a' Choire Ghairbh, after all! We'd only descended half the way, then wandered blissfully up Meall Dubh, an awkwardly placed subsidiary top of Meall na Teanga's! An easy mistake in thick mist, but an embarrassing navigational *faux pas* all the same. All we could do was retrace our steps, then continue to the real col. From here, Sron a' Choire Ghairbh was a steep, fast climb. No hanging about in the icy wind, but straight back down the glen, reaching the car after dark, our muscles stiff from the battle against the wind.

Alastair was in the car – we could see the light on, the windows fogged over with condensation – and Billy had a plan. We sneaked up to the car, then leapt up screaming at opposite windows. Alastair's expletives filled the night air.

Walking in to Invermallie, Alastair plotted his revenge. First he told us ghost stories, and then:

"I dare you to go upstairs with just a candle – no headtorch – and go into each and every room."

We did this, one by one. There is something about an empty bothy in November – carrying a candle flickering set to go out, and a pair of practical jokers in one of the rooms below – that puts you on edge.

When I returned, there was no one in the room. *"Ha ha, very funny, guys,"* I said loudly. Nothing. I put my headtorch on and looked outside but it was too dark to see anything beyond the circle of light cast by the torch. They could have been anywhere out there. I returned to the room, waiting for them to come back, wondering what it was they had planned, but not much caring so long as they were shivering out there in the cold and I was warm here in front of the fire.

"*ARRRGGGHHHHH!!!*" screamed the furniture, as Billy and Alastair burst from two cupboards in our room, laughing at my shaken reaction.

A'Glas Bheinn *(a glass ven)* – *bagging in Kintail* 918m OS 25/33 NH 008231

It was six o'clock, dark, and the wind was rising. We shivered, waiting for the club bus. It had been a hard week, but this was our time now. The shiver was anticipation. It was Friday night. It was time for our weekend fix.

I had a bottle of cheap whisky. Andrew, Alastair and Brian had brought beer. We sat in the dark at the back of the bus, swapping banter and alcohol, ran out of drink by Balloch, and nipped into the off-license for more. Chips in Fort William, fireworks fired out of the minibus windows at the Loch Garry layby, the club driver trying to ignore us, youth off the leash, playing our favourite tunes on the stereo. Tales of what we had seen and done, and plans of what we were going to do, filled our heads. We arrived in Kintail and headed straight for the pub, talking to the locals, talking to the newbies in the club, talking to the wise old heads like Alan, Susan or Pete, hoping for a weekend of great experiences, Monday morning a lifetime away.

If it was November, and it was the club, it was Kintail. Kintail was amongst the favourite meets of the year, with a good pub, plenty of Munros, and the first snows of the winter. Saturday was spent in a heroically long walk traversing the snowy length of the Three Brothers and Five Sisters. After this, a gentle hill was required for Sunday before driving back down the road. A'Glas Bheinn, only 918m high and a solitary Munro, fitted the bill perfectly.

A small group of us drove round to Morvich, and took the trails through felled forest to start the walk. It was a cold day, with plenty of snow on the tops. We made good time up the nearest ridge, and I decided I wanted to be first to the top. I raced ahead of the rest of the group as we approached a likely rise, but on breasting it, I realised that the summit itself lay some distance ahead. As I stood there, despondent, the solid, confident figure of Matt powered past me to claim the top first. Snow was everywhere, especially impressive east and north over remote, uninhabited and trackless country past Sgurr nan Ceathreamhnan. Sgurr Gorsaic – a Corbett of respectable height – looked like a toy hill, a nothing, tacked on as an afterthought to the side of mighty Sgurr nan Ceathreamhnan. Black Loch Gorsaic at its base was a cold, abstract shape in a world of whiteness, the steep, snow-plastered cliffs of Beinn Fhada rising in buttressed and fluted ranks above the Gates of Affric. It was a good, if chilly, place to be on a Sunday afternoon.

We bantered and told stories all the way down to the bottom, when I saw Alastair in the distance. He had headed off himself for Beinn Fhada, and I shouted abuse joyfully at his distant figure. Alastair approached. Except it wasn't Alastair. It was instead a tall, well-built stranger, with a thunderous scowl on his face.

Stob a' Coire Odhair *(stob a cor-ee oar)* – *gear*
947m OS 50 NN 257460

At first, I didn't have a torch. I didn't need one – I was always down the hill before dark. But what if I got stuck somewhere? And why was I always borrowing other people's torches in tents, huts and bothies? I was too much of a cheapskate to get one, though when I finally did, it brought an unexpected benefit. Having a torch enables you to deliberately stay out late, catching the sunset from a summit, which is far more spectacular than that from the glens.

Near the start of my second season, still torchless, I headed for the club hut at Clashgour with Billy and Alastair. I had been in the French Alps during the summer but this glen, smaller in scale, was wilder and surprisingly no less beautiful. Stob Ghabhar rose above all, brown and russet red rising to black crags, a white slash of waterfall falling from its symmetrical corrie, with red deer stags roaring in straggles of pine trees. As we rounded the shores of Loch Tulla, this scene drew us eagerly on.

At Clashgour we dropped our sleeping bags, then headed up the old mine track for Stob a' Coire Odhair. Everyone who frequents Clashgour eventually ascends these hills several times, especially Alastair. If there was work to be done in the doss, he would head up Stob a' Coire Odhair and wander the hills until it was safe to come down.

Late autumn is perhaps the best time of year to visit these hills. The glen is full of roaring as the stags rut, and even on dull days the hillside seems to be on fire thanks to the changing colour of the moorgrass. If you have a good look at a single blade of this grass in autumn, you'll see it consists of an entire spectrum of colour – white near the root, then spring green, dark green, orange, brown, and black at the very tip. No wonder the hillside is bursting with colour, far more interesting than high summer's uniform green.

We headed up the zig-zags to the top of Stob a' Coire Odhair. The stony top flattens out a little after the steep path, with a view over to Stob Ghabhar and its remote corrie lochan. Stob Ghabhar as well? We descended, the big wall of Clach Leathad to the right, the trail meandering between eruptions of rocky crags at the col between the two hills. The pull up to Stob Ghabhar is steep and loose: but once on the ridge, the rest of the ascent is entertainingly narrow. The descent from Stob Ghabhar itself however is unrelentingly steep, and we came down at the side of an interesting rockface with a waterfall. This face looked eminently scramblable and more fun than the path – information filed for a future visit.

Back at the doss darkness came and we made tea, settling in for the night. We discussed the pub a couple of miles walk away at Inveroran. Suddenly, pre-planned, Billy and Alastair disappeared down the track with their torches. *"Hey, guys! Wait for me!"* I struggled with my boots, but they were away. It was a pitch-black night: full cloud cover, moonless and no stars. Opening the door after them, I couldn't even see the Land Rover trail that goes past the doss.

Bastards. I had a good idea what they were up to. I stood outside the door in a vain attempt to acclimatise my eyes to the dark, then stormed down the trail after them as best as I could. Sure enough, a couple minutes from the doss they ambushed me, jumping out of the ditch and dragging my struggling body in. Once disentangled we all had a good laugh, and walked on to Inveroran in high spirits. I pushed open the pub doors. Everyone inside turned to see who it was, and the place erupted in hoots of derision. I looked at myself in the electric light. I was dripping, head to foot, in thick ditch mud.

After this, I bought a torch to take away at the weekends.

Chno Dearg *(chroh jerrig)* – ghost voices
1047m OS 41 NN 377741

A trip to Nancy's hostel at Fersit was an experience not to be missed. Nancy was legendary, her exploits all round the globe well known in Scottish hillwalking circles. I'd heard others talking of Nancy's hospitality, of being snowed in at Fersit and having to take food from the emergency larder she always stocked, putting money in the honesty box. Being snowed in somewhere was my youthful dream, as was meeting Nancy in the flesh. Sadly, she died shortly before I visited Fersit. Although I was not destined to meet Nancy, there was something else about the hills above the hostel that excited.

There was something above these hills that – according to the laws of physics as expounded by my school geography teacher – shouldn't exist. The dendritic drainage pattern, scribed into our malleable teenage minds, was how rivers behaved – streams meet to form larger rivers. But not here! Here, on the northern slopes of Chno Dearg, the streams diverge to form smaller ones! Perhaps, totalitarian-style, our teacher would have tried to cover up the evidence, and released maps with big blanks where the northern slopes of Chno Dearg are. Copernicus himself had said things less heretical than OS 41.

With this in mind, it was with some eagerness I ascended Stob Coire Sgriodain with Ally. I could barely wait to gain altitude to one of the split river phenomena littering the slopes above Fersit. Wonder what they looked like!

We reached the first bifurcation on the river. I stood there, the river racing downhill, splitting left down one stream, right down another and eh, it was an underwhelming experience. Really, what was I so excited about? If you can imagine a stream splitting in two, you have the northern slopes of Chno Dearg sussed. I would have expected the defiance of the Laws of Nature to look a little more spectacular. Bloody swizz.

Higher up, the snow hardened and we donned crampons. The summit of Stob Coire Sgriodain took a surprisingly long time to come, but it may have had something to do with the thick, disorientating cloud we had now entered. It was the same shade as the surrounding snowy slopes, and the horizon was undefined, with perhaps twenty yards visibility at most. We did not drop out of the cloud at the col between Sgriodain and Chno Dearg, and started to ascend the south-western slopes of the higher hill.

I heard Ally – all teeth, bottle specs and reckless enthusiasm – running behind me. I turned and looked, and the sound stopped. He was exactly the same distance behind me as he was last time I looked.

"Were you running there?"

"No."

"Oh."

I pondered this eldritch phenomenon.

"What?" said Ally.

"Eh?" I replied.

"You were saying something," he said.

"No I wasn't".

I stopped and Ally came up close. "I definitely heard voices . . ."

We looked around and listened to the pea-soup whiteout.

Nothing.

Nobody.

Clearly, something supernatural.

But sound on the hill can be a funny thing. Although it was unusual to meet folk on a hill like this in winter, there may easily have been a party of people only yards from us. In this mist we couldn't see them.

"Hello?" I shouted.

No reply.

The cairn on Chno Dearg was hard to find, the summit area a small, unexpected plateau, and we had to quarter the ground for a while to be sure of having reached the actual top. Then we descended west on steepening slopes, and decided to bumslide. The map indicated an absence of cliffs, so we lay on the ground and slid downhill, into nothing, moving fast, experiencing the rush of snow beneath our bodies, ice-axes poised for an arrest, seeing nothing but whiteness, blank whiteness everywhere. I could hear Ally whooping lower down ahead of me, but could see nothing. It was the most exhilarating bumslide ever.

A heavy snowfall on Saturday night continued into the morning. The club decided to leave on Sunday morning while the minibus could still make it out to the main road. In fact, the snow was already lying so deeply that we had to push the bus for a bit, then walk behind it all the way down: the driver didn't think he could make it with a full bus. Almost snowed in! But we were going to escape. Where was the adventure in that? Wasn't that the whole point? I had Monday lectures to miss.

Cairn of Claise – *the argument*
1064m OS 43 NO 185788

Western civilisation has taken hundreds of years to reach today's pinnacle of democracy. Hard-won rights from the Magna Carta, through the French Revolution and American Declaration of Independence, to the Chartists and Suffragettes: the right to vote, the right to a *demos*, is not a prize to let go lightly. Yet sometimes majority rule doesn't work. Sometimes one person is right, and everyone else is wrong. Sometimes people need to be told, not asked. But how do you know when that time has arrived?

Well, a good start would be on the top of Glas Maol on a snowy winter's day of low cloud, and lower visibility. These flat-topped Mounth hills make for difficult navigation, and midway through a club meet to Braemar Matt and I, having found the top of Glas Maol, were having an argument as to the best way onwards to Cairn of Claise. A cadre of inexperienced freshers were in tow, dependent upon us. I was in second year, only eighteen. Matt was a little older, and crucially with a more forceful personality. A cold wind was howling.

At the time I was quietly proud of my navigational ability. This was not the result of any great skill, but a product of natural caution over getting lost, coupled with hours and hours of poring over maps of the Highlands, drinking in every detail. As a result, I had built a virtual representation of many Highland hills in my head.

Matt wanted to head directly for Cairn of Claise, following the compass. This was 3km away, I argued. We were bound to miss it: a blind compass bearing 3km across a plateau is too far to guarantee accuracy. 1km blind was about the most you could hope for, and I proposed we take a couple of doglegs.

We were at loggerheads, each convinced he was right. Matt changed tactics, taking the argument away from being able to find the next summit, and changing it subtly to discuss the effort expended in reaching it. He appealed to the freshers –his route was the direct route, the one needing less effort. They were swayed, standing around in the cold. They wanted to move and get some warmth into their chilling limbs instead of listening to this argument. He was persuasive, dammit! How frustrating – believing I was right, but being unable to convince the group! I went with them rather than strike on alone, as apart from Matt I was the only other member of the group with any experience at all. They would need me when we, inevitably, became lost.

We headed off on our 3km-long, 45-degree (minus magnetic variation) bearing.

Whiteouts are funny things. On level and lightly sloping ground, all senses become blunted, and the impression is of a floatation chamber – made not of warmth, darkness and water, but of cold, whiteness, and snow. There is no horizon, no distance, no sense of up or down except on steeper slopes, communicated through extra strain on the legs. A sense of bearing is only possible if a strong, constant wind is blowing, and even then it cannot be relied upon not to change direction. Footsteps are placed onto white nothingness with the awkwardness of a lunar astronaut, and you must trust your map and compass despite the contrary evidence of your senses.

We walked in single file, navigator front and navigator back using the line like a giant compass needle – the front swallowed in the mist, invisible from the back. About half a kilometre in, the steepness of the descent was registered in our thighs, as our direct route took us off the plateau; and about 1.5km in, the steepness was with us again, as we reached up the other side of the shallow corrie we had descended. After that, it all went wrong. Twenty minutes after the reascent, we were supposed to be at the summit. The minutes ticked by, ten, fifteen minutes overdue at the top. It seemed we might be going back downhill again. "Where were we?" wondered Matt, surrounded by anxious freshers.

I knew where we were. We were lost.

On a misty plateau, it is hard to tell the difference between up and down, especially in the snow. It would be difficult to reach the top now. Fortunately, this part of the hill had a slope that was just detectable. It was clear that if we were heading downhill, we needed to head back uphill instead. Downhill has an infinity of possibilities, but uphill leads to just one point. The map said the top itself was flat, but we would worry about that once the contour lines were exhausted. We changed direction – and came across a stumpy line of old ruined fenceposts poking up above the snow. Jackpot!

The others didn't realise their significance, but having pored over enough OS maps in Glasgow University Library, I did. This was the county boundary, and it ran straight through Cairn of Claise. All we had to do was follow this line of posts and we would reach the top. We followed, and the top came in only a couple of minutes. Relief all round. Matt and the freshers followed me back down. Democracy? It's overrated.

The Cairnwell – *the snow a beach of sparkling diamonds*
933m OS 43 NO 135773

The Cairnwell, by general consensus, is the easiest of all the
Munros, thanks to the A93 that rises to 665m at its base. The
general consensus is wrong; nearby Carn Aosda is not only
slightly lower, but also has a Land Rover track running right
to the top. A fit walker can be up Carn Aosda in fifteen
minutes if they really tank it.

We weren't tanking it up the Cairnwell: we were in a small
club group on a day of incredible snow and sunshine, savour-
ing everything about the day. The Braemar meet in February
was usually one of the best of the year, as good as Kintail. We
walked directly up from the ski-centre car park, stopping once
to soak up the sunshine and exhilaration of being not at our
desks or in our labs, but outside – and up a snowy hill. We
soon reached the summit, and traversed the ridge between the
Cairnwell and Carn Aosda.

Here it felt positively urban with all the skiers and ski
paraphernalia about. But we soon left it behind for a vast,
quiet landscape with just the occasional cross-country skier for
company. Skiing across this backcountry landscape looked a
lot more appealing than the regimented runs on the roadward
side of Carn Aosda. The next hill, Carn a' Gheoidh, seemed an
effort after the easy ascent of the Cairnwell, but it rewarded us
with a view of Glas Tulaichean and vast, flowing, multi-ridged
and mysterious Beinn a' Ghlo. With the snow a beach of a
billion sparkling diamonds, we descended into the shallow
bowl of the Baddoch Burn towards the steady plod up An
Socath. Bumsliding directly off the eastern top provided an
exhilarating 200m run, for me ending painfully as the friction
burnt a hole through my trousers!

A fine day on the hill, iceaxe clanking off heathery rocks
lower down, and a night in the pub with friends to follow.

Creag Leacach *(crayg lec-ach)* – *"You are very fit,*
Mr Alastair"
987m OS 43 NO 154745

Alastair was a few years older than me, and had returned to
the club in a purely social role after some time abroad. He was
gainfully employed, and had even been able to afford to climb
Kilimanjaro in Tanzania with Billy. As I waited at the railway
station one Friday afternoon to meet the club, I saw him
leaving a train, dressed in a smart suit. Not wanting to pass up
the chance to embarrass him in front of the massed ranks of
commuters, I – dressed in a shabby checked shirt and ex-army
trousers – pointed my finger at him and laughed loudly. But if I
hoped he would be embarrassed, I was to be disappointed.
With a grin he lifted his briefcase, and drop-kicked it across
the platform for me to catch.

Alastair was my companion today over the Munros south and
east of the Cairnwell Pass. I had already been over Glas Maol,
Cairn of Claise, and Carn an Tuirc in a previous expedition
with the club from Braemar, and was back to finish them off.
The only Munro in the whole of the Mounth area east and
south of the A93 that I hadn't visited was Creag Leacach; so
Alastair and I headed over the four Munros east of the
Cairnwell Pass – Glas Maol, Cairn of Claise, Carn an Tuirc:
and our first summit of the day, Creag Leacach.
    A club minibus dropped us off halfway down the Devil's
Elbow, and we set off to ascend the scree-grey slopes above. A
few hundred yards from the road we stopped to fill our bottles
with water, and my rucksack strap broke. *Scheisse!* I rigged up
a makeshift strap using the spare bootlace I always carry for
events like this, and it held fine for the rest of the day.
    The weather was in our favour. Though cloud cover was 19/
20ths, the cloudbase kept well above 3000ft, making navigation easy over this brindled, snow-patched landscape of moss,
heather, and dead grass. We headed south-eastish towards the
southern end of Creag Leacath, steepening and slippy with ice
near the top. And then we were there – a ridge appended to a

huge plateau. From here, Glas Maol is not far and, following a good wall, we arrived on the summit of this wide swelling dome in good time. There were other groups about, and a fit-looking bunch in Ronhills and Goretex set off sharply as they saw us approach, looking keen not to let us overtake. Alastair's competitive edge was fired.

"Let's burn them off," he said.

We yomped for Cairn of Claise as quickly as we could. The boggy bits had frozen: the ground was hard and slippery, the best grip on tufts of grass poking above the ice. The key to winning was to use these tufts as efficiently as possible. Not far from the lowest point between the two hills, in the largest expanse of ice, we passed the other group who, to give them their due, had been fairly motoring. Looking back, we saw with grim satisfaction that they had slowed down considerably.

We had 'burned them off' – walked at such a speed that they could no longer keep up. It was a regular game we played when young and fit. So many hillwalkers seem to be of this breed, proud of their fitness, alert and self-sufficient, disliking being overtaken. No words pass between the competing parties – everything is done subtly through body language: the way someone reacts to spotting you coming, then the perceptible increase in his pace. These days I am more relaxed about things: perhaps young tykes are burning *me* off without my even realising it!

We walked straight over the top of Cairn of Claise and headed for Carn an Tuirc – a stony, concave-topped outlier whose summit never seems to come. From here we could head back for base, but it was early enough in the day and Alastair and I still had a little bit of go left. We disliked returning to the village hall too early – far better to arrive late, later than everyone else, and have them think we had done an epic.

Thus we headed on over the Mounth.

Tolmount came first – and we considered our options. Down Glen Callater from here? Onwards over Fafernie to Carn an t-Saigairt Mor? This was the Mounth plateau, and no hill here has a huge reascent, though some are further away than others. The one hill we didn't want to do was Tom Buidhe – well off in the wrong direction, unwanted, standing in the corner like the class dunce.

"I can't be bothered going over there," said Alastair.

"Me neither," I admitted.

"Let's do it then," he grinned wolfishly, cheered by the thought of someone else's suffering.

Thus we headed for Tom Buidhe, and took an unfamiliar line back across a couple of shallow river valleys to Cairn of Gowal, Cairn Bannoch, and finally down the path to Loch Callater at the side of Carn an t-Saigairt Mor. The sun was setting, and we walked past Loch Callater, ice floes on the water.

We pounded the last few miles along the A93 from the end of Glen Callater to Braemar in the dark, feet sore and glad to get back.

The Merrick – *Brian recommends*
843m OS 77 NX 428855

"There are no hills in Southern Scotland!" said a German student to the assembled crowd at the club's regular Tuesday night pub meet.

"Of course there are – let's go there this weekend and prove it!" I said. I was three-quarters of the way through my regular two Tuesday night pints, and feeling quarrelsome. They declined, in favour of some Highland folderol another club member was promoting. But inspired and enthused for Galloway – an area I had yet to visit – I went alone.

Brian had told me about the bothy at Culsharg that lay beneath the Merrick, so late on a March Friday evening of high windy drama I arrived in Glen Trool to wander up the path to the bothy. The trees were disturbingly dynamic in the dark, branches reaching out to touch me in the wind. Culsharg finally appeared, but it was an empty shell in a clearing, just a ghost of a house: four walls and part of a roof without windows, doors, or a floor. Fortunately it wasn't raining, or it could have been an uncomfortable night as I spread my sleeping bag out on the dirt and watched my candle burn itself out.

I needed an early start. The dawn views were incredibly clear heading up Benyellary, and I carried onwards to the frost-capped summit of the Merrick, the highest point in Southern Scotland at 843m. It was maybe a degree or two less vertical than a West Highland panorama, but the terrain was rough and unfrequented, and there were ridges and lochans aplenty. The Lake District was perfectly visible, beyond several other ridges; the Pennines, Ulster too and even the Southern Highlands. The weather can make a big difference, and this was a special day. I headed north for Kirrieroch Hill, from which the Merrick and its mildly stimulating northern ridge and corrie can be seen to best advantage. Back on top of the Merrick, a couple of gruff Belfast men were swearing unmusically. Parts of Galloway are nearer the urban areas of Ireland than those of Scotland.

East of the Merrick lies the most amazing tramping area in the whole of Southern Scotland – an area of lochans at various levels, deep dangerous rivers, sucking flat bogs, granite hillsides, rough land reminiscent of Rannoch Moor: yet ill-frequented and unknown to most hillwalkers, let alone tourists. I bathed at a small beach on cold Loch Enoch, admired its offshore islands, and walked down past Loch Neldricken and Loch Valley into the burgeoning spring. It had been one of the best days on the hill I had yet had, whether such a thing as *a hill* existed in Southern Scotland or not.

The Cobbler – *scrambling with the club*
884m OS 56 NN 259058

The couthy auld Cobbler is the favourite hill of many Scots. It crouches above Arrochar like a troll's head or Viking helmet, calling you to climb its remarkable outline, the most outrageous shape in the southern half of Scotland. Once up the path past the Narnain Boulders, the hill is suddenly smaller than it first appeared from a distance: and you are soon on the top. But there is a sting in its tail! The lower, subsidiary peaks look formidable from a distance, and the summit OK – but once on top, a short pillar of rock forms the very summit, and only the level-headed scrambler, crawling up a narrow ledge, can conquer the topmost point of this mountain. I can't remember how many times I've climbed it, though it must have been a fair few. Thanks to high wind or ice, not all of them involved the very summit. Ah, the Cobbler in the evening, moon rising over Ben Lomond: wild, lumpy, and whose smell to me is the smell of the hills of home.

Only once have I visited all three peaks, not an easy task given the level of difficulty of the South Peak. I'd been up a few months previously, heading for this formidable peak, making good progress, until halfway up a steep hard section, a step over a huge drop made me pause. The crux. I hesitated – and spotted the eye-level plaque. *RIP* it said. Who had died? I looked down – stepping onto the crux would expose me to the risk of death far below – and my nerve gave out. I would have to return with someone bolder and more experienced.

"Matt? Fancy the Cobbler?"

A while later Matt and I returned. At the crux Matt led and, confident through his presence, I followed his moves onto and up the rock. It was easy enough – if you didn't look down. The rest of the peak is steep but easy, a fine airy perch to contemplate the North Peak and complexities of the hillside architecture beneath the summit. There are caves in these cliffs, according to *Mountain Days and Bothy Nights*, caves where climbers could doss away from everyone and everything.

Descent from the South Peak is not easy. Unlike so many British scrambles, there is no 'back slope' you can stroll down. We continued onward over a less than obvious route towards the summit col, Matt going one way, me the other, but both getting to the col unscathed. Matt had spotted a balaclava, so dropped down to retrieve it – and I watched him recoil in disgust when he reached it. *"A pair of Y-fronts!"* he shouted, scurrying up. Who would leave their undercrackers on a hill?

After the South Peak, the summit by its normal route is a

formality. I left Matt to the purer, more difficult, and direct route to the summit, whilst I marvelled at the way the summit ledge always appears narrower in descent. We were back on familiar territory, completing the traverse with a visit to the North Peak. From below this is the most intimidating of all the peaks, but unlike the South Peak, it *does* have a back slope – we were able to wander up it with our hands in our pockets, lying on the edge at the top to peer over the overhang. A fine day on a fine hill, and I was happy to have been here with a more experienced climber, as I would never have had the courage to tackle the South Peak alone. This is one of the benefits of being in a mountaineering club with a wide spectrum of interests and abilities.

I loved the club.

Inaccessible Pinnacle – *dark rampart of mountaineering desire*
986m OS 32 NG 444215

The Black Cuillin is Britain's ultimate mountain range. Not the highest, but the steepest, fiercest, rockiest and most naked. The continuous traverse of the whole range – which in winter takes two days – is unanimously held to be the finest mountaineering expedition in Britain. Admittedly this is a small boast, hardly in the same class as the challenges of the Alps or Rockies; but then neither of these ranges combines island views, sudden disorientating sea-mists, magnetic gabbro, 4m annual rainfall, or history of bloody clan battles fought at their foot.

No, the peaks of the Cuillin are not *real* mountains, but they remain braes apart from the rest of well-tramped, couthy auld Scotia: impossibly summitted, dark ramparts of mountaineering desire.

So what better place to test yourself with club friends on your first mountaineering summer? Could I manage these fearsome peaks? In the morning I would find out. The excitement and fear kept me awake, and I felt so very alive.

We wandered up from Glen Brittle, Matt, Billy, Dave and I, up through hard going moorland to Coire Lagan. Sea-mists revealed little except still Loch Lagan, steep rocky shorelines plunging into the water from high imagined summits. Dave had been here before, and led us to some unpromising looking screes on the far side of Loch Lagan. Here we ascended.

In the mist it was clear we were climbing some kind of chimney: dank black beetling walls rose to disappear into the mist on either side, narrowing as we climbed. The screes in the chimney became more denuded and dangerous with altitude – this was the famous Great Stone Chute, which the Cuillin pioneers had recorded as a grand scree run. Now it is a threadbare, dangerous gully, devoid of charm: with some evilly poised boulders, all too easy to send hurtling downwards onto your companions' heads if the utmost care isn't taken. It was still the easiest route – in fact the *only* easy route – to the top of Sgurr Alasdair, summit of Skye, and we reached the top of the screes and the final knife-edge of Sgurr Alasdair, solid and immovable, with relief.

A grand viewpoint perhaps? Not in today's mist. Back at the top of the Great Stone Chute, Sgurr Thearlaich was next. We roped up for a short, steep section that needed only confident scrambling skills, before attaining the summit ridge and Sgurr Thearlaich itself. We were enjoying ourselves immensely. This was what it was all about! I trusted in the others' ability to lead me safely over this hardcore landscape. Dave went scouting for a safe route onward.

He returned, and we followed him down a wee gully that turned into a walk over a short, outwards sloping ledge that appeared to end in nothing at all . . . and, a few heart-stopping steps later, we reached safer ground and the Bealach Mhic Coinnich.

Above was the steep impossible nose of Sgurr Mhic Coinnich. How would we climb it?

"Easy," promised Dave. One hard move, and we were on Collie's Ledge, the sort of lucky break that makes one suspect that the hand of the scramblers' god has intervened in the Cuillin. Collie's Ledge leads spectacularly but easily around the side of Sgurr Mhic Coinnich, away from the steep direct route to the summit, and onto its much less fearsome back-slope – a backslope that we then climbed to the tiny summit. We laughed. This was the business!

Ahead of us however lay the hardest Munro in Skye, and indeed all Scotland: the Inaccessible Pinnacle. We clambered purposely over gabbro towards it. A short gap appeared in the mist for the first and only time, lending a heroic aspect to our endeavours as we glimpsed, through this mist-rent hole of rock and sky, some of the bare-chested landscape in which we were moving. A basalt intrusion lay crumbled below our feet, and this seemed to be the only walkable way up: stroking the base of the Inaccessible Pinnacle on our ascent, the Inaccessible Pinnacle which towered above us, a rose-thorn jutting from the stem of the main ridge, a thin wall reaching up into the sky with only this basalt ledge between it and a 1500ft drop to Coire Lagan: and on the farther side, a near 3000ft drop to the waters of Coruisk.

Matt and Dave unfurled their rope for the Inaccessible Pinnacle's long, extremely exposed southern edge. Billy and I continued uphill on the basalt ledge, to find the Pinnacle's shorter northern edge. The southern edge is rated Moderate, barely a rock climb at all. The length and mountain exposure however, render it a serious proposition for all but those with the steadiest of heads. The northern edge is much shorter and less exposed, if more technically difficult, but it is still only graded V Diff (though harder in the wet, which it was today). Either route should be well within the capacity of the climber who spends their time on an indoor wall or training crag, even if they remain unfamiliar with the awesome change of scale on a proper mountain route.

Matt and Dave arrived at the summit above us, and let down their rope to abseil off. Billy attached himself to this rope and ascended. He went the wrong way and ended up in a difficult, slimy gully, devoid of good holds, and was either fortunate or skilful to reach the top. I followed, but took instead the easiest possible line to reach the summit, and struggled to touch the highest point, a precarious block above our heads. And we had made it! I abseiled off, Billy following: revealing once down that he had replaced the fixed karabiner on the summit with one of his own for his abseil, due to the rusted piece of metal I used bending excessively on my descent.

Now if you are wont to seek out the easiest route on every hill, if your idea of exposure is to stand on the edge of a city kerb, and you never try some scrambling or simple climbing, the Inaccessible Pinnacle will remain just that. But its reputation and name are both more fearsome than reality. I managed it, albeit in the company of people who knew how to climb, and with a reduced sense of exposure due to thick mist. But if a non-climber like me managed it, you could too.

I was very happy to have 'conquered' this hill, and we celebrated in the pub afterwards. Sgurr Alasdair was my 48th Munro, Sgurr Mhic Coinnich my 49th, and the In Pinn (as it's familiarly called) was my 50th. By that point I knew for sure I was a confirmed Munro bagger.

We spent a few days in Skye, adjusting our minds to the heady exposure. Once you are used to the Black Cuillin, technical difficulties on the mainland hills seem ridiculously easy: mere plods in comparison. Or as one of the characters in Peter Kemp's *Of Big Hills and Wee Men* puts it more succinctly: 'See efter Skye, evrythin else is a' shite!'

Beinn nan Aighenan *(ben nan ay-eh-nan) – a flower between the abysses*
960m OS 50 NN 149405

Our hardest honours exam was starting in an hour, and my coursemates and I tried something we'd discussed, but had not – yet – implemented. Settling into the Glasgow University Union's Beer Bar, we took a good quarter-gill bracer, before walking up the short steep hill to the imposing Victorian Quadrangles of Glasgow University. It was Aeroelasticity, our hardest and most baffling engineering subject, and we had taken a drink beforehand. It worked magnificently: we approached the hall with great confidence, a confidence that dissolved only on opening the exam paper and digesting its contents.

I hated my course. Four years of a subject I'd initially been enthusiastic about, but had soon become disillusioned with – a vocational course in an area I now disliked, leaving me an uncertain future. Fortunately, the Lord rarely sends us burdens greater than we can bear – and at this, my final year exams, the time of greatest trial, a window of opportunity presented itself. I wrote it triumphantly in my exam diary. *May 30th*. With a clear six days between Aeroelasticity and the next exam, this was going to be my rose in the desert, my flower between the abysses. My one day in the hills during exam or study time.

It was late May and I had been deskbound for far too long. Billy and Dave had taken the Clashgour key. I would join them. I packed my bag in the late evening and drove off full of anticipation for Clashgour – but disaster! I had barely left the street when the car's lights gave out. I fiddled around under the bonnet, but this time they had really gone. In despair, I drove back into the street and parked, crushed.

"What's up?" asked Dad.

"The lights have died for good. I can't go."

Dad heard my sheer disappointment, bless him, for he drove me in his car the fifty-mile-plus journey to Victoria Bridge, and arranged to pick me up next evening from the Inveroran. With renewed happiness, I walked at half-past midnight under a fat, full moon for Clashgour, where the others were asleep. *"Who's there?"*

In the morning we spoke briefly, then I was away early, eager to be in the sunshine, the outdoors, exercising, the feeling of freedom on my face and in my limbs. Spring is my favourite time of year, and the warm sun encouraged hopes of a wonderful summer. Brown fish lazed in the murky water of the river on the ascent to Loch Dochart. I'd never been further than Loch Dochart before, and the continuation of the track into Glen Kinglass is fascinating. Rocky hill architecture is spaced around a vast, open area, giving a feeling of being benignly surrounded by mountains. Another rickety bridge, and I was in completely virgin territory. Not a soul about for miles, on a beautiful sunny day. It was hot and bright.

I stripped off completely, wearing only boots, rucksack and sunhat. The feeling of freedom was wonderful! Exams might well be another lifetime away. The hill from here is a steeply convex, grassy slope, constantly interrupted by whalebacks of steeper black slabs. I scrambled and climbed awkwardly and directly upwards, enjoying the hands-on work until the steepness relented and I was established on the ridge.

The continuation of the route upwards was hard going, a maze of slabs and ups and downs, and it was with glad relief the summit area was reached. But unfortunately, the top was shrouded in mist despite the day's heat, and there was no view. I didn't linger, and, clothed again, headed down the way I'd come up, taking a detour into Coire na Caime halfway down the ridge. A day on the hill was exactly what I'd needed: and then, in a steep, shadowy ravine, I came across a tiny, beautiful, delicate flower. I sat in the cool shade and contemplated its beauty. My heart filled with wonder at this little marvel: so fragile, yet able to withstand the elements and survive in this harsh landscape. This wee flower in the corrie made my day.

Brimming with tender sensibility, I walked the long way back out the glen, coming at Loch Dochart across a miserable-looking mixed venture scout/guide group trudging the other way, each teenager laden with a huge rucksack – packed, no doubt, with the unnecessary and pleasure-sapping accoutrements of comfort insisted upon them by their leaders *just-in-case*. They were heading into this wonderful wild area; I was heading back out to lower ground, the hills falling away with the miles, the river benign and land thick-grassed as I reach the forestry, the bridge, the Inveroran. Ordering a pint, I lay outside on the tarmac sipping contentedly, waiting for Dad, looking far up the glen towards the dark shape of Beinn nan Aighenan in the evening light. Exercised, relaxed, supremely, rarely content: a feeling of satisfaction untinged by worry or sorrow. Beinn nan Aighenan, my hill saviour, had cured me.

In four days, I had my final-ever exam. I no longer cared.

PART TWO
Daft Days

Some boys go a bit crazy in their early teens, drinking,
smoking pot, sniffing glue, but hopefully emerging more or
less unscathed. I was a late developer, working my daft streak
out in the hills, with not all of my scrapes involving the club.
We sat outside drinking whisky in a national park, not the
local park; remote bothies hosted our house parties, river
crossings were our games of chicken, and cornices our railway
lines.

At least we weren't hanging around street corners, mena-
cing old ladies.

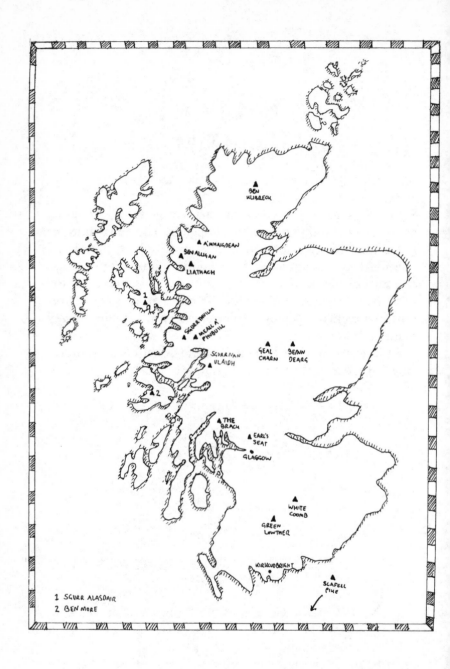

BEN
KLIBRECK

A'MHAIGDEAN
BEN ALLIGAN
LIATHACH

1

SGURR A'MHILM
MEALL A'
PHIOBUILL

SGURR NAN
ULAIDH

GEAL
CHARN

BEINN
DEARG

2

THE
BRACH

EARL'S
SEAT

GLASGOW

WHITE
COOMB

GREEN
LOWTHER

KIRKCUDBRIGHT

SCAFELL
PIKE

1 SGURR ALASDAIR
2 BEN MORE

Sgurr Alasdair *(skoor ala-stair)* – *axe murrrderers*
993m OS 32 NG 449208

Billy and I arrived late in Glen Brittle, heading for the Mountaineering Council hostel. We had stayed before, so booking-in difficulties hadn't clouded our minds, but the new warden was a jobsworth.

"Are you members of the BMC?" he enquired with suspicion. We hadn't pre-booked, so were obviously not members of the British Mountaineering Council – an organisation that, to our young minds, made the Royal & Ancient at St Andrews look like a bunch of spontaneous hippies – and therefore could not be trusted.

No, we informed him: we were members of a club which was possibly affiliated to the BMC, although we weren't sure. Either way, we were well-mannered young men, there was space in the hostel, and we were there to take the burden of empty beds off his hands.

The hostel warden became agitated. "You can't stay here!" he explained. "You aren't in the BMC!" He wasn't going to budge, despite our protestations, despite the empty beds. "You could be anybody!"

"You're right," I said, glowering, defeated by petty officialdom, sarcasm my only weapon: "we could be axe murrrderers."

The hostellers who *had* gained a bed for the night, and who were following this drama with interest in the background, failed to stifle a laugh.

Billy and I, cheesed off, about-turned and stayed at the youth hostel instead. There is nothing wrong with the youth hostel. It just isn't quite as good as the Mountaineering Council hostel.

However, you can just as easily reach the Cuillin from the youth hostel as from the Mountaineering Council hostel, which is the whole point of this story.

Next morning we walked down Glen Brittle to the campsite, across the flat grass, through the gate, packs taut on our backs and ready boots on our feet. The path above the campsite took us high quickly, the serrated rocky skyline of the Cuillin drawing us on. The scenery improves the higher you climb into Coire Lagan, and we couldn't help but stop awhile at the loch, heads swivelling, trying to absorb the whole awesome scene. It is too big, too close, to grasp in one glance.

Coire Lagan! Is this the finest spot in Britain? Our eyes sought routes in the complex architecture, and we trembled with anticipation. *Come climb us*, whispered the Cuillin. We answered their call, contouring around Loch Coire Lagan for the start of our second ascent of the Great Stone Chute. We made sure to climb very close together.

When we reached the top of the Chute, we took the short, pleasant scramble for Sgurr Alasdair's tiny summit. It was a beautiful summer day, on the best hills in the country, with mountains and islands all round in the glittering sea. We couldn't help grinning, and took photographs with which to taunt Dave later. We headed back to the top of the Chute and investigated the big wall above us – Sgurr Thearlaich. Scrambling pleasantly and safely upwards, we attained the ridge and Sgurr Thearlaich's summit. Dear Lord, the verticalities! The Cuillin's extreme exposure takes some getting used to, but we had done this route before, and enjoyed it in the knowledge that nothing here was beyond our capabilities.

We traversed Collie's Ledge – possibly the handiest ledge in mountaineering history – for the backslope of Sgurr Mhic Coinnich, doubling back for the summit. This is a sharp, tilted slab, falling away into nothing on both sides, and our senses were extra-heightened by the exposure.

The descent to the top of the An Stac screes was much longer and involved than we remembered, and the ascent of Sgurr

Dearg was similarly long. Not carrying any ropes, we didn't fancy tackling the In Pinn – in fact, I'm quite comfortable never to tackle the In Pinn again – and descended back down to the An Stac screes, almost rubbing our hands in anticipation of the scree surfing that was to follow: find the right rock, balance on it, then ride a wave of loose stones all the way to the bottom. Somehow, though, these screes didn't seem as good as they had been. It had not been that long since our first visit, and already the An Stac screes were drying up. One day, these will be as denuded as the Great Stone Chute – and at the bottom we looked up, grateful to have experienced them, something future generations will be unable to do.

We stopped for a paddle in Loch Coire Lagan in fine evening sunshine, then took the path down via the huge waterfall above the Glen Brittle Hut. Boots scuffed, hands ripped, we were glowing, tingling with exposed Cuillin pleasure.

Sgor na h-Ulaidh *(skor na oo-lay)* – *mountain rescue* *994m OS 41 NN 111518*

Sgor na h-Ulaidh is Glencoe's forgotten hill. The Buachaille! Aonach Eagach! Bidean nam Bian! Beinn a' Bheithir! Surrounded by such excellence, no wonder Sgor na h-Ulaidh remains neglected, visited only – and only through a sense of requirement – by Munrobaggers. Yet from near Glencoe Village, this hill appears exciting: a sharp, conical ridge complementing Aonach Dubh's bands of cliffs. Sgor na h-Ulaidh is also the most historic hill in Glencoe; for it was below this hill, rather than around the more atmospheric spots higher up the glen where the tourist buses pause, that the infamous massacre took place.

Duncan, Pam, Alastair and I were camping at Clachaig, in the days when this was still permitted; and while Duncan and Alastair headed for a repeat ascent elsewhere, Pam and I decided to head for Sgor na h-Ulaidh, the only Munro in Glencoe neither of us had visited. As we were so close to the hill we walked straight from the campsite, across a footbridge on the River Coe in squirrel-heavy forestry, past the remains of the old Glencoe Visitor Centre, and on to the track leading up Gleann leac-na-muidhe. Rather than tackling the intimidatingly steep cone of Aonach Dubh a' Ghlinne straight on, we did as every other hillwalker surely does: wandered onwards up the glen for a suitable breach in the side of this ridge, then headed hard and steep up high green slopes to become established on the ridge half-way along.

From here, the hard work of the day was done, and the double-topped summit can be reached without much extra effort. The very summit is perched above some impressive cliff faces, but it was viewless, mist covering the last thirty to fifty metres. We descended the way we had come up. It was early autumn, the hills just turning from green to brown, the nights noticeably longer.

Back at the campsite after tea, we swapped stories with Alastair and Duncan, until Duncan pointed out something directly above us. A headtorch in Clachaig gully – and yes, it was flashing S.O.S. in Morse code! Somebody was in trouble. Should we help? Should we call mountain rescue? Does anyone have a mobile phone? By chance, we bumped into Fiona Muriel, another club member up with a separate group. She had already called the police.

Half an hour later a police car parked in the Clachaig car park, accompanied by a rescue van sporting a giant loudspeaker. The loudspeaker was turned on, and an electric humming filled the air. Whatever was about to happen was going to be loud.

"THIS IS GLENCOE MOUNTAIN RESCUE!" boomed the voice of God, echoing up and down the dark banded cliffs of Glencoe.

"ARE YOU INJURED? ONE FLASH YES, TWO FLASHES NO."

The torch flashed twice.

"CAN YOU MOVE? ONE FLASH YES, TWO FLASHES NO."

The torch flashed twice.

I bought another round and we settled down to enjoy the
spectacle. Everyone in the campsite stood around their tents,
watching and wondering.

Another van arrived, and people with headtorches dec-
anted, then ascended the hill. The two in the lead were
astonishingly rapid – they must have been running – and four
others followed close behind. The headtorches met where the
S.O.S. was called. We watched as the walkers – who had fallen
into Clachaig Gully and become trapped, though fortunately
not harmed – were retrieved and brought down to safety.
Amazing stuff from the mountain rescue volunteers. I wondered how often these guys were called out – probably almost
every weekend. I would have been tempted to leave the
stranded but unharmed walkers until daybreak!

After the excitement of the rescue, a bunch of strangers
gathered round a campfire. One fellow brought out his guitar
to sing 'Caledonia' before the flickering flames, in a voice
sweeter and more musical than that of the song's author,
Dougie Maclean, and with greater musical dexterity as well.
We told him that the last time we camped at Glencoe, a drunk
started a fight by borrowing a guitar and smashing it in the
river. Our man was horrified at the thought, and clutched his
instrument more tightly.

Liathach *(leea-hach)* – *car trouble*
1055m OS 25 NG 929579

I arrived at Glen Torridon campsite in my Russian-built Lada,
parked at the top of a slope, and killed the engine. Billy and
Dave were relaxing in the evening light, talking to a stranger
with a nice reliable Volkswagen Golf who, on seeing my
parking technique, fondly reminisced about when he too
had an unreliable car. I wondered if he might have forgotten
what it's like, so I gave him a list of reminders:

  1. I parked facing downhill, as the car always needed a
     push to start.

2. One night along a fortunately deserted and moonlit Highland road, the lights packed in completely. I rewired them directly to the battery in order to continue my journey.
3. The driver's door window-winder mechanism broke, so I pulled off the door facing and shored up the window with a prop of wood. If I wanted to wind down the window, I pulled the wooden stake out, and the window dropped like a guillotine blade.
4. There was the odd time when switching off the engine made no difference and for reasons still unexplained, I had to put the car in neutral, get out, and disconnect the battery for the engine to stop.
5. The first time I drove it alone after passing my test, I ran out of petrol at Arrochar. The few coins in the glove compartment weren't enough to buy petrol from the (fortunately nearby) garage, but a scavenge through the flotsam at the head of dirty Loch Long provided enough deposit-return ginger bottles for me to be able to afford petrol to get home.
6. One wintry day whilst overtaking on the A9, a sudden ice storm froze the windscreen and I couldn't see a thing as I hurtled the wrong side down this dangerous road at high speed. I pulled the wooden stake out and stuck my head out the window. My whey-faced passenger never came on another club meet again.

But after hearing this, just a fraction of the tribulations suffered with my Lada, Golf Man grew misty-eyed.

"Ah, those were the days! When getting to the hill was as much of an adventure as the mountain itself!"

I generously offered to swap cars but, for some reason, Golf Man – who had been in the raptures of nostalgia only seconds earlier – strangely declined.

Despite trouble with the car, at least I had access to one; and here we were in Torridon, looking forward to Liathach the next day. Or at least I was – my companions had changed their minds and opted for Slioch instead, leaving me nervous.

Liathach's Am Fasarinen pinnacles have a reputation for exposure and technical difficulty, and I just hoped I would cope with them without the support of their experience.

Next morning found me powering alone up the track to Liathach, on a safe, well-tramped, if exceedingly steep route threading through the impressive tiered cliffs of this giant hill. Before you know it you're a kilometre above the road, head popping out onto the main ridge, a sinuous, muscular series of curves rising to the rocky grey arrowhead summit. Although narrow and airy, the ridge holds no difficulties, providing a grandstand promenade to Spidean a' Choire Leith, the main summit of Liathach. Here I stopped for a sandwich, and to consider the difficulties to come on the infamous Am Fasarinen pinnacles. Several other people were in a similar situation, and we hopefully eyed up one man boasting that he had been here before and knew what he was doing. Yet when I finally made to set off, his confident façade slipped, and he asked if he could follow me. Dammit – I had hoped to follow him!

Am Fasarinen turned out not to be too bad – no harder than the hardest part of the Aonach Eagach and shorter than it in total length, though of a more sustained nature. All too soon the scrambling was over, and my heightened awareness took in the final slope to Mullach an Rathain with a feeling of relief, but also anticlimax.

On the top sat a man with a bloody cut on his head, which had happened, he explained, by banging it on his car door in the morning. We sat for a while as the sun turned in the sky, and he produced a bottle of whisky which was gratefully shared. I was amused that every passer-by saw his cut, assumed like me it occurred on the hill, and asked in concern if he was OK, to which he again sheepishly recounted the same story. (It was perhaps the whisky, but I warmed exceedingly to him.)

The quickest descent was down a steep scree gully directly above Torridon village. I started to regret this route, which was so steep I couldn't avoid making small avalanches of stone. I stopped, looked upwards, and tensed. A deer stood directly above, poised, watching. I feared it might kick scree down, but the deer moved gracefully and quickly across the gully, dislodging nothing, an impressive display of sure-footedness. However fit I was, I had nothing on the deer.

I sat down, blood stilling in my ears, listening to the silence. But there was a noise, a background noise: I couldn't work out what it was. Was it distant traffic, echoing up and down the glen? Was it the rivers, sound mingling in the air? Was it something out on the large reflective pan of the loch? Perhaps it was all the noises mingling: the voices of the people, the swish of the wind, the rushing of the water, the calling of the birds, even the rocks themselves moving and settling. Whatever it was, it was a constant, low, directionless, profound hum: the sound of a living mountain.

My companions on Slioch were later back. It had been a satisfying day over the finest hill in Scotland, and after comparing stories with them in the pub, I slept the sleep of the justified.

Beinn Alligan *(beyn al-ee-gin) – the surprised hitchhiker* 986m OS 19/24 NG 865613

Beinn Alligan is one of the most beautiful hills in Scotland, especially when seen from the south across Loch Torridon. Its graceful form rises in steep banded tiers from the moorland, perfectly proportioned, stands of Scots pine at its base. We climbed Beinn Alligan in September, harvesting a lazy, Indian summer day.

Billy and I ascended via a steep scrambly ridge, chiding Dave who took the easy way up the corrie to the first top. We walked together past the gash of An Eag to the summit, a fantastic viewpoint over the horns of Alligan to the rest of Torridon. The horns provided the best entertainment of the day: easy but enjoyable scrambling reminiscent of Hallival on Rum, with superb views over Torridon and back to the impressively steep wedge of Beinn Alligan's summit. Descent was long, steep, and heavy on the knees, but it had been a fine day, Billy and Dave cracking constant jokes of the highest quality.

At the campsite at the bottom of the hill we parted ways. I

counted my pennies and discovered that I had miscalculated the petrol money, with the result that last night in the pub I'd drunk what I needed to get home. However it had been too satisfying a weekend, over two of the finest hills in the country, for something as minor as this to ruin the good feeling. I was unfashed, sure something would turn up, and something did. As I drove down the road with the fuel gauge hovering near red, two Dutch hitchhikers appeared who were surprised – but more importantly willing – to fork out money to pay for petrol to reach the Central Belt.

Beinn Dearg, Atholl *(ben jerrig)* – *even the boring ones*
1008m OS 43 NN 853778

Brian, Billy, and I climbed this hill from the south, having arrived in Blair Atholl the previous night and slept in an unlocked railway hut. In the morning the cloud was down very low, and as we climbed a dry mist revealed nothing except little trackside details. We ascended the long landrover track that goes most of the way to the top: a navigationally easy task, so there was little to keep us occupied mapwise. We chatted and paid little attention to our surroundings. I recall very little from the day, except for a rant Brian started near the top about all things Scottish, concluding with:
  "The Scottish hills are the best hills in the world!"
  "What," we chided him, "even the boring ones?"
  "Aye," he replied, *"even the boring ones."*

White Coomb – *tales of Galloway*
822m OS 79 NT 163151

Alastair's parents' house in Kircudbright was an urban bothy: up an 18th century close, it had an open fire, stone walls, old rugs, Greenmantle ale in the fridge, a comfy sofa, driftwood, interesting books, and model sailing ships on shelves. It wouldn't be hard to spend a whole winter there, but Alastair, Bonny, Pete and I were only down for the weekend. Alastair entertained us with spooky stories – some of them even true. The close had featured briefly in legendary B-movie 'The Wicker Man' and he was proud of this, endlessly quoting from the movie, assuming everyone had seen it (it must have been shown in the schools in Galloway, such was his astonishment at finding anyone who hadn't). His grandfather told us about the murder of the lighthouse keeper on Little Ross, the innocuous looking light just offshore. He pulled out the newspaper cuttings to prove it. Pete blanched, perhaps affected by Alastair's relentless eeriness. "That was exactly the same day and time as I was born . . ."

We walked along the rocky coast, rough green fields above, low broken seacliffs below, and took to the stony beach, looking out to Little Ross. We visited Torrs Cave on the shore, dark inside and coated in a carpet of bird shit. Further along the coast were smugglers caves. This area was a popular landing spot with traders in French contraband during the Napoleonic Wars. Alastair told us that one of these caves even led directly into the wine cellar of the Balcarry Hotel!

On the way back to Glasgow on Sunday, we visited White Coomb in the under-appreciated area of Tweedsmuir, the high hill country in the centre of Southern Scotland where the rivers Clyde, Tweed and Annan rise. A vertiginous 270m slope next to the Grey Mare's Tail waterfall was tackled in ten minutes (eight by Pete, who stopped at the bottom to adjust his shoes), calves on fire, tendons fit to burst – the fastest ascent I've ever done. The remainder of the ascent took a fair bit longer, as we wandered across snow-slushed peat hags and wiry heather, following a fence on a compass bearing to the wintry summit. No views, but a feeling of – how can I put it? *Experiencing Southern Scotland.*

The Brack – *on meeting Herne the Hunter*
787m OS 56 NN 246031

One winter, Alastair and I headed for the Ardgoil Peninsula, or 'Argyll's Bowling Green' as it was known. This nickname is a corruption of the Gaelic 'Bo Ghriana' – *sunny cattle fold* – and is deliberately ironic, because few landscapes could be less like a bowling green (or intriguingly, a sunny cattle fold) than rough, knarled, knobbly Ardgoil. It lacks public roads or habitation except for a single, empty cottage at its southern end, used as an adventure base by Sea Cadets. Its proximity to home – yet ruggedness and inaccessibility – made it irresistible.

We parked at Ardgarten, and took forestry tracks to the base of The Brack. The ascent is simple and brutal – straight up the northern slope, avoiding the large summit cliff by turning it on the left. I put my foot in a deep, hidden hole that, in descent, would have caused a sprained ankle at best. It was a sobering reminder that these chaotic schistose Arrochar hills are riven with caves, holes, and ravines. One such split in the rock near the summit was large enough for Alastair to crawl into and call a cave, and we were entertained by similar rock scenery until the summit.

The southward descent passes a huge crag that, were it visible from the road, would be popular with climbers. Instead, it is unknown. We traversed boggy moorland between The Brack and Cnoc Coinnich towards ill-frequented country, really getting into the walk. Cnoc Coinnich is another fine summit, although the quality of the tops diminished as we continued – despite being closer to the tip of the peninsula, the views from the lower hills are not quite as good.

Beinn Reithe was our third top, with southward views down Loch Long and the Clyde to the Lowlands and Arran; but also an unusual aspect down the Gareloch to Faslane and Ardmore. Alastair brought out his tin whistle to play a tune that stirred a couthy nostalgia for woolly jerseys, bothy fires, fragile folk music on car tapes, wind blowing through denuded trees. We descended towards the next top and passed a small drumlin about twenty metres long, Alastair on one side and me on the other. I could still hear the sound of his footsteps and therefore knew he was as far down this hillock as me.

I could hear Alastair on the other side of the drumlin, and when he came into view again a prickling of horror overwhelmed my senses: *somehow, in this remote and unvisited spot on a dead winter's day, he had turned into a multi-pointed stag.*

I stood immobilised. The stag, a few yards away, stared at me: but then in relief Alastair appeared, just a few feet from the stag, catching it completely unawares. It suddenly noticed him and bolted, and I laughed in relief that Alastair had not transmogrified into Herne the Hunter. It sounds ridiculous, but that was what my senses told me for a second on the southern slope of Beinn Reithe. The cold dread of the impossible disappeared with the retreating stag, and my body returned to normal, senses in sweet agreement.

The view from our final summit, The Saddle, was not quite as good as that from Beinn Reithe. Although we hadn't reached the tip of the peninsula, there were no more major tops, so we dropped down to a useful forestry track that took us back to Ardgarten, revelling in the grandstand sunset views up Loch Long.

Meall a' Phubuill *(myal a poo-bill)* – Hogmanay
774m OS 41 NN 029854

If you are going to celebrate Hogmanay, then do it properly. Don't sit around at home waiting for the bells being counted down by the comedy turn on TV (a show probably recorded in July); don't stand on the streets of Edinburgh on the most miserable night of the year, herded into a tiny space with every pickpocket north of Manchester and thousands of drunk Australians you've never met before and never plan to meet again. No, if you are going to celebrate Hogmanay, there is only one proper and correct way to do it, as far as a hillwalker is concerned – a night in a bothy.

Thus a small group of us headed for Glen Suileag for a party, laden with coal, food, musical instruments and – most importantly – alcohol. Each of us had a full bottle of whisky (weighing less than beer, whisky is the backpacker's preference) and in one Bacchanalian night, it was all gone. Some even brought that precious elixir, Single Malt, Pete's 16-year old Lagavulin the crowning glory.

The fire was lit, and food prepared. We played at table traverses – a bothy favourite. Lie on top of the table, then try to traverse all the way underneath it and back up onto the top, without touching the ground! The band of Susan, Alan, Stevie and Bill played their fiddle, guitar, accordion and tin whistle, chairs pushed to the side of the room as we danced to ceilidh tunes. The single malt was passed around continuously – a waste after the fifth dram as tastebuds lose the power of discrimination – and our dancing and carousing became bolder. The fire dimmed, and Brian threw his gas cooking cylinder onto the embers in an attempt to relight it. Never has a room evacuated so quickly, Andrew returning to drag Brian out too. Miraculously, there was no explosion. We returned, threw an entire sack of coal on the fire, retreated to the back of the room as the heat built up, and barred Brian from going anywhere near it.

The heat had us half-naked, and Brian and Billy wrestled on the floor while Alastair headed outside to howl at the moon . . .

The evening was rescued by Bonnie's sweet singing. We sang for hours – extemporising on 'What Shall We Do With the Drunken Sailor', inventing cruel and unusual punishments for Andrew as he lay collapsed and dribbling in a corner. Brian stayed up late after everyone else had retired, stoking the fire despite his ban, and singing tunelessly the entire content of Alan and Susan's songbook.

Next day most of us headed in bluff windy conditions for Meall a' Phubuill, a steep Corbett of wind-distressed tundra grass and gullies full of bumslidable snow. I found a rusted hatchet, and puzzled over its presence halfway up a treeless hill. Beinn Fhada to the south was bleak and cornice-rimmed, the above-freezing weather filling the glen with thick, tangibly moist winds. Gulvain, a Munro, lay higher to the west: gripped in dreich cloud, its snow-frosted sides looked huge and intimidating in the short daylight.

Back down we played the ice-axe game – grabbing an axe

placed in the ground and spinning around it before standing up and dizzily trying to retain balance – before walking out to face the challenges, disappointments, new experiences, and friendships of the New Year.

Green Lowther – *golf ball hill*
732m OS 71/78 NS 900120

The plan was to visit the Southern Uplands from Glasgow, get a hill and a quick blast of fresh air, then spend the rest of the afternoon in the pub, watching the Five Nations. A fine plan, especially for the one not driving and therefore able to drink (me).

Brian and I headed for the mist-clamped, snowy Lowther Hills above the twin villages of Leadhills and Wanlockhead, former lead mining villages. Wanlockhead is the highest village in Scotland, and it certainly felt like it this bleak winter's day. We ascended into cloud for the low summits on a service road, passing local children playing with sledges – no hardcore Highland peak this. It was cold and bluffly windy on top, but enjoyable, as we were well wrapped and planning no huge effort. These hills host huge radio transmitters in geodesic domes, and a well-made road along the ridge between the two hills brought a surreal aspect to the walk for us, familiar only with untainted hilltops. Other countries often have human structures built high into their hills, but it was rare then in pre-windfarm Scotland.

Once down we headed to the only bar for miles, in the hotel in Leadhills, where the Five Nations was being shown.

Inside, four tough looking men sat by the door and, at the opposite end of the small bar, a woman with two children.

One of the men cursed.

"Ssh!" chorused his companions, *"the weans!"*

The childrens' ears pricked up, a new swear word learnt.

More people entered the bar, some there like us for the rugby and a couple of pints, most for a bit of banter with the barman or the men by the door. There was a problem with this door – it wouldn't shut properly. By now it was snowing violently, and the cold wind whistled past the ill-fitting jamb. Each time a punter opened the door, a hurricane of snow blew in, flakes swirling round the room. Eventually the man nearest the door threw down his pint and shouted "right!" before striding out of the pub. Assuming he had gone home in annoyance, I couldn't believe my eyes when, ten minutes later, he returned with a tool kit to perform carpentry on the pub door mid-blizzard so that it would shut properly.

"Bugger me backwards!" I exclaimed.

"The weans!" hissed Brian, through gritted teeth.

Geal Carn, Drumochter *(jeel karn)* – *whiteout*
917m OS 42 NN 598783

Of the four Munros called Geal Carn – famed each for dullness – the most memorable for me was the one above the Drumochter Pass. For the wrong reasons, it gave one of my most memorable ever hill days.

Billy and I had parked at Balsporran Cottage for a jaunt over the hills west of Drumochter. Snow lay thick by the roadside and the tops were in cloud, but we headed for Geal Carn, hoping that we could bag, perhaps, three Munros. Higher up, the wind increased with every step, visibility worsened, and spindrift tore across the smooth contours of the hill. We sat behind one of the numerous cairns on the ascent, arguing over whether or not it was the top, spindrift streaming round the cairn and eddying back to blast us icily in the face.

Finally we made the summit of Geal Carn, buffeted by wind-blown snow and visibility less than ten yards. After descending for a couple of minutes I decided to use my axe and, calling out to Billy that I was doing so, threw off my rucksack, unclipped the axe, and straightened up again.

Billy was nowhere to be seen.

I called out, as loudly as I could, but it was a hopeless task: the wind snatched the words from my mouth as they were formed, tearing them into scraps of white noise. I blew my whistle, carefully avoiding the six-short-blasts distress signal, to no avail. What would Billy do on discovering I was gone? I returned uphill to the summit cairn, but he wasn't there. I didn't want to hang around long in this inhospitable environment. Perhaps he had headed downwards to the col between Geal Carn and the next Munro? Yes, this would be a good idea: it was possible that the cloud base would be higher than the col and we might see each other. So downhill I went.

The situation at the col was no better. I hung around for a while, chilling, then decided that the best course of action would be to get off the hill entirely.

Thus I headed downhill, away from any potential cliff faces and away from the prevailing wind into a thick, deep bank of snow. It was still hard to see anything – even harder than before in fact, as there were no landmarks, exposed rocks, or any visual bearings at all in this giant snowdrift – and I stumbled and fell everywhere. As the map indicated an absence of cliffs in this direction, I continued blindly on. Each step sunk me deeper and more immobile into the snow, and I crawled, roly-poly, half in, half over the snow. This first kilometre from the col took an hour and a half, but gradually, the terrain and visibility improved, and the wind lessened. By the time I dropped out of the bottom of the cloud there were only another four kilometres to go, and these took only an hour.

It was cold and I was looking forward to getting into my car, a lonely looking Lada rocking in the wind. However there was one more surprise in the day – the locks had iced over completely. I breathed to no avail on the keyhole. I had been moving constantly in difficult terrain for several hours and this, combined with my current predicament, suddenly made me need the toilet very badly. So I did the only logical thing: I peed on the keyhole, which melted the ice enough for me to get the key into the lock.

I sat in the car for nearly another hour, darkness starting to fall. Just as I was really beginning to worry, Billy appeared in the distance. He had wondered where the hell I had gone.

When he realised I was missing, he returned to the summit, but I hadn't waited long enough at the summit and we had missed each other. He had heard some of the whistle blasts, but in the wind it was impossible to tell where they had come from. Concerned that I might have slipped and fallen and been unable to move, he had started to quarter the hillside, only to eventually have to give up and battle his way back down the hill as I had done, except fearing the worst.

It had been my fault for not making absolutely sure Billy knew I was getting my axe out. We drove back humbled, stunned that we had become separated so easily. What if we had been on a hill with cliffs or narrow ridges? Thankfully, Geal Carn is an easy hill, without great difficulties or inherent dangers. "Just as well we weren't up the Cairngorms today, eh!" I said as the car warmed up, and we shivered at the thought, then laughed with relief.

Except it wasn't funny. Because, as we read in the papers a couple of days later, someone was up the Cairngorms that foul day, and lost their life.

Earl's Seat – *in the footsteps of Tom Weir* *578m OS 57/64 NS 569838*

According to Tom Weir's *Weir's World*, the man himself used to like wandering over the Campsies and back from Glasgow entirely under his own steam. Wouldn't you love to follow in his footsteps? I knew I did, and the thought of wandering out of my flat in Glasgow's West End, up Maryhill Road, out by the Switchback, along the West Highland Way, up the Campsies, and all the way back, filled me with a strange longing. Finally, one raw March weekend it happened.

There had been a student party the night before, and on a grey Saturday morning I dropped in to a newsagent for Irn Bru, crisps and rolls before continuing along Maryhill Road hungover, head throbbing and legs dragging. Thankfully the weather was dull and cool; I couldn't have coped if it were sunny or warm. Having been to Milngavie before I knew where the West Highland Way starts and, more importantly, where it actually goes that first confusing mile or two round the back of Milngavie. Soon I was out of the country park, past the Carbeth huts, and walking in Strathblane.

Strathblane is not a large strath. A mile or so across and widening towards Drymen, steep sided with the Kilpatrick Hills west and Campsies east, Strathblane is a scenic place, with the first glimpses of the Highlands in the distance and the curiosities of the Whangie, Dumgoyne and Dumgoyach immediately around. I left the West Highland Way for a neglected prehistoric stone circle beneath Dumgoyach, and climbed this artificial looking volcanic hill on a whim. In an area of grass and moorland, its steep, stumpy, tree-clad, motte-like profile attracted my attention. Yet at the top there was nothing: no old forts, no ancient walls; nothing for a tourist, only perhaps some vestigial remains for an archaeologist, thousands-year-old ruins buried in the roots of hundreds-year-old trees.

In my imagination, the citadel of an ancient and forgotten civilisation once crowned this point.

A steep descent of Dumgoyach, then once down, the steepness was in ascent, as the worn horn of Dumgoyne was approached. Whilst Dumgoyach is a fancy, a folderol, Dumgoyne is a proper hill, with no chance of there being any ancient settlement on its blasted summit. It is too high, steepsided, and small-topped to have supported anything human. I peched all the way to the top, the initial gradient steepening to a ladder-like intensity, before standing on its tiny summit. The descent towards Earls Seat is short but equally intense, and I decided that Dumgoyne – sticking out the side of the Campsies like a stumpy rhinoceros horn – would not be easy to descend in winter conditions.

After Dumgoyach and Dumgoyne, Earls Seat proved much more mundane. The cloud had lowered over the escarpment, and a sketchy track in rough heather combined with compass work took me to Earls Seat, highest of all the Campsies. It was a shame in the mist to be unable to see anything: not the north-facing corries, the Highlands beyond the escarpment, or the meandering Forth below. But, views aside, there was a more pressing problem. I was knackered and wanted to stop, sit down and take a rest, but there was nowhere to go except onwards, and the jungly terrain at 1700ft is tougher to traverse than tundra-like Munro tops. Through the mist I navigated a course: following an old fence, I trudged through peat hags, tough heather and oozing bogs – hard terrain before Dumbreck.

The descent steepened near the southern face of the Campsies, and after the purgatorial bogs an unexpected treat was revealed on breaking out of the cloud. This was the Spout of Ballagan – a tree-lined, V-shaped feature, a graceful and airy waterfall – and I followed it down, then took the back road to Milngavie. It was dark by the sodium-lit outskirts. Yes, I was tired; and had not fully recovered all day from the previous night's excesses. Switchback and Maryhill Road? My feet ached. No, I took the train; sinking gratefully into the plush, cushioned seat that took me quickly back to Glasgow.

Tom Weir, you win.

Ben More, Mull *(ben mor)* – *spring in the islands* 966m OS 47/48 NM 526331

Mull is a beautiful and interesting island. Combined with Iona and Staffa, it is one of the best holiday destinations in the country. So it is a shame that hillwalkers are likely to visit Mull for a quick bagging raid, returning to the mainland unaware of its wider beauties. Just as Skye is far more than the Black Cuillin, so Mull is far more than Ben More – a good quality Munro, but just one hill amongst many interesting things to see and do. It is almost certain that if the club had ever visited Mull, the foreign exchange students who only joined as a cheap way of seeing a bit of the countryside would have loved visiting Duart Castle, Iona Abbey, Fingal's Cave or the Carsaig Arches.

Anyway, to the hill! The SMC recommends an ascent from Loch na Keal but, carless, Harry and I took the Fionnphort bus. We jumped off the bus and ascended from Ben More farm and, such is the quality of the route, I doubt the approach from Loch na Keal is any better. Ben More's serried lower tiers and black upper parts are seen to best advantage from here, especially with some April snow lingering on the tops. Harry and I headed toward A'Chioch, from which a sporting scrambler's ridge connects with Ben More. The ascent took ages, but gave us all the more time to take in the small yellow flowers, fescue-bristled outcrops, bog-cotton, and volcanic-slag upper slopes on the way up in the rare spring sunshine. Above us, the ridge from A'Chioch to Ben More looked increasingly interesting. Would it prove too much for us? Would our legs turn to jelly? Would we become cragfast?

Eventually, we reached A' Chioch, and the intimidating ridge. Along it, the nearer we approached Ben More, the steeper, narrower, and more notched it became. But this excellent ridge is less difficult than it looks. I was in my element. Its rock is rough, an incredibly textural friable black rock, a ridge with a profile like Harry Lauder's walking stick or the Aonach Eagach set at a thirty degree angle. But easier, if just as much fun.

The summit was covered in a deep crust of old, hard snow, one that could be sunbathed upon, and the view was disappointingly hazy. Still, Ben More is a proper mountain on days like this, and the descent south over snowpack, steep volcanic scree, then a dogleg southeast avoiding a cliff face, demanded concentration and attention to the map.

We waited at the head of yellow-flowered Loch Scridain for the bus as the tide came in over the kelp, skylarks in the distance filling the broom-perfumed air with song.

A'Mhaigdean *(a vyay-un) – queen of the Fisherfield wilderness*
967m OS 19 NH 007748

A'Mhaigdean. The Maiden. Of all the legendary hills in Britain, this seemed to us to be the most mythical, unobtainable, and highly prized. The SMC guide in Glasgow University Library stated that it was the remotest hill in the country. Hamish Brown asserted in *Hamish's Mountain Walk* that it was the best viewpoint in Scotland. The map showed it cliff-girt, rising above tiers of multi-level lochans in untrod isolation. Given this information, we decided before even setting foot on it that it must be the finest hill in the British Isles. We couldn't wait to visit! And then, Dave came up with a proposal: he was thinking of taking part in Cancer Research's *Boots Across Scotland* charity event, which aimed to get a person on top of every Munro in the country on the same day in early May. We were sold; all that had to be done was decide upon a driver. As nobody was keen to go for a long trip in my unreliable car, Dave volunteered.

On a fine evening we pulled up near Dundonnell, Billy showing off his ability in the pole trick – a game of strength popular with climbers, that involves grabbing a lamppost and holding your body horizontally outwards. Initially the walk in to the bothy was a sweaty trudge up dry stones, but the track eventually degenerated into one of the boggiest pieces of fiction ever perpetrated by the Ordnance Survey. As we picked our way around the morass, weighed down by heavy packs, I hoped the effort was going to be worth it. And then in the evening light, Beinn Dearg Mor appeared over the pass, looming massive and dark in front of us, with Shenavall – one of the most beautifully situated bothies – in a sunny hollow below. It was surprisingly busy, with every room full of bustle, and our hard-carried coal unnecessary. According to one of the old-timers present, the blame for the busyness lies squarely at the door of people writing about and popularising bothies – something I am aware I'm only adding to here.

At dawn an elderly gentleman in our room stirred himself, donned full waterproofs, and headed out the door.

Much later, we three dragged ourselves out of our scratchers, cooked a leisurely breakfast, and made for the river below the bothy. There are areas in the Highlands where rivers must be forded to reach the hills, and this is one. A full river now – or worse, a day of torrential rain – and we would be stuck, unable to cross. However the weather had been kind, and the river was clear and barely calf deep in the shallows. We removed boots to cross, then sat on the opposite bank, drying feet and contemplating Beinn a' Chlaidheimh.

This ascent was the hardest work of the day, and we pulled on branches of heather to haul ourselves up over slabs of Torridonian sandstone hidden in the undergrowth. A nice narrow summit with a prospect of hard work and good hills to come, and then down and up Stob Ban, fanning out to plod up blocky quartzite as other groups were spotted and the weather closed in. Mullach Coire Mhic Fhearchair was the highest top of the day, and we took a self-timer photo of ourselves, hoods up, mist closed in, holding the Cancer Research flag. A shame about the views – we had been looking forward to A'Mhaidgean.

But then, descending the Mullach, the clouds lifted. After an argument over whether to go over or round an intervening top, Beinn Tarsuinn provided the highlight of the day. Miles from our starting point, further still from the road, Beinn Tarsuinn is capped by an entertaining ridge of weird shapes, and we traversed in delight.

Now A'Mhaigdean lay before us. The long ascent was a chore on what had become a hot sunny afternoon, but eventually we arrived at the summit cairn perched dramatically at the edge of cliffs looking west, far out to the coast. A'Mhaigdean! Why did it feel like an anti-climax, even though the cloud had now cleared? Perhaps we should have ascended this hill from the west, as below us, the lochs at multiple levels and numerous cliff faces looked as if they would provide a complex and interesting route. We continued over to Ruadh Stac Mor, a marginally better viewpoint than A'Mhaigdean in my opinion, then down in late afternoon sun to the track in Gleann na Muice Beag.

There was one final uncertainty – would we be able to cross the Abhainn Gleann na Muice? It looked impassable. But at Larachantivore in the flats of the glen, the river broadened and shallowed and we crossed easily, heading directly for Shenavall and the Abhainn Srath na Sealga we had crossed earlier in the day. It was time to relax and cook in the open, enjoying the late sunshine, chatting to others in the bothy, feeling happy with life, content after the exercise and achievement of the day's six remote, high-quality Munros.

Much later, as dusk fell, the elderly gentleman returned, still clad head-to-foot in waterproofs. We hadn't seen him on the hill, but he informed us before collapsing into bed that he had done the same walk as us today – only in double the time.

Sgurr Thuilm *(skoor hoo-lm)* – *lost*
963m OS 40 NM 939879

The Ordnance Survey is one of Britain's greatest institutions. The Royal Mail, for example, keeps official transactions flowing; the BBC keeps the masses entertained, informed, and educated; and the Queen goes about her business with a dedication to duty and inscrutable aloofness. Yes, these constitute the glue that binds us together, the institutions that make us think, 'I may actually have something in common with people who cried at Princess Diana's funeral!'

In a similar way, the Ordnance Survey is the underlying stratum, the bedrock linking hillwalkers in Britain. "Surely not!" you scoff. "What about the weather forecast?" But weather forecasts are inherently unreliable; the Ordnance Survey, with a few small exceptions, is not, and the appropriate map shields walkers against fog, mist, or low cloud. Furthermore, a map's graphical representation of a landscape looks good as an artistic artefact in its own right, and it can be read for hours on end, plotting journeys, weekends, and adventures. The Ordnance Survey rules. I long ago realised that I feel as naked on the hills without a map and compass as a fireman would feel attending a callout without a hose.

So what happens when you decide to head up a hill then discover, well into your drive north, that you have left a critical map of the area at home? Fret not. If you are lucky – as we were – you will be heading for a hill like Sgurr Thuilm above Glenfinnan, and you will have stopped in Fort William for chips when you discover the map is missing. This is lucky, because Fort William boasts one of the finest navigational reserves in the whole of these isles: a massive mural in the downstairs bar of Nevisport, covering a considerable extent of wall. The mural is made from pieced together Ordnance Survey maps, covering a choice slice of country from Skye to Aberdeen, and from Glencoe to An Teallach. It is the finest single piece of map I have ever seen. To stand in the Nevisport bar, pint in hand, and rove the country by eye from island shieling to Cairngorm corrie to Aberdeenshire croft is a grand pleasure.

It is just as well this incredible mural existed, because no one had brought the map for Sgurr Thuilm. In transit through Fort William late one evening and halfway through our chips, Billy dropped the bombshell – he didn't have OS 40 (Mallaig and Loch Shiel) either!

No map! It was late and the shops were closed! What would we do?! Ah, what would we do? A cunning plan presented itself, and I blurted it out:

"Let's see if the Nevisport Bar is still open . . ."

and Billy immediately caught my drift. He grinned and, chip papers binned, we descended on Nevisport's basement bar, paper and pen in hand. "OK, so this is the area we need . . ." I started, and began to sketch.

"You'll need to put this in as well . . ." said Billy.

. . .

and eventually we had copied, free of charge, a reasonable representation of the area of interest around Sgurr Thuilm and Corryhully bothy. Satisfied, we left Nevisport, drove to the roadend of the track leading to Corryhully, and walked up the track to the bothy, the only one I have ever seen with electric light (the meter took 50p pieces). Next day we wandered up the cloud-covered hills, following our Nevisport-copied paper & pencil map on the steep descent of Sgurr nan Coireachan to safety, congratulating not only the magnificent accuracy and detail pursued by the Ordnance Survey, but also our own ingenuity in copying the map – which thanks to today's mist was essential – from the wall in Nevisport.

At the time of writing, Nevisport has dismantled this fine mural. Let us start a campaign for its return, as an emergency resource!

Ben Klibreck *(ben klib-rek)* – *the elemental mountain* 961m OS 16 NC 585299

In mid-June in the north of Scotland, semi-darkness descends for only a couple of hours on a clear night. People can go a little crazy, leaving the pubs on a Friday night when it is still light and forgetting to go to bed, heading out fishing on some peaceful loch somewhere and not catching any sleep until Sunday afternoon. We were not as badly affected as this by the simmer dim, though I was tickled to see well enough to drive without lights after midnight. We arrived late at a quiet spot on the A836 near the Altnaharra Hotel and set up camp.

Next morning I woke around 4am, the sun already well established in the sky. It was a GLORIOUS morning! This weather awakened vigour in me, and I ran around the fields with my arms outstretched, bathing my limbs in morning sunshine. I attempted to wake the others, only to be told where to go. Waiting until they woke at the sinfully late hour of 8am was torture. *C'mon c'mon c'mon!!*

Finally we broke camp and headed for Ben Klibreck. From the west this is a large, simple hill above Strath Vagastie, formed of elemental wind-blasted shapes. The summit revealed a panorama that can hardly have changed since the Bronze Age: a land from a time, it seemed to our traffic-choked eyes, when the earth was still young. We were at the centre of a vast bowl, more spacious than anything in the Grampian Highlands, with distant, snow-flecked green hills rimming the horizon in every direction. The only sign of humanity was the Altnaharra Hotel and a tiny ribbon of single-track road threading its way through the hills. It is a film set, awaiting a suitably epic story. I wondered aloud if anyone was planning an adaptation of the Tain Bo Cuailnge, or wanted to make a porridge western filmed in Scotland; and we descended to the car back to more pressing matters, of what to do next, and of where to get a bite to eat, and a drink tonight.

Scafell Pike – *the Three Peaks Challenge*
978m OS 89/90 NY 215072

Well now. To date I've only been up the highest hill in England once, and it was as part of the Three Peaks Challenge. This is an unorganised, unofficial concept (my favourite kind of challenge), a walk anyone can try at any time. The idea is to climb Ben Nevis, Snowdon, and Scafell Pike in 24 hours. The route you take, and how you do it, is up to you. Some people decide to take a minibus with dedicated drivers, walkers, cooks, aides-de-camp, and create training schedules and so on and so forth for this achievement. However, Jeremy and I had just finished our final year exams, we had a couple of days free, fine summer weather was forecast, and he put it to me: how about the Three Peaks Challenge? Jeremy was a coursemate rather than a club member, and we had only been up a couple of hills together. But in his spare time he competed in off-road rallies, so Jeremy was ideally suited to the driving part of the challenge, while I lived for hillwalking. It was an excellent partnership: we had the right experience, and could travel light and fast. We set off in his car the next day. Our thinking went like this. Glen Nevis at 6pm: plenty time before sunset to climb the Ben in the coolness of the evening. Then a late-night, traffic-free romp down the A82 and M74 to the Lake District and Scafell Pike: we could climb it at dawn after the short summer night. Finally, the M6 and A5 to Snowdonia and Snowdon itself, where we would have until 6pm to summit on Yr Wyddfa. Travelling light and fast, just the two of us in Jeremy's car, a long-legged, second-hand Ford Sierra. We had no idea if we would do it, but it seemed possible in theory: and thus we set off from Glasgow one afternoon for Fort William, spirits high.

Jeremy dropped me off at the bottom of the tourist track up

Ben Nevis at 6pm. "Good luck," he said; "I'll be back at ten." I was wearing boots, shorts, t-shirt, and had a jersey wrapped round my waist: a few barley sugars in my pocket. I intended to travel light. I was fast, bouncing up the track without a rucksack. I stopped for four minutes at the halfway burn to greedily gulp water and suck a couple of barley-sugars, and then it was uphill again, limbs free and back unencumbered.

An hour and a half after setting off I was on top. I lingered for four minutes, catching my breath and enjoying the ambience of the highest point in Britain. Ironically, despite being the highest, this would prove to be the easiest summit. I let myself rip down the tourist track, running where I could, and ended back at my start point two and a half hours after leaving. It was only just after 8:30pm. Oh no! I'd told Jeremy I'd be back down around 10:30pm! (Tonight's walk was two hours quicker than my previous best time.) We would squander this unexpected bonus. And then, almost on cue, Jeremy drove up and opened the passenger door. "I thought you'd be quicker than expected," he explained. With forward thinking like that, no wonder Jeremy graduated with a first from our degree course, whereas I only managed a lower second.

We drove down the road. I relaxed. It had been dark for a couple of hours by the turn-off for the Lakes. Jeremy pointed the long bonnet of his 1.8 litre Sierra down the empty country roads and pressed his foot on the accelerator. Dream-like, the car ate up the miles. It was late and Jeremy had been driving at maximum effort for several hours. There was no doubt that his part of the task was the more onerous. Fortunately we reached Wasdale Head without incident, earlier than expected. The moon was out. It was tempting to walk now. But daylight was only a few hours away. We rolled the car seats back and tried to sleep, which was just as well. The moon set shortly afterwards, and the rest of the night was pitch dark.

Early morning at Wasdale Head – around 5am – I stirred. Damn! I'd thought I'd rise at four! Every hour was a prisoner! Jumping out of my sleeping bag I laced my boots and raced out of the lay-by. "See you soon!" I said to Jeremy, who caught a little more kip, before making breakfast.

Scafell Pike was a troublesome hill. Although lower than Ben Nevis, the track is stonier, not as good; my feet pounded sharp rock, complaining by the summit. Dawn was breaking over the Pennines and Lakeland fells. It was breathtaking. I could have watched this for hours, wave upon wave of hills coming at me from the sun. Instead, I briefly circled the summit, discovering a waking couple in bivvy bags going 'huh?' They had had a romantic western sunset, but hadn't moved, and were missing sunrise. Then I descended, clattering down Lord's Rake to meet the Lingmell Gill path I had ascended. At Wasdale Head I stripped, sweaty, and jumped naked in the river – Jeremy was brought out the car by my yells of mortification. It had taken two and a half hours to do this lower hill, the same time as Ben Nevis.

Jeremy drove off along twisting roads and, on reaching the M6 and a petrol station, we had only fate to decide whether or not we would complete the Three Peaks. We were well ahead of schedule, but who knows what roadworks, car break-downs, twisted ankles, or Acts of God might happen between now and the summit of Wales?

We jumped in the car and roared off across Westmorland in pursuit of further adventure, arriving in Wales with plenty of time to climb Snowdon.

We had so much spare time, Jeremy wanted to climb the hill too. Billy had recommended the Crib Goch ridge as a fun but very easy scramble, so rather than slog up the tourist path, we tried Crib Goch. Up we went, slowly in the heat – in summer, it is far harder to climb a hill in the middle of the day than at 4am.

The route steepened and steepened. At one point, we were definitely performing some moves that were gradable as an easy rock climb. We assumed this was the hardest part – after all, Billy had told me it was easy! I reassured Jeremy on this point. We wouldn't have to attempt to descend this way. But on reaching the top of Crib Goch, our jaws dropped. The ridge continued onwards like a tightrope, a piece of Cuillin exca-vated from Skye and deposited in Snowdonia. The technical difficulty was low, but the sense of exposure was more like

Skye than anywhere else on the mainland. Yet not wanting to descend what we had just climbed, what could we do but carry on?

I led and Jeremy gingerly followed, and Crib Goch took us a while. But once it met with the tourist track the walking was easy, and after touching the overcrowded summit (Snowdon has a railway station and cafe at the top) we descended the well-worn Pyg Track back to the car and a celebratory pint in Llandudno. We had arrived back at the base of Snowdon and completed the Three Peaks Challenge with about an hour to spare.

I confronted Billy next time we met. "You told me Crib Goch was easy!"

"Did I?" he said. "Why would I say something like that?"

PART THREE
Munro Fever

There was one thing I knew when I first set foot in the Highlands and became aware of some of the sad geeky types ruled by lists of hills. There was no way I was going to become a Munrobagger. No way! But by my 50th Munro, I knew I was hooked. What better way of curing the obsession than climbing all the Munros? The problem with such a single-minded approach to life is that it crowds out the other things a body needs – a career, a relationship, a place to call your own: things all neglected in my drive to climb the Munros. I went where I needed to go, not where my friends wanted to go. I couldn't get a decent job, I lived with my parents, I walked alone. I wasn't happy, and what I was doing seemed essentially pointless.

But I did it anyway.

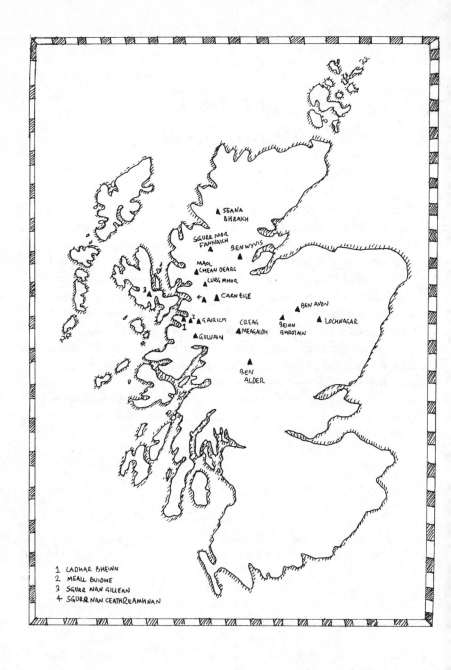

1 LADHAR BHEINN
2 MEALL BUIDHE
3 SGURR NAN GILLEAN
4 SGURR NAN CEATHREAMHNAN

Gulvain *(gul-ven) – lost in a haze*
987m OS 41 NN 002876

Trout in the river, pollen in the air, lush greenery bursting forth, blue dragonflies everywhere . . . lost in a warm summer haze, I walked up the flat glen to Gulvain. What was I doing here, alone with myself in the hills? I'd graduated, couldn't get a job, and had no idea where my life was going.

Once out of the forestry at the end of the track, the steep green bulk of Gulvain confronted me: consuming my thoughts in hard uphill grind, my mind blessedly blanked with pain, cursing as I went – cursing Gulvain, cursing my legs, cursing this ladder of earth, cursing Sir Hugh Munro, cursing any reason I had to be here. On the tops, the second summit is the higher: so I walked towards it, taking note of the rough view, before descending the way I came, returning home to stew in frustration. Back home, I filled out a job application form, wondering now I'd graduated how I was going to move on with my life.

Ben Avon *(ben ann) – big walk*
1171m OS 36 NJ 132019

Two of the largest hills in Scotland (in both height and extent) are Ben Avon and Beinn a' Bhuirid; they form part of the Cairngorm massif, yet remain isolated and unfrequented compared to the rest of the Cairngorms. Perhaps it has something to do with the undeniably long approach walks that must be made to attain these broad, flat, summits. However,

Munros they are, and therefore Must Be Bagged, long approach or not. The day Billy and I staggered over their tops was not only one of the longest walks we'd ever done, it was also one of the hottest days ever experienced in the Scottish Highlands.

We slept rough at the Glen Quoich car park, and woke to a disconcertingly warm morning. Glen Quoich is a Chinese watercolour of a glen, with wild yet easily accessible river scenery, perfectly proportioned amongst rocks and trees. This sylvan perfection is temporary, and it wasn't long before we were out of the shade of the trees and pounding past shrivelled heather on the hard, dusty landrover track, exposed to the sun, our t-shirts employed as kafiyas.

After 8km, the river took a bend and we entered a pathless stand of trees. This was perhaps the loveliest part of the walk, a remnant of virgin forest, full of anthills and birds and fallen logs across the river. The approach to these hills is long, but it is a walk-in that goes easily spent in beautiful surroundings like this. After the forest, the Glen Quoich route joins up with the Glen Slugain track, and finally we reached the approach to the hills proper. We kept our eyes peeled for the 'secret bothy' mentioned in *Mountain Days and Bothy Nights*, but to no avail – although it wouldn't be very secret if it could be spotted from the path!

The sun was merciless: as we passed underneath the impressive cliffs of Beinn a' Bhuird the ground steepened, and a heat haze clamped down, filling our minds with doubts. We felt delirious, immobilised, directionless. We staggered slowly towards the col. Neither of us had known heat like this in the hills before, and it worried us to be exerting so much effort. I wanted to stop and turn back but kept pushing, afraid to say anything. At the col we left our rucksacks, and Billy admitted that he too wanted to turn back due to the heat. Like me, he would have done so had either of us spoken.

Fortunately it was cooler up on the plateau of Beinn Avon, a 9km2 expanse of gravelly ground and tufts of tundra grass, with granite tors erupting from the surface of the plateau at random points. The summit is one of the larger tors: it holds the possibility for some bouldering, and has a strange seat-shaped depression near the top. There are weatherworn cup-holes, mirror images of the famous punch bowl in the River Quoich way back at the start of the walk. We returned to the rucksacks and looked north over the deep glen of Slochd Mor to a wild and unfrequented landscape.

Beinn a' Bhuird is an even bigger hill than Beinn Avon, with an impressive cliff-girt corrie for keen climbers, but no summit tor to hold a walker's interest. There were two more summits to come, the lesser heights of Beinn a' Chaorainn (as high as Snowdon or Stob Ghabhar, but a bit-player in the Cairngorms), and Beinn Bhreac, but already we were tired. We stopped to gather energy and enthusiasm for the long, drawn-out steppe between Beinn a' Bhuird and Beinn a' Chaorainn, and the third summit was finally reached.

It had been a hot day, and we had walked a long way. In fact, we had walked enough. We wanted to head down and go home. Unfortunately, the shortest route back lay 15km over Beinn Bhreac, via further miles of monotonous moorland. The monstrous whaleback of Beinn a' Bhuird loomed large to the left, and Ben Macdhui's granite-edged cliffs to the right – but we had no eyes for this grand stage, only curses for each weary footstep. It was a blessed relief to finally reach Beinn Bhreac, and begin the downward journey.

Then something magical happened. The heat of the day relented, and the evening's mellow light gave golden views across the forest of Glen Quoich to the heights of Lochnagar. Once down on the edge of the forest and finally into some shade, a grouse thrummed by, threading through the twilight trees, and we heard a capercaillie. The rest of the walk passed in weary relief, and we reached the car tired but otherwise in good condition. We had walked a little further than we would have liked, but the result of the trek was that the Munros – and the memories, already acquiring a glow of pleasure now the grinding effort was over – were in the bag.

Sgurr nan Gillean *(skoor nan gil-ee-an) – the eternal sgurr*
965m OS 32 NG 472253

I was in Skye, bagging my remaining Cuillin Munros. The previous day, I had attempted Sgurr nan Gillean by its West Ridge. But alone in early evening on a tightrope of rock above the reeling depths, gravity tugging at my feet, I met fear square in the face. I quailed, legs shaking, sick with awe, having to be content instead with Am Bastier and Bruach na Frithe.

And so I came to try Sgurr nan Gillean via the easier tourist route. Early, I set off from the Sligachan Hotel, following the rough, boggy path along the Sligachan River; the day fine, warm, and full of promise. As the track progressed up Glen Sligachan, Pinnacle Ridge slowly unveiled itself. Obscured in roadside views by being head-on, Pinnacle Ridge consists of four huge pinnacles, each bigger than its neighbour: culminating in the fifth pinnacle of Sgurr nan Gillean itself. The path in the glen continued on for some way below these sunlit pinnacles, until the summit itself was passed and the path turned uphill. As I climbed this steep section uphill – four points of contact necessary at times, and not the easiest of trails to navigate – I wondered what else lay above. This 'tourist route', I had heard, was not exactly easy.

Eventually the southern ridge of Sgurr nan Gillean is reached at its col with the lower peak of Sgurr an Uamh, a sharp and characterful end to the Cuillin main ridge. I headed upwards for Sgurr nan Gillean and, each time I thought the ridge couldn't get any narrower (controlling my breathing, telling myself "slow and steady gets you there"), another even more exposed section appeared. I kept my head however, even over the hardest part: an awkward, ridiculously undignified step over a ledge perched precariously above huge drops. It is easy though, compared to the West Ridge.

After this, the difficulty was over, and the tiny summit was reached with a sense of relief and achievement. This is one of the very finest summits in the British Isles, and surely the airiest outside a seastack. The entire main ridge of the Cuillin stretches away west and south, a complicated, densely sculptured area where the ordinary 1:50,000 scale Landranger map is entirely inadequate (I personally was only able to navigate successfully over the Cuillin with the help of a special 1:12,500 scale map sold only in mountaineering shops).

East of Sgurr nan Gillean, across the deep trench of Glen Sligachan, lie the smoother, rounded Red Hills, and the long, jagged spine of the Blaven massif. I looked at it. It was early enough in the day. I fancied climbing it too.

Thus I gingerly retraced my steps over the 'tourist route' on Sgurr nan Gillean, breathing more easily the lower I descended.

Once down the steep gully and into Glen Sligachan, it was a fast yomp out to the road, and the long drive around the coast to Torrin.

Ascending Blaven was hard work in the afternoon heat. I stuck to the shade as much as possible, and made rapid progress uphill. It seemed a travesty to climb such a fine mountain by this most direct and uninteresting of routes – for preference, surely, the southern ridge all the way from Camasunary bothy, or even better, the climbers-only Clach Glas traverse of the entire massif? But this was the shortest and easiest route up Blaven, a real 'tourist route' despite the occasional hands-out-of-pockets moments near the top, and I wasn't complaining at the opportunity of visiting a second Munro in the same day.

The view from the top of Blaven was fantastic: hills, sea, and peninsulas in every direction. I soaked it all in. West: the whole Cuillin, including Sgurr nan Gillean. North: Trotternish, Portree and Applecross. South: Minginish, Sleat, Rum and Canna. East: the western seaboard of Scotland and the roughest part of all, Knoydart. Each numerous peak and corrie, each fold in the hills, each ripple on the ocean, was picked out with great clarity in the late afternoon light. No single quadrant catches the attention – it is a three hundred and sixty degree prospect of incomparable scenery. Another group arrived and I requested a summit photo, revelling in the situation. It was hard to take my eyes off the views, but eventually it was time to descend, and I was well pleased with my day on two of the finest hills in the country. I was also elated for a different reason. These were my last Skye Munros. Now I *knew* they would be finished. The technical difficulties were behind me, and only plodding remained.

Lochnagar *(loch-na-gar)* – *job satisfaction*
1115m OS 44 NO 244861

"My favourite hill name," said Ally, "Lochnagar. Not been up it yet, but what a name."

He has a point. Loch-na-gar. Dark, mysterious. And yet the story behind the name is even more interesting. For in the original Gaelic, Lochnagar is Cac Carn Mor – Big *Crap Cairn*. Yes, that really is this hill's name! When Queen Victoria bought Balmoral at the hill's base, the Victorians were embarrassed by its name, so they changed it to Loch na Gearr – Short Loch – the name of the hill's corrie lochan. Not even the name of a hill! Truth is stranger than fiction in the case of the proper name for Lochnagar.

It was on a trip to restore Loch Callater bothy that I first became acquainted with Lochnagar. It took the keen, but impractical students of the club an entire summer to make repairs to Clashgour; by contrast, it took MBA volunteers just a couple of hours to build an entire floor for Loch Callater bothy. In three weekends they turned this hut from a roofless, nettle-infested, two-and-a-half-walled ruin into a habitable bothy. Their workrate was astonishing. On this particular trip, all the volunteers except myself worked in the building trade; they were joiners, brickies, and roofers. There was no way I, willing but bookish, could keep up.

Eventually, after two days of ceaseless toil I cracked, and told the team that I was heading for the hills. If truth be told they probably welcomed the decision, since the only part of Loch Callater bothy that wasn't well built was the short section of roof it was my proud duty to put together.

I headed along Loch Callater through increasingly wild territory, past Loch Kander in its corrie nest, and up a short, sharp slope to Tolmount and the Mounth Plateau. This is an oppressively flat area of high mossland, inhospitable in winter, free of birdsong in summer, part of the historical barrier between Northern and Southern Scotland. From Tolmount it is a simple task to head for Tom Buidhe; and once there, you might as well head for the Munros of Cairn Bannoch, Broad Cairn, and Carn-an-t-Sagairt Mor.

However, my unease was building. Eventually, at some indeterminate point, the oppressive flatness of the high plateau took a grip. I couldn't shake off a strange feeling of walking without moving forwards at all, the vast sky pressing down on me. It sounds stupid, but it was no joke to bear this heavy, suffocating, inescapable sky. I had to break into a jog to shake the feeling off: a common feeling perhaps in the Cairngorms and Mounth hills, and perhaps a contributing factor to the eerie tales associated with this area.

On reaching the summit of Carn an-t-Sagairt Mor a startling change in the monotony broke the spell, as I came across the remains of aircraft wreckage: but this mangled reminder of death hardly dispelled the eldritch air around these elevated flatlands. It took the final ascent towards Lochnagar past White Mounth to break free of the strange feeling that can grip the walker on this most featureless of mountain landscapes.

Lochnagar itself is an interesting hill: steep-sided cliffs at An Stuic, and one of Scotland's most celebrated climbing areas around the summit of Lochnagar itself, a huge pile of stones buttressed by famous ridges towering above the black depths of Loch nan Gearr. Approaching from there would give a very different day on the hill, one of verticality and excitement. I ate my emergency oatmeal as my energy was low after the day's exertions. Back at the bothy they were still working, despite being on the go since dawn (and it was now nearly sunset, in summer, for their third day in a row). Seven Munros was an easy task in comparison.

Loch Callater bothy was in the news the very next winter, as a woman who had become lost in the hills found it and sheltered there overnight. She was quoted as saying that it probably saved her life. On hearing this, an unfamiliar, tingling sensation passed over me – Job Satisfaction.

Lurg Mor *(lurg mor)* – the job and the hill
986m OS 25 NH 065404

I was in Kyle of Lochalsh for a job interview. They were looking for someone to pilot, maintain, and repair ROVs used in the Navy torpedo range in the Inner Sound. When travelling all the way to Kyle on expenses, why not make the most of it? Thus immediately on conclusion of the interview, I stripped out of my suit, donned my bothymongering gear, and headed for Achintee on Loch Carron for the walk in to Bernais bothy.

I had been through this general area before on an Ardnamurchan to Cape Wrath trek and was impressed by it, but this was the first time I'd seen Bernais from the west. This tiny cube of a building in a wide vista of nothingness gives a human scale to the wild Strathcarron-Kintail interior. There were two people inside, one a lorry driver from Inverness who bemoaned tourists' misuse of single-track roads (always give way to a lorry thundering up behind you).

Next day, I headed up the steepening flanks of Bidein a' Choire Sheasgaich to the narrow summit ridge, enjoying its incredible view southwest to Skye and the Inner Sound. In some ways this is a finer top than better-known Lurg Mhor, which is renowned for its remoteness, but little else. The trek over to Lurg Mhor and back was a formality, although with a good view of the head of Loch Monar and the unvisited slopes opposite. The deer must be left in some peace on the southern flanks of Sgurr a' Chaorachain, a candidate for loneliest spot in Britain.

The return journey over the flank of Bidein a' Choire Sheasgaich – avoiding the summit – was hard work, as was the bash through the gentler (but boggier) lower slopes towards Bernais – but I was invigorated by a chilly dip in the river next to Bernais, and walked back out to the car in good spirits. Lurg Mhor: a hill that I had imagined might be a long, dull slog had turned out to be anything but. At the top of the pass out from Bernais I looked back at the hills glowing in the late sunshine, and was well satisfied with these two new ticks.

I didn't get the job.

Sgurr Mor Fannaich *(skoor mor fan-ich)* – *a bubble of grace*
1110m OS 20 NH 203718

The Aultguish Inn is one of my favourite inns in the Highlands. The hospitality of the host is the stuff of legend, and it
remains to this day the only pub I've visited where the landlord
has stood the bar a round (on the condition that each of us gets
up and sings a song). On this particular night a large, stocky,
kilted drunk was slurring his words, falling half off his table,
and looking at the world through half-shut eyes – and yet the
rest of the bar continued to buy him drinks when he should
clearly have been packed off to bed with a jug of water.

Next day I rose to face what I had expected to be, if I am
being honest, a chore. The five eastern Fannichs were unbagged Munros that had, some time, to be tackled. Looking at
the map I saw nothing to excite me, with long, pathless walks
in and out, presumably through thick difficult heather. None
of my friends were interested in such an unexciting walk, so I
had come alone. Resigned to the task, I set off for the first
Munro of the five, plodding slowly up the heathery slopes. It
was hard work to reach that point, but then on the misty top
something happened, something magical. Despite worsening
weather, the day suddenly seemed effortless.

I had raised my hood, and walked in a bubble of comfort,
protected from the weather by my jacket, boots and over-
trousers, moving effortlessly over the land like a ghost. Sgurr
Mor Fannaich was a genuine peak, sadly cloud capped and
viewless but snowy, steep and with the impressive cliff-girt
Loch Fannaich at its base. From here on the walk held a
dreamy quality, with visibility stretching all day only to the
introverted but easily navigable middle distance; and although
I was expending energy with legs pumping like pistons over
the hard landscape, it felt as though I were gliding. A strange
walk, and not a feeling I've had before or since.

By the fifth and final summit I felt a sense of profound calm
even as the wind howled. The descent past multi-tiered lochans was beautiful, and there was even a discreet path by the
meandering riverside, unmarked on the map, following the

streaky river, full of interest and beauty. One particular set of rapids made me smile. To think I had feared that this walk would be a dull chore! I laughed at myself and the spell was broken.

A day later I was back home and opened the newspaper. To my surprise, who should be pictured but the kilted drunk from Aultguish! It turned out he had been wandering up the hill in his kilt and probably little else that misty Saturday, and found a hillwalker who was lost, disorientated, and hypothermic. Without hesitating, he had called mountain rescue on his mobile with exact coordinates, whipped off his kilt, wrapped it round the by now lost, disorientated, and severely confused hillwalker, and enveloped him in a big, warming bear hug until the cavalry arrived. An unsung hero, this story is dedicated to him; and if this book happens to make any money at all, I'll stand him a round myself.

Beinn Bhrotain *(beyn vro-tan)* – *a Cairngorm whiteout* *1157m OS 43 NN 954923*

I'd been up Beinn Bhrotain before with Alastair, but Billy hadn't. Sometimes he came with me to Munros he had climbed before – this time it was my turn to tread old ground. It was easy enough that first time in summer with Alastair, so I had no fears about it this winter day.

It would be easy.

Beinn Bhrotain and Monadh Mor are two lumpy hills tacked onto the end of the long plateau bounded by the Dee, Spey, Feshie and Lairig Ghru. This vast area can be intimidating on a winter day like today, with low cloud, disorientating snow, and high winds. How cold would it be on the tops?

We walked along the landrover track, bantering as far as the Allt Garbh, where the real work begun. Up the steep, heathery hillside we climbed, following rushing water over dark rocks, to the snow. Then into thick cloud, and things immediately became less obvious. The burn disappeared under a shallow, disorientating bowl of snow, and we headed vaguely upward, cloud thickening with altitude, whiteness all around. Eyes searched for tiny details, something to gain some perspective with, some orientation . . . the burning had gone from my thighs, and our motion was less work. The slope must be easing. We must be on the summit plateau now.

"Another fifteen minutes in this direction?" I suggested.

Twenty minutes elapsed, then twenty-five. We must have missed the top. But where were we exactly? The summit might only be a few yards away, but we couldn't see that far. Fortunately it was marked by a trig point so we should at least recognise it.

"Let's set up a search grid," Billy suggested, and we quartered the ground. Twenty minutes of this, and we were close to quitting. The wind was strong and, though we were safe for the moment in our warm clothing, this was no place to linger. A metallic taste of defeat filled my mouth. I didn't want to give up! "Five more minutes" I said. And then, what was that? The summit cairn! Disappointment immediately turned to exhilaration. We had found it! We had navigated to the top! It felt like a huge achievement.

Five minutes earlier, defeated, we had planned to head back down the hill, bagless. Now, buoyed by our successful discovery, we headed onwards for Monadh Mor – an equally plateau-like top. The col between these two hills is easy to find from Beinn Bhrotain, but the top of Monadh Mor might be a more elusive target. We set a bearing and headed upwards, more in hope than expectation. Then, nearly 2km later and bang on the estimated time, a cairn materialised out of the fog. Bingo!

"What skill!" I boasted.

Billy was more realistic. "We got lucky," he said.

The side of Monadh Mor is steep, so we continued northward until it was safe to descend at Loch nan Stuirteag, which atmospherically appeared right as we broke out of the cloud. Tendrils of mist lay across its waters, surrounded by snowy slopes; and we dropped into dark Glen Geusachan and the long walk back to my car.

"I'm tired," I said as we began the drive. "Talk to me."

"No, you talk," said Billy, and fell asleep.

Back home, the Jobcentre sent me on a course. I had been unemployed since leaving university six months previously, and they were giving me a kick in the pants. The course leader treated us like children, and some of the other people on the course had a chronic lack of self-esteem. It was a desperate environment.

"Now, CVs," said the course leader, as if I hadn't been filling them out every week. "You need to put your achievements on here – now, I know we Scots aren't so good about blowing our own trumpets . . ."

"There's nothing wrong with being Scottish!" yelled one man, jolting us awake. He picked up his chair, threw it across the room, and stormed out.

How did I get mixed up with people like this? *Get me out of here!*

I went back to the Jobcentre. I had a minimum wage job doing data entry by the end of the week.

Seana Bhraigh *(shan-na vray)* – *the stupid ploy*
927m OS 20 NH 281878

The Kingshouse Hotel – with a band in – was a fine place to bring in the New Year: the drink flowing until well after midnight, and a large cheerful party dancing to the band. Bonnie didn't drink, so drove us all back to Clashgour where the festivities continued.

Next day, restorative walks were planned in the Black Mount by all except Billy and me. We drove north through the eerily empty landscape of New Year's Day Scotland for Seana Bhraigh. One of the remotest Munros on a cold January 2nd? It was a stupid plan. It was cold that night, sleeping in the car park of the Aultguish Inn: approximately –10° C, and there was ice to scrape off the inside of the car windows before we could drive the short distance for Inverlael.

On one of the shortest days of the year, with thick snow

down to sea level, we didn't finally start walking until 11am, two hours after sunrise – even though we needed all the daylight we could get for this walk. However, in good spirits, we set off up the glen, the snow varying between ankle and knee deep. Breaking the trail was hard work.

We slowly covered the uphill miles. A group of lochans stand at a point that would mark, in terms of effort expended, the summit of any normal big hill. This was only halfway up Seana Bhraigh, and there were further ups and downs to follow. On a cliff edge overlooking the final piece of descent before the pull to the summit, the sun set. Hopefully we could negotiate this area in the dark! Our pace increased, to wring maximum benefit from the remaining glimmer of light in the sky. The summit was reached an hour and a half after sunset, six and a half hours after setting off. Grinning in the glare of each other's torches, we shook hands in the style of gentlemen climbers on a month-long ascent in the Himalaya, not ordinary Joes on half a day in Scotland.

Retracing our steps was easier than expected. The sky remained clear with a glitter of stars – a grey beach of them – and our footprints in the snow made for easy navigation. However it was disconcerting to find the downhill effort no easier than the thigh-burning ascent. We stopped a couple of times to marvel at the stars and eat the last of our rations, and were chilled to the bone within a few minutes of each stop. "What would our chances of survival be if one of us broke a leg?" we wondered, and pushed the result of the calculation to the back of our minds. My glove stuck to the metal of my axe, and the cold drained the power from my torch. Fortunately I had a spare battery. It was cold, much colder than the previous night. It was 11pm by the time we finally reached the road and the car.

When we woke next morning, the bottles of Irn Bru in the car had frozen solid. The inside of the car windows were covered in ice. I was wearing everything including ski mitts and a balaclava. I didn't want to get out of my sleeping bag. If only there was a hole in the bottom I could put my feet through and drive! But a cup of tea at Tarvie truckstop –

the first place we had seen open in two and a half days in this vast snowy landscape – stilled our chattering bones.

And that is the story of our ascent of Seana Bhraigh on the 2nd of January.

Creag Meagaidh *(crayg meg-ee)* – *predisastered* 1130m OS 34/42 NN 418875

One spring there was a good fall of snow, and Ally and I agreed to head for an easy winter route in Coire Ardair. It was to be my first proper roped winter climb, and I was nervously anticipating it. But when two people fell to their deaths in Coire Ardair a few days before our trip, I phoned Ally to express serious doubts about the wisdom of our plan.

"I don't know what you're worried about," he responded with the cheerful sang froid of one blessed by an underactive imagination. "It's been *predisastered*; we'll be OK."

We never did the route, and I never saw Ally again. He headed off to America soon afterwards and now has children there. But I went up Creag Meagaidh myself the next year.

The sun shone bright on high snow and gold-brown lower ground as I stepped out of my car beneath the Moy Corrie. Sunshine, unaccustomed sunshine after a couple of weeks in the grey city, flooded my body with Vitamin D. Yet clouds were already gathering, and winter days are short. I pushed myself hard up steep ground to get high before the sun went. High around Moy Corrie, the cloud jellyfish joined into one solid grey mass; but it didn't spoil the beauty of this round bowl of a corrie, a pure black lochan nestling at its bottom, walled by white-snowed cliffs. I climbed steepish mixed rock and snow, working with the axe, but without exposure: the best of terrain.

Once established on the ridge above Moy Corrie, the view down the other side into Coire Ardair took my breath away: Moy Corrie, for all its grand beauty, is a mere appetiser for the monstrous bite out of the land that is Coire Ardair. A line in the snow above this abyss led to the swelling white dome of

Creag Meagaidh's plateau. The sky turned grey, then dark blue, threatening thunder perhaps. The snow was tinged green and dirty yellow. Creag Meagaidh's primevally perfect summit dome has a shape untainted by irregularity, and the snows on its sacred summit subtly changed colour as I ascended. There was something transcendent about the day; the barrier between Two Worlds seemed wafer-thin on the summit of Creag Meagaidh, late on a winter's day in a threatening thunderstorm. It felt like the summit of the world, just a few metres below the roiling cloud.

I descended Creag Meagaidh's southwest ridge into the Moy Burn as the sun set and walked along the road back to my car in the dark, the heavy rain and lightning never quite materialising.

Meall Buidhe (myal boo-ee) – the misery of Knoydart
946m OS 33/40 NM 849989

Whenever I looked at Meall Buidhe on the map, I assumed I'd climb it one day from Carnoch or perhaps Inverie. In the end, we approached from the north, from Barrisdale.

Barrisdale was a dive, a cold, heartless private bothy that the walker must pay to visit. However, it is uniquely well situated for the remote hills of Knoydart, hills that are almost impossible to visit in a daytrip except by the fittest of walkers, and then only in summer. For this reason, Barrisdale becomes an integral part of the whole miserable experience of visiting Knoydart. I went with Mark, a friend whom I only met to go walking with. He was that rare creature, a keen rock climber who also liked bagging Munros.

Mark parked at Kinloch Hourn and the pair of us walked in to Barrisdale. The 10km walk up and down the side of Loch Hourn is a chore, but the islands in Barrisdale Bay are quite singular – I imagined a castle on the steepest one. Arriving in gathering darkness, Mark announced he was off for a swim. What? It wasn't exactly warm. But Mark has to be clean before getting into his sleeping bag for the night, so while I cooked dinner, he went skinny-dipping with his headtorch in the nearby river. Hardcore.

The next day was wet but I was determined, having walked so far in, not to miss out on Luinne Bheinn. The peculiar darkness of Knoydart – caused by the thick deadness of the ever-present clouds and closeness of the crowding mountains – is oppressive on short-of-light winter days like today, but hard exercise is the answer to any depression brought about by the weather. We steamed up the stony, wet path in Gleann Unndalain, past solitary birch and rowan trees, on to the col, then powered up to the summit. Bagged! A relief. In barely more than an hour and a half from the bothy.

The ground between Luinne Bheinn and Meall Buidhe is classic Knoydart country: rough, knobbly, time-consuming, hard going, and a nightmare to navigate in mist. Mark started to pull in front, his superior fitness showing. Our second Munro of the day eventually came, but it was hard work. All we had to do now was return to the bothy; but it was difficult finding an easy descent line on the northern slopes of Meall Buidhe. Once down, I wanted to sink into the thick grass at the head of the Gleann an Dubh-Lochain, but instead we pounded on and up for the Mam Barrisdale, and a straightforward descent, boots and bodies wet, back to the bothy.

I lay on my sleeping bag for a few minutes rest, exhausted: whilst Mark took himself off to the nearest river to purge his flesh in its freezing waters.

Ladhar Bheinn *(lar ven)* – *I bagging hate*
1020m OS 33 NG 824040

Ladhar Bheinn gave one of the most unpleasant days on the hill *ever*.

I was in remote Barrisdale for the weekend with Mark, the hardy gentleman who bathes every night in the nearest suitable river in the absence of a real shower, but even he baulked at ascending Ladhar Bheinn that wet and stormy Sunday. I had the Munro to bag, so felt duty bound to head, by myself, for the summit.

It was a long wet slog, and on the summit ridge a wet, battered crawl thanks to the wind and stinging, ferocious rain. Navigation was a serious issue. All the way up, I had ample time to question my motivation. I was earning peanuts in a mind-numbing, repetitive job, and lonely through not being involved in a relationship. What was I doing wasting my time climbing some random hill, miles from anywhere, in appalling weather? Munro bagging made me think like this a lot, but I can date my disillusionment with hillwalking, subsequent move to England, and ability to relax and get a life, to ascending Ladhar Bheinn.

At least I got down and home safely. Back down at Barrisdale, soaking wet, weather-beaten and miserable, we still had to shoulder our damp packs for 10km of a walkout over a rough path before reaching the car.

Soon after, I had a job interview with British Aerospace in Preston. They are one of the best employers in the country and I decided I would love to work for them. I had passed the initial interview, various tests in the assessment day, and had been called back for a final interview. It was going well, until the trick question was asked:

"How do you feel about the fact we manufacture weapons?"

Be honest, I thought. "The country needs to defend itself," I said, and they nodded. "We need to stay at the forefront of technology if that is to happen – we don't want to become dependant on the Americans. But –"

No Craig, no!

"– we shouldn't sell weapons to dodgy regimes that oppress their own people."

And with that, my potential career at BAe was over – although I prefer to think it was because they interviewed a better engineer.

Gairich (gayr-ich) – on top of the world
919m OS 33 NN 025995

It's a drive of a hundred and fifty miles to Gairich from Glasgow. Not a hundred and fifty smooth motorway miles; but a hundred and fifty twisting, wheel-clenching miles through the mountain-crowded roads of the West Highlands. We arrived four hours later at the dam at the base of Gairich, and peered out of the windows at the hill, hidden by mists, wiping the windows free of condensation. Alastair, Billy, Brian and I had a good look at the hill, somewhere in the clouds on the far side of the reservoir, rain hammering down like the Deluge.

Twenty-eight minutes we sat in that car, jackets on, ready to go, turning to each other for motivation.

"Naaaahh," we said, simultaneously, and about-turned for a nearby bothy instead.

Thus Gairich remained unbagged, so the next spring Billy and I made sure of it.

We parked at the same spot, but it was unrecognisable: a clear day of blue skies with the hills laid out before us, tops in snow, the loch striated by wind. We crossed the dam in sunshine, the high water line cutting an ugly rim round the reservoir, and walked through the bog looking for the shortest route onto Gairich itself. Gairich is an uncomplicated hill, a steep but simple lump. Once past the dam and onto the hill proper, we peched up steep slopes, stopping gratefully to sunbathe in deep brown heather.

There were a number of things on my mind at that time – job applications, parental and peer pressure, my love life, my future – but they all melted away in the wonderful amnesiac sunshine. What else was there in life except sunbathing half-way up Gairich, the timeless bliss of closing your eyes in the first warm sunshine of the year? Stress poured out of my body into the ground.

We continued on up to the snow-clad summit, the gathering cloud knitting the sky into a grey holey mass; sun shafting through the gaps, views of the rest of Knoydart before us, sun and backlit clouds picking out each peak. Billy raised his axe triumphantly. We were on top of the world.

Of course, the only way to go from the top is back down. I'd left my data entry job, but still didn't know what I was going to do with my life. Perhaps I should go back to university to do a Masters, or join the armed forces? I decided that I would apply to join the navy or RAF should I fail to find a job by the end of the summer.

Sgurr nan Ceathreamhnan *(skoor nan kyeroonan?)* – *backpacking over Sacred Mountain* *1151m OS 25/33 NH 057228*

In *Hamish's Mountain Walk*, the book that inspired my early hillwalking more than any other, Hamish Brown states that his favourite British map is OS 25. Unfold it, and the scar of a single-track road cuts diagonally from the middle of the left edge of the map to the middle of the top edge. Apart from that, it is wall-to-wall, hardcore contours: hills, and lots of them, untroubled by evidence of human presence, and with a few lochs thrown in as a bonus.

It's not my favourite British map (that's probably OS 41), but I see where he's coming from. Some of the best wild country in our otherwise overcrowded island is described in this map: wide, empty heads of glens where it would be possible to go backpacking for a week and not meet another soul.

Sgurr nan Ceathreamhnan lies at the southern end of this area. Poring over the map at home, I decided I would visit this hill.

It was late afternoon when I arrived at the Cluanie Inn, and wandered north into the wilderness up the faint track to the pass of An Caorann Beag. I travelled light: shorts, boots, t-shirt, thick woolly socks, and a small rucksack with food and overclothes were all I took. Tied to the outside of the rucksack were my sleeping bag and mat, and I never carried a stove or pan. Dry oatmeal, chocolate, a water bottle (a reused plastic Irn-Bru bottle), apples and sandwiches were all I needed.

In an earlier club expedition – my first in Kintail – we'd wandered over the Five Sisters and Three Brothers in winter conditions, and Ciste Dubh had been missed out entirely (although super-fit Mark had made the detour himself, catching up with the rest of the group later). So I headed for this entertaining crest of a summit: green fringed on one side with black cliffs on the other, much steeper and narrower than expected. After summiting I continued northwards down more difficult terrain. The descent is steep, but when I reached the wild, trackless glen floor, looking down Upper Glen Affric in the evening light, the feeling was of being in another realm. The road lay far behind, and this long, empty green glen glowing in the late sunlight was all mine.

At Camban bothy I dropped the sleeping bag and continued uphill for Beinn Fhada, sweating as I pounded up the steep slopes as quickly as I could. Once up on the long ridge of this hill (it isn't 'long hill' in Gaelic for nothing, being by itself the same length as the Five Sisters across the glen), I made good time, arriving at the atmospheric summit at sunset. Pointy hills rolled off in every direction, dark ridges crowding like stormy seas to the west.

There was a pair of hillwalking boots, in reasonable condition, sitting at the cairn. Who would leave their boots behind, especially on a hill with such a long walk out? In the gathering gloaming, it remained a mystery.

Back at Camban I slept on the wooden floor of the upstairs loft, hanging my food on a nail in the wall so the bothy mice couldn't reach it.

Next morning dawned bright – unaccustomedly so for Scotland – and the world seemed young, a sense of vigour in the air.

I walked down Glen Affric to remote Alltbeithe Youth Hostel, and took the easy-angled path up Coire na Cloiche, dropping the pack to detour up the small hill of An Socath. A simple summit, but the day's other hills would be more effort, and I re-shouldered the pack to head up Sgurr nan

Ceathreamhnan's long east ridge. This hill looked positively huge. It is defended on all sides by barriers of other hills, far from any road, and I fancied for a short time that I was not climbing a hill in Scotland, but one somewhere else, somewhere three times as vertical. Eventually I reached the tapering spire of the summit, and saw another top – the twin summit – half a kilometre away. Feeling light and happy to be up here, I headed for this second summit, ridges flung everywhere.

Sgurr nan Ceathreamhnan is a complex hill. One of my favourite stories is that no one knows definitively how to pronounce its name – even native Gaelic speakers disagreeing. I don't know if this is true or not, but the thought that *Ceathreamhnan* is some kind of unsayable sacred word adds to its general appeal.

Back on the summit top, I headed steeply down, carefully picking my way through little crags on a path that wends and jumps between small level areas, before heading along the stony ridge of Mullach na Dheiragain. Looking around, it amazed me that the hill opposite, Stuc Bheag, is not classified as a Munro – it is just as prominent as the Mullach. This is a good 18km from the road in Glen Shiel. It is about the same distance to approach from the west, so despite their appealing aspect, walkers must hardly ever visit these remote slopes above Glen Elchaig.

On the way back, I contoured above the loch round the inside of Coire nan Dearcag, and headed back down to Alltbeithe. It was hot, and I could feel that I would suffer from sunburn next day. Twenty minutes immersion in cold water was required to ameliorate the worst effects of the sun. There were a couple of other backpackers at the hostel, the only other people I'd seen all weekend, and they watched me douse myself in the river next to the bridge over the Affric.

All that remained was to walk out, but this is not an easy task. The 'path' quickly deteriorates into a boggy morass. The walker struggles beneath giant green hills on the long walk to the road, surrounded by magnificent scenery perhaps, yet unable to enjoy it, stumbling, slipping and schlopping because of the terrible underfoot conditions. High above, deer effortlessly contoured around the steep slopes of A'Chralaig, and I envied their solid footholds, gritting my teeth at this boggy, ankle-to-knee-deep morass. I reached the road tired and dehydrated, with scratched legs caked in dried mud, but with a sense of pleasure and achievement at the last two days' work.

Ben Alder *(ben al-der)* – *an impromptu plan*
1148m OS 42 NN 496718

One summery Friday evening in Helensburgh, I consulted the West Highland Line timetable, looked at my list of unclimbed Munros, and a plan jumped into focus. Perhaps I could take the train to roadless Corrour station, walk over the hills to a bothy, and reverse the journey on Sunday? The number of potential new Munros excited me, and I packed my rucksack with a feeling of anticipation.

Thus I arrived at Corrour station on Saturday afternoon and walked over the easy Munro of Beinn na Lap. The top wore a mist cap, flowing lightly over the hill. Back down by Ceann Loch Ossian the low cloud had burned off, and the hills revealed themselves in late afternoon sunshine around remote Strath Ossian. Idyllic. I sat by the river. It was tempting to simply walk through Bealach Dubh to the bothy and forget the hills entirely. However, a fast ascent of the remaining four Munros of the day had to be made, and my mind went blank with the effort of the ascent.

These four Munros lay along a high ridge, so it was just a matter of continuing along the ridge to tick them all off. Once up, the cloud dropped again, and the tops were mysterious, affording only occasional glimpses through the mist into deep northern corries or away to giant distant hills.

By Carn Dearg, the last hill, gloaming was well advanced. I wanted to linger: its deep, lochan-filled corrie has an outstanding situation, walled by the Lancet Edge, but instead I descended with as much haste as my tired legs could manage, looking back up at this large, heathery prow in the final light of day.

Culra bothy was the destination, and I could see lights and activity from a distance. I walked into the main room and my glasses steamed over completely, dim blurry shapes of countless bodies in the fug. As to their expressions, I could only guess, but a general murmur and tittering suggested that my presence was unexpected and, at best, a source of curiosity. "Sorry mate," informed a voice, "this room's full. But the back room is free."

I went to the back room, to find a smaller but similar situation, steamy, crowded, and disorientating. "Full up" was the mantra. I silently cursed them all. Who did they think they were, taking over an entire bothy? Did they know nothing? Bothy etiquette says a group should always leave space for strangers. Well, they'd better make room for me! I made a beeline for the fireplace, removed my boots, hung up my socks above the fire, asked a teenager on the bench to budge up, and sat down. 'Try to move me now,' I thought.

We chatted.

They were on an exercise with the Air Cadets, and perfectly pleasant – quite a contrast to the first impression they gave. They'd come up from England on a week-long exercise and the officer knew about this bothy – though obviously not how to use one, as he'd crowded it out. I took an instant dislike to the bothy-etiquette-ignorant officer, although he was transparently keen to establish a rapport between himself and me, the new unknown quantity, so that I would be more amenable to his large group and his leadership. He asked where I had come from today. I told him, and he pretended to be impressed.

I dismissed his loud exclamation of "wow, you must be fit!" as insincere. He looked a lot fitter than me. Perhaps he was saying this as a way of ingratiating me into his group? Or perhaps he was hoping to stroke my ego by making me look big in front of the cadets? For this I perversely liked him even less. I rolled out my mat and lay down on it, covering myself with my jacket.

"Where's your sleeping bag?" he asked, perturbed.

"Don't have one."

"But what are you going to do?"

"Have an uncomfortable night."

It was true I wasn't looking forward to a cold shivery night, but it was only going to be for a few hours. It saved carrying the weight of the sleeping bag, and it wasn't the first time I'd done this. This time the leader was appalled, but at last the emotion he expressed seemed spontaneous and genuine, and not cribbed from the Bumper Book of Military Cadet Motivation. I finally warmed to him. He generously offered his bivvy bag, a new lightweight design that he had been asked to test. It was definitely better than the jacket, though still filled with condensation by next morning.

The Air Cadets were woken reluctantly by the officer's alarm, and then by his noisy moving around, his ghettoblaster with unfashionable music, and general encouraging and chivvying noises. I lay in bed and secretly enjoyed the spectacle of *Cadet Field Reveille, Plans A-D* in action. They banged cooking pots and rustled in rucksacks for an interminable length of time and I sat up, chewed a handful of dry oats, donned my boots, rolled up my carry mat, thanked the leader for his bivvy bag, and was gone.

It was cloudier, cooler and greyer than the previous day, and the way up Beinn Bheoil unclear. The map was unequivocal however, and the summit quickly reached. Rather than continuing to the Bealach Breabag, I descended partially back the way I came so I could head up the Short Leacas, one of the two scrambling ridges on Ben Alder.

Cliff faces disappeared into mist all round, with a long, green-fringed mountain loch at their base; scenery's basic building blocks. The Leacas was rocky only at its uppermost part, but it was an easy and entertaining scramble once there. The remote summit of Ben Alder, one of the largest hills in Scotland, was a place I had wanted to visit for a long time, but unfortunately the top held little excitement. There was some snow, but otherwise only a vista of featureless, misty terrain. I walked across the plateau on a compass bearing for over 2km before breaking out of the cloud, glad to be where I expected to be, having had to fight the disorientating feeling that comes with walking for a while without reference points.

After big Ben Alder I felt that the last two Munros, much lower, would be easy. This was not to be, with the awkward, unavoidable bump of Beinn a' Chumhainn to go up and down first, and I descended gratefully from the summit of the last Munro, more tired than the previous day, collapsing occasionally into the heather, having to psyche myself up for the continued moorbashing. Finally the track along Loch Ossian to Corrour station was reached, and with an increased, easier stride I headed for a rendezvous with the train, well satisfied with the weekend's efforts and with nine new Munros in the bag. Not bad for an impromptu Friday night plan.

Carn Eige *(karn ay-kih)* – *a big round*
1183m OS 25 NH 123262

It was a Friday evening in early summer at the Kingshouse Hotel. We congregated often at the Kingshouse, as Brian, who'd done temp bar work in summer, had been working there full-time since graduation. It seemed like the ideal spot for a hillwalker, but the isolation and lack of things to do had been driving him crazy. Visiting him seemed like the best way of cheering him up, though in retrospect, watching us all get drunk on his watch can't have been much fun.

This particular night, I boasted to assembled friends that I was going to do a Big Walk. I was reasonably fit, and in determined enthusiasm drove all the way to the dam at Loch Mullardoch, sleeping in my car.

Next morning I rose early to tackle the four Munros to the north of Loch Mullardoch. These hills went fairly easily. I wasn't rushing as I wanted to conserve energy, but at the same time I didn't hang around. My memory of them is blurred, an impression of summits and graceful ridges, with late-season snow clinging to the corries and north sides of the higher ridges. I dropped down from the last Munro to the river at the head of Loch Mullardoch.

Most days, this would be plenty. It was about 20km into the walk and felt like a remote spot – a flat, grassy, pathless area surrounded on all sides by hills, closer to the tracks coming from the west coast than the head of the dam on Loch Mullardoch. Fortunately it hadn't rained for a while, and the river here was easy to cross, its dark, peaty banks exposed by the low water levels. The sun was well up by now, and I indulged in some skinny dipping by a pretty, white-walled gorge in the Abhainn a' Choilich, enjoying the moment as the heat of the day really began. It was to be the last enjoyable part of the day, as the rest was just Hard Work.

Above, Beinn Fhionnlaidh looked intimidating in the heat haze, and the 2500ft reascent up its brutal northwest slope crushed my spirit: turning me from a fit walker floating over the tops in a delight of movement to a plodding curser, sweltering in the heat, leaden and helpless in gravity's merciless grip. And it was no relief to reach the summit, as a 500ft drop led to the ascent of an even higher hill (the highest hill north of the Great Glen); the twin tops of Carn Eige and Mam Sodhail (pronounced, wonderfully, Mam Soul). I looked ruefully back at Beinn Fhionnlaidh, legs aching and salt staining my brow, and encountered a large, enthusiastic group accompanying a fit-looking woman in her 50s or possibly even 60s. They were there to celebrate her 200th Munro. I congratulated her, keeping quiet that it was almost my last.

And there were more Munros to come – Tom a' Choinich was OK, but Toll Creagach really sapped my spirit, as by this point I was running out of energy and had eaten everything, including my emergency oatmeal. I descended the rough northeast side of Toll Creagach, having to sit down to rest a few times – especially once I reached the heather, whose deep, snagging branches I cursed and stumbled through.

By now I was running on willpower alone, and the final straw was the dam. It is actually double-bottomed, with two separate rivers coming out of the base, and I threw a strop when I realised on the far side of the first river that I had to descend down into the second river and back up again to the road. But as soon as I reached the car the pain was forgotten, and I drove back to the Kingshouse with weary limbs, light heart, and bragging rights intact.

"Ah, Mr Craig," said Alastair at the bar, imitating his Kilimanjaro porter, Mr Zachariah. "You very fit. Mr Zachariah give you boiled egg."

Maol Chean Dearg *(myal kan jerrig)* – balance
933m OS 25 NG 924498

I arrived early in the evening in Strathcarron, where the close-knit ridges of Knoydart and Kintail give way to the singular, regal summits of Torridon and Fisherfield.

It was cool, late and bright. Perfect hillwalking weather. The smell of bog myrtle in the air. I walked up the track leading towards Coire Fionnarich bothy. On a lovely evening and without a heavy rucksack it seemed practically effortless, quite different to carrying a sack of coal in the dark and rain over a boggy pass to Kinbreck. Coire Fionnarich is a handsome, substantial two-storey building, and I investigated approvingly – two large, clean ground floor rooms with fireplaces, and a wooden panelled upstairs sleeping space. This would make a good doss for the night. Its situation by the river is exquisite: elevated, open to the sun, with steep hills close by at the back. I plunged my hand in the river outside, enjoying the sensation of the cool rushing water. Water, rock, heather. A Feng Shui expert would very much like Coire Fionnarich.

I filled my bottle and continued on up the path past the Clach nan Con-Fhionn, a phallic white rock around which Fingal once tethered his dog. There are places in Ireland with the same legend, evidence of a common Gaelic culture. I entered the cooler shadow of the Munro above, and ascended the path. Once established on the ridge, it was a matter of putting the head down, and plodding steadily up steep stony slopes to the summit, grey quartzite giving way to marbled sandstone. The prospect here an hour or two before sunset was extremely fine.

The shadow of Maol Chean Dearg crept up the big blank flank of Sgor Ruadh opposite to the east. Rock-girt lochans are situated at various levels below to the north and west, with the shadowed horn of An Ruadh Stac impressively close to the west. To the north was Liathach's distant serrated, sun-kissed ridge, all Torridon laid out, with a deep, dizzying rent of a corrie below. The sun was setting to the west, and complicated ben and sea views were all around. A good old linger, and then I headed down before the last of the light went.

I brewed a meal of rice and tea in Coire Fionnarich, content in the beauty of the situation and the day's exercise, though a restlessness bubbled through me, refusing to die down. A Feng Shui expert would like Coire Fionnarich, but would have words to say about the imbalance of my Munro-obsessed lifestyle. My feverish bagging – though nearly over – had been interfering with my social life and emotional and financial health.

Ben Wyvis *(ben wiv-iss)* – *the compleationist* *1046m OS 20 NH 463684*

Ben Wyvis, my last Munro.

It is a hill whose smooth bulk had brought nothing but disparaging comments from Billy and me, and whenever a plan was hatched to visit Ben Wyvis, some more interesting alternative always arose to scupper our plans. Finally, I had visited every other Munro, and only Ben Wyvis remained.

As Ben Wyvis is quite a drive from Glasgow, only a select group of Brian, Alastair, Mark, and I were free on my chosen weekend to head north to the Aultguish Inn. Once we dropped our stuff at the bunkhouse, we headed for the hill. It was an unappealing, rainy day, with a cloud base two feet above sea level; but we were there, so might as well climb the thing.

A boggy path led to an eroded zig-zig up a steep shoulder, to the summit plateau which was a revelation – beautifully soft moss which could and should be walked barefoot, were it not for the torrential freezing rain and by now, driving wind. A quick-as-possible stop at the summit to partake in bottles of celebratory whisky and port, and we retraced our steps without lingering.

Brian took a short-cut and ended up a good kilometre behind, cursing the peat hags above the forest. Catching up at last he told us that he'd bought a computer, and was going to combat his boredom by writing a history of the Kingshouse.

The Aultguish bunkhouse had huge, steaming baths of peaty whisky-coloured water and, relaxed, we took to the bar. It closed early as the owner – an entertaining host when on form – had been carousing all the previous night and still felt the worse for wear.

"What are you going to do now you've finished?" people asked out of curiosity. 'Keep going up the hills' I thought. I had just turned 23, wasn't long out of university, and was too young to hang up my boots. However, there were other things missing from my life that needed addressing. "Get a woman and a decent job!" I half-joked.

Shortly afterwards I was in Aberdeen, being interviewed for another ROV post.

"It says on your CV you like rugby – what position?" asked the interviewer.

"Second row," I said – even though I hadn't played since school, or bulked up since then either. He leaned back in his chair.

"I think we'll take a chance on you. The works team is short at second row . . ."

PART FOUR
The Marilyns

The Marilyns are the Real Ale of bagging – only the hillwalking equivalent of bearded, half-pint quaffing supernerds get into bagging the Marilyns, those bumps of Britain with an all-round drop of 500ft, no matter their actual height.

Having finally got a decent job offshore, I had time on my hands when at home. Rather than sit in my local pub like other single offshore workers, I decided to travel round the country, taking pictures for my new website loveofscotland.com. In the meantime, I learned about the Marilyns: they are everywhere, in all sizes, and can be great fun. If you can't be bothered with a big walk, there is a Marilyn nearby for you. If you want to write an outdoor column, and worry that there are not enough hills to last more than a couple of years, then the Marilyns offer a near-inexhaustible supply. The Marilyns are wonderful, a list big enough and flexible enough with which to do whatever you want. My hillwalking friends, most of whom still treated 3,000ft as some kind of minimum requirement, indulged my enthusiasm for this new list in a bemused but kindly manner.

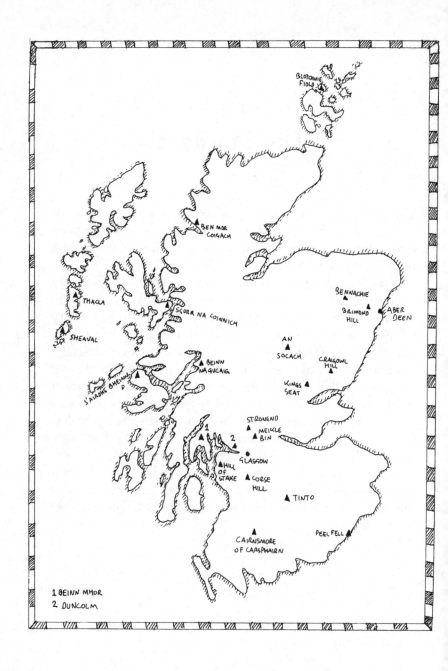

BLOTCHNIE
FIOLD

BEN MOR
COIGACH

BENNACHIE

BRIMOND
HILL

ABER
DEEN

THACLA

SCURR NA COINNICH

AN
SOCACH

SHEAVAL

CRAIGOWL
HILL

BEINN
NAGUCAIG

KINGS
SEAT

S'AIRDNE BHEINN

STRONEND

MEIKLE
BIN

1

2

GLASGOW

HILL
OF
STAKE

CORSE
HILL

TINTO

PEEL FELL

CAIRNSMORE
OF CARSPHAIRN

1 BEINN MHOR
2 DUNCOLM

Peel Fell – *the start of 'The Walk'*
602m OS 80 NY 626997

I rarely visited the Borders. As a Munrobagger, there was no reason to do so. But this was a chance I couldn't miss. Dave Hewitt, author of *Walking the Watershed* and editor of *The Angry Corrie*, had asked me along to Peel Fell in the Cheviots, right on the border, to commemorate the tenth anniversary of his huge walk along the entire watershed of Scotland, from the border through the Lowlands and Grampians, into Knoydart and finally up to Cape Wrath.

I drove down through ill-frequented country, all trees and low featureless ridges; as empty of people as the Highlands, and just as full of echoes of the past. The land itself seemed to sigh. Without obvious wilderness landscapes, the emptiness is even more remarkable. At the lonely hamlet of Saughtree, I turned onto an even less-travelled road. The start for Peel Fell lay just over the border. I was in rare company – Andy Wightman, author of *Who owns Scotland?*; Alan Dawson, compiler of *The Relative Hills of Britain*; arch Marilynbaggers Ann and Rowland Bowker; super-keen hillwalker Richard Webb; and others. We set off up a forest track in warm April sunshine. We continued up to a burn at a bend in the track, and beat on through young Sitka spruce forestry. Once on the top, only Richard bothered to head over the Border fence into Scotland.

"Ah, my kind of country!" he said.

It was a bit flat-topped for me – but it was a nice day and good to be out with a unique group. Dave had the most poignant memories: ten years ago, time-rich and penniless, he had set off from here for his big walk to Cape Wrath. We walked round a ridge of sorts rather than heading straight back, and found another track taking us down through the forest to the road at our starting point. Dave talked about walks in the Keilder forest and picked up some litter from the path. I had heard about people doing things like this: picking up other people's litter, walking right up the middle of a muddy track (to avoid the spread of erosion); but this was the first time I had seen it in action, and it encouraged me to do likewise in future.

"How many Marilyns have you done?" asked Dave, and I had to tell him I had no idea. I had only recently come across them in *The Angry Corrie*, and had just a vague notion of what and where they were. He gave me a copy of Alan's book, its dry, terse lists an Aladdin's Cave of promised experiences. Just as I was coming towards the end of the Munros, a whole new world of bag-and-tick hillwalking opened up to me.

Brimond Hill – *offshore life*
266m OS 38 NJ 856091

I was working in the oil industry. My first trip offshore was a disaster. I'd been seasick for a whole week – imagine a never-ending, world's worst hangover – and the crew nicknamed me 'Sally' for my rapid dashes for the gunnels to puke. The boat was elderly, a trawler refitted for surveys, and the exhaust from the engine seeped into the cabins for the survey crew. These cabins had been built above the top deck, but the ship's funnel had not been lengthened accordingly, and its fumes choked us when the portholes were opened. The boat was infested with cockroaches. They scuttled out of the cutlery drawer when I opened it, and the first mate suggested 'you might want to fumigate your bags for cockroach eggs before you leave.' I had a lot to learn about the job, and to top it all, the team leader was a bully. This was not the lifestyle for me. But I needed the money, and fortunately every subsequent trip offshore was better than this hellish introduction!

Staying in Aberdeen for my offshore training, I had a car for a couple of weeks, and once work was over there were still a good couple of hours of daylight. Deciding to make the most of it and explore this new part of the country, I headed for Brimond Hill. When I stopped at a garage outside the city for directions, the owner pointed to his teenage daughter.

"You can take her," he cackled, "she'll show ye the way." She blushed. I *think* he was kidding.

Brimond Hill didn't take long, an elevated carpet of beautiful heather blooming in the late August air. All around were rolling green fields, leading to higher heathery hills and the dark massy line of the Grampians in the distance, black against the setting sun. In the other direction, Clochnaben with its summit tor, and the curiously named Tyrebagger Hill. To the east was Aberdeen – my new home. As the sun lingered on the city while everything else fell into shadow, I wondered what life in Aberdeen would bring. Driving along the narrow country backroads, I noticed the local architecture. The castles were different here.

Back at the hotel, we newbies discussed which night that week we would hit the pubs. Some grizzled sailors were also at the bar. They were discussing which night they would stay *in*. Welcome to the offshore life!

Bennachie *(ben-a-hee) – a strange effect these stones on me* 529m OS 38 NJ 662227

It was summer in Aberdeen, but the tops of the high hills had already started to change colour, the purple heather gone. It was a good time to leave work and head along the criss-crossing roads of the Aberdeenshire countryside for a hill. Bennachie, a prominent landmark with its unusual summit tor, was my target.

The hill is celebrated in legend and song, but looks unprepossessing from the map. Before visiting, I wondered what the fuss was about. After all, it is only 1733ft high. But the name of its unusual summit tor, Mither Tap (Mother Top) speaks of an ancient reverence for the hill. It rises out of the fat fields and woodlands of old Pictland, surrounded by prehistoric monuments, and Mither Tap provides an unsurpassed panorama of the entire Grampian area. The view from the tor takes in the Mounth in the south, Aberdeen to the east, the Cairngorms and foothills to the west, and the rolling farmland of Aberdeenshire and Buchan to the north, all the way to another small but prominent landmark, Mormond Hill.

I headed up a dry forest track beneath the Mither Tap, broached the forest, and was soon on top. Relaxing on the sloping edge of the granite tor, I nearly slid off to my death. Scare averted, I held on a bit tighter for a full appreciation of the view. The wedge-shaped shadow of Bennachie glided like a shark's fin across the Lowland fields of Aberdeenshire, with the high flats of the city gleaming in the evening sun. Bands of high cloud advanced across the North Sea, but my gaze lingered northwest, on Ben Rinnes and the mysterious, mist-shrouded Tap o' Noth. Some tendrils of mist were beginning to creep up the sides of Bennachie too, so I headed for the actual summit, a short distance from Mither Tap and only marginally higher. Dusk came and I left, racing darkness to the forest and the road back to Aberdeen and a pint with my new colleagues. I had glimpsed the soul of this reserved and taciturn part of Scotland: not in the bright lights and bars of the city, but in touching the granite of Mither Tap.

Alone on top of Bennachie
A strange effect these stones on me
Snake in heather, hind in trees
"I am ancestor – come join me."

Tinto – *my Lanarkshire*
711m OS 72 NS 953344

Lanarkshire? Neds, Buckfast, sectarianism, Old Firm football fans, the wreck of heavy industry, corrupt local politics, great indie music. These images are hard to reconcile with the other

Lanarkshire: country backroads, green vales, Clydesdale horses, the Falls of Clyde, Lanark Ridings, a UNESCO World Heritage village and flowing Southern Upland hills.

This is my Lanarkshire. Not the Lanarkshire of machine politicians and modified hot hatchbacks and Mr Universe contestants and Daily Record models: no, the eternal fields and hills, neglected medieval castles standing on crags above the Clyde, and pastoral lands bounded by stands of ancient trees. These Lanarkshires are congruent; yet we only ever hear of the former.

Tinto lies in the latter.

Climb any prominent height in the once-great city of Glasgow and look south, there – there beyond the last high-rise flat is Tinto, its swelling form delineating the southeast horizon. Tinto is a magic hill, visible from most of the Central Belt, an icon like Ben Lomond or Eildon, though for some reason less recognised. I drove southeast on the M74 on a clear autumn day, cocooned in my car, looking at Tinto all the while. It grew and grew in my windscreen, and I wondered why I had not noticed it before.

I turned off through the backwoods village of Rigside, past a couple of tracksuited single mums pushing their weans in chairs, chatting nine-to-the-dozen, with a solitary, defiant pub the focal point of the village, elevated in the moors. Tinto lies above, smooth-sided and flowing, a line of trees marching up its spine, smaller and more manageable than Highland hills. A local hill. And then Wiston where I parked, a strange ghost village materialising from a stand of forestry with no one about.

I headed up muddy slopes to the end of the trees, and Tinto itself rose directly above. The going slowed, thanks to a steepening slope that ends in a spur of cliff, scree fanning the base. This cliff gives Tinto its most recognisable outline from the east or west, and walkers must go around it to reach the rounded, wind-blown summit.

On my first visit, northwest was the only familiar aspect, the rest an unfamiliar jumble of hills. But the second time round I was living in Edinburgh and more familiar with the Borderlands, able to spot new friends, the Pentlands to the northeast with Biggar at their base. Tinto, though moated by the Clyde, is actually closer to Edinburgh than Glasgow; with the Moorfoots east, Culter Fell south, and the Lowthers in the distance. Tinto's secret as a viewpoint is that it is a Central Belt outlier of the Southern Uplands, separated from them by a curve of the Clyde. The large cairns have a prehistoric air, giving the impression this was a popular hill with the first people of the area. For my first time on Tinto, I descended via Fatlips Castle (which is nothing more than some foundations in knee-high heather); on my second visit I climbed it with an Airdrie-raised astrophysicist and a transvestite called Keith.

That's Lanarkshire for you. Buckfast, neds, sectarianism: only 10% of the real story.

Beinn na Gucaig (beyn na goo-cayg) – boring hills and boring hillwalkers
616m OS 41 NN 063653

Beinn na Gucaig is a hill nobody climbs. 600-odd metres high in an unfashionable spot round the corner from Glencoe, it is surrounded by much higher hills, both in terms of altitude and quality. No one is likely to give Beinn na Gucaig a second glance. I didn't, and neither did any of my hillwalking companions, until one night we stayed at Inchree and found ourselves looking for a walk to do on a miserable, wet Sunday.

"Look," I said, "the hill behind the hostel, Beinn na Gucaig, is in my Marilyns book!"

And so up Alastair, Duncan and I went.

The hill provided little more than perfunctory exercise, until for some reason I removed my boots a mile from the top and, barefoot, raced the others to the trig point (they won). We descended to the forest road, with an unexpected view of Lochan Lundavra, and lower down a large, handsome, and to me completely unknown waterfall on the Abhainn Righ. There is a saying that there is no such thing as boring hills, only boring hillwalkers; and we weren't bored – not today, anyway.

Hill of Stake – *in search of a view*
522m OS 63 NS 273630

Hill of Stake is the highpoint of the Renfrewshire Heights, an area with which I was briefly obsessed. I was grappling with the problem of finding the best viewpoint of the Firth of Clyde for my website, and pencilled in a few areas (Dunrod, Hill of Stake, Quadrocks above Largs, Bishops Hill above Dunoon, the hills above Rhu, *und so weiter*) for investigation.

Camera in bag, I pulled up at the Muirshiel Country Park on a fine late-summer day. I was soon away from the visitor centre and surrounded by trees. Crossing a bridge and emerging from the wood, I bade farewell to the rough track and headed on to the open moor.

Above lay a spur of Hill of Stake, and I plodded up it in the sunshine, ground squelching beneath my feet. Mossy bogland. I was looking forward to getting higher up.

The summit was little more than a half-hearted rise in the general lumpy moorland. I was glad to reach it. Schlurping through these bogs was hot work, but the view was disappointing. Whichever way I looked, bogs filled the view. Arran can be glimpsed in a gap to the southwest, but there is no wide panorama.

As it turns out, the best viewpoints I've found for the Firth of Clyde aren't at the top of hills after all.

Kings Seat – *Shakespeare and stones*
377m OS 53 NO 230330

King's Seat is aptly named. On this hillside Dunsinane, Macbeth's fortress, once stood – at least, according to Shakespeare. There really was a King Macbeth, but Shakespeare's story takes huge liberties with the facts: the Duncan of history was a young and unsuccessful early 11th century king, who died invading Macbeth's powerbase of Moray. When Macbeth ruled, he was considered a capable king. Shakespeare was being *politick*, not accurate: James VI of Scotland, who became king of England shortly before the creation of *Macbeth*, was descended from Duncan and his son Malcolm.

There is also a legend that the Stone of Destiny is hidden in this hillside. One of the many tales regarding this Coronation Stone of the ancient Scots has it that, informed of Edward I of England approaching with his army in 1296, the Stone's guardians – the monks of Scone Abbey – hid it somewhere in a hole on King's Seat, replacing it with a worthless slab of Perthshire sandstone for Edward to carry triumphantly away. According to the legend, this is why the Scots demanded but did not pursue the return of the stone after Bannockburn had put them in the ascendant. Unfortunately, in the confusion and bloodshed around the Wars of Independence, the keepers of the secret location of the real stone died before they could pass it on. So – or so they say – somewhere in this hillside lies the real Stone of Destiny: a carved slab of black marble, possibly of meteoric origin, said to be the pillow Jacob lay on when he had his vision recorded in the Bible. A stone with properties analogous to the Black Stone set in the southeast corner of the Kabba, and matching key points in the history of the Dome of the Rock. Kings Seat could, perhaps, be the site of the Jews' messianic Third Temple.

But despite keeping a keen eye open, I saw no black monoliths inscribed with ancient symbols. I saw sheep, grass, deep heather, grey stones, a little bit of snow and, on reaching the summit, Dundee.

S' Airdhe Bheinn *(sayr-ee ven)* – *the wasted weekend* *292m OS 47 NM 471537*

This unusually named peak is not really a peak at all, but the rim of a tiny volcanic crater, 300m x 800m across – or at least, it *seems* to be a volcanic crater. It is a minor volcano at only 292m high and 300m x 800m across – no Kilimanjaro or Fuji-san, S'Airdhe Bheinn – but this area is renowned for past volcanic activity, and so could well be the remains of a volcanic crater or vent-hole. It even has a miniature crater lake and is a pretty cool place despite its tiny size. Even the dense mists that obscured any views at all on our rampart walk failed to dampen the sense of being somewhere special the weekend Alastair and I visited.

Alastair wasn't feeling too well, and had brought work to do from his stressful job. It was just the two of us. Alastair wanted to work, so back at the car he pulled files from his briefcase, poring over them. This wouldn't do! The Bright Lights of Tobermory were calling! We drove into town for a pint in the Mishnish – a place that was filling up with folk musicians and a place I would willingly have stayed – but Alastair was having none of it, so we drove to Glenforsa and walked the cold miles to a dingy Tomsleibhe bothy, ten kilos of coal on my back and ten tonnes of worry on Alastair's. Sitting there, miles from the action in Tobermory, no real hills getting climbed, we could barely be bothered to get a decent fire going, never mind a conversation. I watched him fret and took a silent pull on a can of cheap lager. Waste of a ferry fare and weekend, really.

Corse Hill – *a day's escape*
376m OS 64 NS 598464

Early one frosty Sunday morning, I set off on my bike across the centre of Glasgow from the West End to Eaglesham. The roads were blissfully traffic-free, but the air was so cold I had to stop at Woolworths in Shawlands to buy extra fleecy gloves, before continuing uphill through a city that was slowly awakening and going about its groggy-eyed business.

It is an uphill ride all the way from the bridge over the Clyde to the end of the track on Corse Hill's summit, and I was feeling it. My bike was a neglected second-hand model, heavy and rusty-chained. But the final few miles of forest track went quite easily, and I met a rambling club coming down. I rode to the very summit, pedalling over the last few trackless yards so I could touch the trig point without getting out of the saddle.

What a view! Glasgow laid out to the north, with the

Campsies behind, the Highlands behind even them; more snow on the Ochils than the Western Highlands. To the southwest, Arran and Ailsa Craig, and I hurt my eyes staring into the sun at the Galloway and Lowther hills. I laughed delightedly at the quality of the view from such a modest brae. The descent down the forest trail took concentration, but it was a breeze freewheeling down the public road back to Glasgow.

A brilliant day, fair set me up for the week.

Meikle Bin – *short walk, old friends*
570m OS 578/64 NS 667822

The 'traditional' Boxing day walk saw me, Billy, David and Cameron drive to Campsie to pick up Brian. He had stayed up all night talking to his dad and drinking Irn Bru and whisky, but groggily joined us for a quick blast of winter air on Meikle Bin.

The cold top was scoured by wind, spindrift-laden and foggy, and we didn't linger, but it was a good walk, and a pleasure to see old friends and get out of the house. In the shelter of the forest we shared mince pies and whisky minia-tures. Cameron told us about the time he caught the train to London and found himself sitting opposite a woman from 'the nice part' of the Raploch, Stirling; an area then in the news due to the anti-social antics of the Haney clan, and its ferocious matriarch Big Mags. On hearing that she was from the good part of the Raploch, Cameron offered:

"You'll no have had a run-in wi' Big Mags, then!"

"*I am Big Mags,*" the woman glowered back.

An Socath (*ann so-cach*) – *spindrift*
944m OS 43 NO 079799

An Socath. It isn't a glamorous hill, but its unpretentious, smooth, easy slopes are fun and welcoming rather than a

The young author: *The Cobbler* (Chapter 1)

Brian: *Pap of Glencoe* (Chapter 1)

Approaching Clashgour Hut: *Stob a' Coire Odhair* (Chapter 1)

Clashgour close-up: *Stob a' Coire Odhair* (Chapter 1)

Looking across Galloway from Benyellary: *The Merrick* (Chapter 1)

In Coire Lagan: *Inaccessible Pinnacle* (Chapter 1)

The Grey Mare's Tail: *White Coomb* (Chapter 2)

The ice axe game: *Meall a' Phubuill* (Chapter 2)

Ben More, Mull: *Ben More, Mull* (Chapter 2)

The pole trick: *A'Mhaigdean* (Chapter 2)

A'Mhaigdean summit: *A'Mhaigdean* (Chapter 2)

Lochnagar summit: *Lochnagar* (Chapter 3)

On top of the world: *Gairich* (Chapter 3)

The heart of Knoydart: *Meall Bhuidhe* (Chapter 3)

Glen Torridon from Maol Chean Dearg: *Maol Chean Dearg* (Chapter 3)

An Socach spindrift: *An Socach* (Chapter 4)

c Pollaidh and Suilven from Ben Mor Coigach: *Ben Mor Coigach* (Chapter 4)

Baling out the boat: *Beinn Mhor, Cowal* (Chapter 4)

Strathmore from the Sidlaws: *Craigowl Hill* (Chapter 4)

Bagh a' Caisteal from Sheabhal: *Sheabhal* (Chapter 4)

Beinn Trilleachan and Kinlochetive: *Beinn Trilleachan* (Chapter 5)

Rois Bheinn sunset: *Rois Bheinn* (Chapter 5)

Table traverse: *Beinn Damph* (Chapter 5)

Cadair Idris summit ridge: *Cadair Idris* (Chapter 6)

Author on Pen-y-Fan: *Pen-y-Fan* (Chapter 6)

Miles on Cairngorm: *Geal Charn Mor* (Chapter 7)

Billy's last Munro: *Beinn Narnain* (Chapter 7)

Bone Cave: *Breabag* (Chapter 7)

On Beinn a' Chrulaiste: *Beinn a' Chrulaiste* (Chapter 7)

Ascending Carn Ban: *Carn Ban, Freevater* (Chapter 7)

plodding chore. Am I alone here? Does anyone else find An Socath such a pleasant ascent?

Billy and I visited one sunny winter day, deep snow lying right down to the road. Garrons gathered by the fence as we prepared to set off up the snowy track. I'd had my best-ever bumslide on this hill – taking off like a snowboarder on a hump and ripping my trousers – and nearly my skin – to shreds. Today was equally snowy, and again a sunny day. We took the track and then followed the burn as far as it would go. We were in a shallow bowl of deep snow, steepening above to An Socath's broad ridge. As we worked our way up the hill in a rising wind, snow crunching and calves burning, the snow disturbed by our feet turned from a pleasant scrunch of crusty powder into something more sinister. Each step released a demon of energy, screaming across the landscape at calf height. Eventually, approaching the broad, shallow spine of the top of the hill, the entire landscape was shifting around us like the surface of the sea in a hurricane. Stinging needles of ice attacked our exposed skin, and we turned heads into our hoods against the onslaught. The spindrift was like daggers, and yet when we eventually lifted our battered eyes a beautiful scene surrounded us: smooth, sculptured hills rendered soft to melting point by their fuzzy surfaces, a vast landscape en-nobled by wastes of blown snow rising into the air, threaten-ing death – well, a severe battering at least – to those foolish enough to wander their otherwise nondescript slopes. The entire world was a confusion of blown snow, bright sunshine cutting through, and something solid at our feet persuading us onwards.

We located the summit, a gentle but unmistakeable swelling to a high point on this hill back, and turned as soon as we reached it for lower, less frantic ground. Eventually we des-cended far enough to drop our hoods, enjoying the exhilarat-ing feel of freezing superstreams of air against our exposed skin, devoid of spindrift in the relative shelter.

"At least the hill isn't trying to kill us anymore!" said Billy.

Stronend – *Campsie exploration*
511m OS 57 NS 629895

Consider the Campsies. Park at Queen's View, the spot on the A806 where Queen Victoria reputedly gained her maiden view of Loch Lomond. What is the most remarkable sight? Guess what – it is not the Highland host crowding Loch Lomond. It is Dumgoyne, a steep, conical volcanic horn in the Campsie Fells. Yet where do hundreds, maybe thousands head out the city for every weekend? The Highlands. And do they cast a sideways glance at the Campsies as they motor past? No, they do not.

That the Campsies are virtually untrodden is proof that people are daft. For the non-heightist, the Campsies are full of little delights, and on Stronend we were about to discover one, which was all the more enjoyable as we were unaware of it.

On a wintry weekend Billy, Brian, Alastair and I headed for a lung-freshening winter half-day from Glasgow. We'd all been up Earls Seat before, so Stronend was chosen as the half-day's objective. With no expectations except a short workout and some fresh air, we parked a couple miles east of Fintry and headed up steepening grassy slopes to a line of cliffs.

There is a line of weakness in the cliffs, so we investigated, climbing higher into a tiny hidden corrie, made of friable volcanic rock. An unexpected treat. But was this the best way up? We were all standing at different levels in this scambler's room, when Brian, off to one side, made a discovery. A cave. He wandered in . . . and up . . . we followed him. I was last. Above me, I saw his head pop over the line of the cliffs. "Coming up?"

In I went. The cave turned out not to be a cave at all, but a steep-floored chimney, the rock of the cliff face flaking away from the bedrock to create a fissure. I pulled on tough heather roots in this dark, claustrophobic space to get to the top, and had to be hauled up the last step by my more nimble friends. And then my head popped up through the heather, and I was on top of the cliff edge with the others. Covered in dirt, we laughed, and headed uneventfully for the summit of Stronend, with a fine wide view of the edge of the Highlands across the Carse of Forth.

Did you know about this walk? No? Neither did we!

Duncolm – *squalid cities of numbness*
401m OS 64 NS 470775

I was bedsitting in Glasgow between jobs, trying half-heartedly to get a music career off the ground after quitting my offshore job, and it wasn't going very well. Walking back from the pub one night nearly crying in loneliness and frustration, I decided that the only thing I wanted to do next day was to get out of the bleak winter city for a hillwalk.

So next morning I cycled along the dual carriageway of the A82 in dull winter weather, the trees bare sketches, the sky a woe-filled hermetical cap, to Hardgate and up a rough track to the reservoir. From here I struck across soggy moorland to the pudding-bowl lump of Duncolm, considerably refreshed yet still feeling millennial angst, the hillside empty of companionship or comfort. However there were clear views north to Loch Lomond that distracted my attention for a while, and Ailsa Craig, and snow-clad Tinto. Some mountain bikers appeared high on the moorland. Half-day cycle/walk combos from Glasgow are the business, and a great many are possible in the Campsies, Kilpatricks, and Renfrewshire/Lanarkshire moorlands.

I ran down the hill and rode back to my bedsit via Maryhill Road, endorphin levels topped up, calmer and more philosophical if no happier.

Cairnsmore of Carsphairn – *Scotland, distilled*
797m OS 77 NX 594980

When you think of Scotland, what do you see? Is it steeply walled Glencoe, the islands of the west, the neo-classical terraces of Edinburgh, or the mean streets of Glasgow? Perhaps it is none of these. Perhaps it is the Borderlands, perhaps it is Galloway? Scientists merged images of a thousand faces in an attempt to find the average human: the face they came up with was an androgynous, bland, universally attractive one.

In the same way, Galloway and the Borderlands are Scotland distilled: nothing dramatic, nothing grotesquely swollen or diminished, but an attractive landscape of rolling hills, modest towns and villages, fishing rivers, towerhouse castles, and a generally rural air. Much of Scotland's story can be told with reference to events in these glens. The architecture is typically Scots; the gross urbanisation of the Central Belt nearby yet distant in feel; the echoing wilderness of the far Highlands glimpsed only in flashes.

With this in mind, a proper appreciation can be made of Cairnsmore of Carsphairn.

I arrived and parked on a muddy verge in the bright light of early spring, the hillforms still clad in winter grass, the green change already stirring in the Lowlands heralded here by brighter, warmer weather. I negotiated a field of wandering cows, then took a Land Rover track leading long and high into the hills. There were plastic tubs of saltlick lying near the track, left out for the livestock. I left the track and headed up steep short-cropped grass, wind and stones increasing with altitude, but the light remained yellowed-green and bright. At the top, I saw that industry had come to the Galloway and Border hills. Eastwards, proper roads snake to the very summits, and there are thick ruled swathes of Sitka spruce and a whole hillside spined with wind turbines. Although I like the individual elegance of wind turbines, I'm ambivalent towards whole windfarms, and the equilibrium of the day was disturbed.

I descended Cairnsmore of Carsphairn to the west, continuing a natural traverse of the hill. I reached the river, a short section of which has been given the intriguing name on the map of Green Well of Scotland. There is nothing remarkable to justify the name, but perhaps that is the point: this is the land with the rough edges smoothed off, and this river the archetypal source of all.

Ben Mor Coigach *(ben mor coi-gach)* – *the forgotten gem*
743m OS 15 NC 094042

Of all the unfairly neglected hills in Scotland, Ben Mor Coigach probably has the best case before the Hill Neglect Panel. Perhaps Beinn Mor Coigach should be given to another country, one that would treat it with more respect: Wales perhaps, England or Belgium. For Ben More Coigach is superior to many Munros, and holds its own against other well-known sub-Munros like Stac Pollaidh, Suilven or the Cobbler: so it is a mystery why no one talks about, reveres, or climbs Ben Mor Coigach.

A glance at Ben Mor Coigach from the Ullapool road turnoff towards Achiltibuie reveals no reason not to climb. Steep cliffs and the singular peak of Sgurr an Fhidhleir are prominent. Who is not drawn towards these heights? Thus Brian and I, en route to Achnahaird campsite, stopped opposite Ben Mor Coigach and started to walk.

The trek degenerates in a matter of yards into unpleasant bog hopping, and we aimed directly for the sanctuary of the nearest steep ground on the subsidiary ridge of Beinn Tarsuinn. Beinn Tarsuinn is a hillside of thick, jungly heather and reddish-grey Torridonian sandstone; we pulled and stepped our way up. But on the flattish tops a change occurs, with flat grey stones, short green grass and dramatic vistas of the jagged hills of Fisherfield, Flowerdale and An Teallach. The going becomes easier the higher one goes. From Beinn Tarsuinn we wandered over to the collapsed, eroded pile of the summit of Ben Mor Coigach, sand in little V-shaped channels amongst the tundra plains. This is perhaps the least interesting of all the hills in the massif it names, yet it has a fantastic view of Stac Pollaidh through a gunsight-like gap between Sgurr an Fhidhleir and Sgorr Deas an Beinn an Eoin. We headed for the narrow, porcupine ridge of Garbh Coireachan.

I've heard it said that Ben Mor Coigach is unique on the west coast in having a steep face plunging directly to the sea, and while there are plenty of steep hills on the west coast, it is true there are few without some intervening coastal platform.

But the feeling from Garbh Coireachan, although higher, is similar to that from the Mull of Galloway or many other concave coastal cliffs. The unique situation on Ben Mor, in my opinion, is the experience of a hydraesque miniature hill massif, each top on the hill providing a different geology and experience. Garbh Coireachan's narrow ridge with its precipitous seaward side is just one aspect of this.

As we walked out picking our way along the ridge, we saw a GUM Club woman in the distance called Fiona Muriel. In truth her name was just Fiona, but with her shock of spiky peroxide hair she was the spitting image of Muriel Gray, doyenne of the Scottish hills, whose *Munro Show* program had inspired our whole generation into hillwalking. I was slightly ahead of Brian; and as Fiona Muriel came closer I composed a greeting. It was with surprise I realised it wasn't Fiona Muriel at all. It was Muriel Gray herself!

She had two other women with her, women in tank tops and skin-tight jogging trousers. They looked in good shape, but gym, not hill shape; there was an air about them of having been plucked from the BBC canteen for a jolly, their hard-concentrating, gingerly balanced steps in contrast to Muriel Gray's fluid, wiry strides. A stoic 'aye' on both sides, and she was gone. I turned round to enjoy Brian's epiphany: the looking up, the realisation, the big grin. Proof, if any were needed, that Muriel Gray not only didn't take helicopters up the hill: she didn't even just climb Munros.

We were back on the summit of Ben Mor Coigach, and as we were returning east we neglected all the western tops (like Cairn Conmheall, which is different again, probably a quartzite pile) so had only the most exciting top in the range left – Sgurr an Fhidhleir. This top is an arrowhead of a hill, rising in walkable slopes from the south and west but plunging as vertically as one gets in Scotland to the north and east towards a deep lochan, the cliff face having a crease as sharp as a paper aeroplane's nose between the northern and the eastern faces. I have heard this is rated an Extreme climb. The situation is certainly extreme, and just standing on the edge of the summit was exposure enough for me.

We descended gingerly, well away from the edge, to find a steep couloir that led down to Lochan Tuath. The situation here is very fine, deep water with steep hills and cliffs all around and mighty Sgurr an Fhidleir cleaving the air. All that remained was to walk out; bashing through a final couple of kilometres of bog a Royal Marine PE Sergeant would give his pension for.

Beinn Mhor, Cowal *(ben mor)* – *a plan and an adventure* *741m OS 56 NS 108908*

Halfway down ribbon-like Loch Eck on a foul summer's day, Billy and I saw a small stand of boats outside the Whistlefield Inn and had A Plan. We were heading for Beinn Mhor on the roadless opposite shore, but if we hired a rowing boat for the day, we could save ourselves a considerable walk halfway up the length of Loch Eck and back. On other days, I have seen people out fishing in boats on Loch Eck, and it can be an idyllic scene, the trees of Argyll Forest Park swathing the steep shores and the still, deep waters of Loch Eck reflecting a liquid sun. This, however, was a different day entirely. After arranging boat hire with the dubious owner ("Pay *if* you get back," he'd said), we rowed out, until halfway across the loch, the wind-blown waves became too strong. We had to turn 90 degrees to face directly into the wind to reduce the boat's rocking, which was threatening to capsize us.

It was at this point we spotted the crowd that had gathered by the shore, attracted out of the bar in the Inn by the opportunity, perhaps, of betting on our chances of making it across the loch in this weather. This did not fill us with confidence. However it did inspire bravado, and eventually we made it across, dragged the boat well out of the water, tied it to a tree, and started up the hill.

This is possibly a good walk, and can be continued onwards once on the tops to Clach Bheinn. Today though the weather was so foul, the wind so strong, the rain so cold and cutting, that we headed straight back downhill. Summer was supposed to be almost here, but the weather was more like winter with grey clouds, low light levels, and bucketfuls of driving rain. We hadn't been gone long, but still had to bale out the rain-filled boat before cautiously navigating our way back across the loch. But wet as we were, we were grinning. We had had A Plan: and it had led to An Adventure.

A pint next to the open fire in the Whistlefield Inn before heading back home was well justified.

Sgurr na Coinnich *(skoor na koin-ich)* – *the folk you meet* 739m OS 33 NG 762222

I was hitchhiking north to Kintail. I'd reached the Commando Memorial at Spean bridge but darkness would fall soon, and I wasn't sure I'd get another lift after sunset. Then an old Volvo pulled up, and took me all the way.

They were heading for Skye. The driver told me about their campaign against the Skye Bridge tolls. I recognised his name, Alastair Scott. Didn't he have a couple of books in my local library? I'd seen them, but hadn't read them. The covers looked boring.

One day, a while later, I decided to go up Sgurr na Coinnich near Alastair's house. A narrow, stringy road connects Broadford and Kylerhea, and the top of this road is the closest point to the top of Sgurr na Coinnich. I abandoned the car and wandered up tough, overgrown slopes to an airy cairn. It was a shame the clouds were flitting about, and that Beinn na Caillich blocked the view northeast; this hill would be a superlative panoramic viewpoint otherwise, with the whole of Skye spread out west and the mainland (Knoydart, Kintail, Applecross) east. The hill had taken more effort than I expected (or maybe today was one of those can't-be-arsed days) and I couldn't be bothered going over to Beinn na Caillich too.

I subsequently borrowed Alastair Scott's books *Native Stranger* and *Scot Free* from the local library – they are excellent reads.

Blotchnie Fiold – *Bonxie Attack!*
250m OS 5/6 HY 418289

Rousay. Grey sea-girt Rousay, with the low hill cloud-capped and the steep heathery shore rising straight into the mirk. I left my bike on the circuiting coastal road for a walk through a prehistoric, processional landscape of great antiquity. It was a grey-skied evening with a restless sea, gulls wheeling and an eerie sound of seals calling off Eynhallow. I liked this atmosphere, standing by the stones of Midhowe broch, breathing the sea air, scanning the horizon, the steep hill to my back. I decided to leave the hill till tomorrow. It was 9pm, and time for my tea at the hostel, an otherwise unoccupied Victorian house.

The pub was quiet, midweek, and I sat nursing a pint by the bar until a local asked a question, bringing me into their circle. The cloud had cleared by the time I left, and so even at half-past midnight I didn't need lights. Cycling unsteadily, I was captivated by the simmer dim and the view across the Wyre Sound to the low, wind-smoothed whalebacks of the Orkney mainland and the clear streetlights of Kirkwall.

The morning dawned clear and bright. I set off past a prehistoric chambered cairn – so numerous here as to be hardly worth mentioning – and up past a heavily wooded dell around a ruined Victorian mansion, then up through heather onto the hill. At a shallow angle of peat hags near the top I decided to sunbathe for a short while, throwing my rucksack down and laying my head on it.

WHOOSH

What was that?

I opened my eyes and sat up, to locate a seabird wheeling round, eyeing me all the time.

It was coming at me. Strange bird. And then – it's about to hit me! I ducked.

WHOOSH!

Inches from my head, its dead, black eye like a shark. The bonxie!

I'd heard of these birds, known outside the Northern Isles as the Great Skua. They attack walkers and kill other seabirds, don't they? *Or is it the other way around?*

It came at me again, and I was angry, my peace disturbed. As it approached, I swung my camera case at it. It saw this, and effortlessly wheeled out the way, reacting fast. At least it wasn't anywhere near my head. But instead of giving up, it just kept on coming. What I would give for a net or airgun!

I like wildlife, but not this bird. Britain is a country of passive wildlife, so the bonxie is something of a shock. Packing up, and not a little concerned – if it hit my head with that beak at that speed, it would make a fair hole – I fled for the summit, and the bonxie did not follow.

A fine summit. Orkney and the other islands surround it, green, smooth, streamlined swellings with browner moors north and west on Rousay itself. I didn't want to head downhill so soon on such a fine day, so continued the walk round to Knitchen Hill, dodging the bonxie again when crossing its territory just below Blotchnie Fiold summit. Knitchen Hill is an even better viewpoint back to the mainland.

Rousay is fantastic. It was my first off-mainland Orkney island, and I had caught this small community on a good day. I walked in the heat of the afternoon round to the island shop, a place with just about everything for sale and adverts for a local dance and many other activities, where I queued with a couple of unattended children, chatting to the shopkeeper. On the walk back to the hostel a car stopped to offer a lift, and I squeezed in the back, the driver a teenager home for the summer from university, his happy, Orcadian-accented granny in the back. The previous night in the pub, a fellow had told me how, if he wanted, he could get the ferry to the mainland, the bus to Kirkwall Airport, then the plane to London, and be there two hours after leaving his croft. Who says Orkney is isolated?

It was only once I left Orkney that I discovered that the bonxie is a protected species. Protected schmected. Shoot them.

Craigowl Hill – *fruitpickers and sheep*
455m OS 54 NO 377400

Craigowl Hill is the highest point in the Sidlaws, lowest of the hill ranges girdling Scotland's waist that gently mock the term 'Central Lowlands'. (The Renfrewshire Heights, Kilpatricks, Campsies, Pentlands and the Ochils are the other ranges.) These hills provide perfect half-day lung-freshening walks from the Central Belt's cities and towns, yet remain uncrowded due to the magnetic pull of the Highlands only a short distance to the north. Neglected they may be; but appreciated by me. Though Scotland with its surfeit of bigger, wilder hills can ignore these Central Belt ranges, I can tell you that a range of hills like the Ochils, for example, would be given proper appreciation if situated south of the border.

The Sidlaws aren't as impressive as the Ochils or Campsies, and lack any steep escarpments or cliff faces. However in the agricultural and arable east coast, they provide high grassy walking just a short distance from Dundee.

One fine summer's evening heading south from Aberdeen, I decided to stop at Craigowl Hill. Off the A90, a maze of unclassified backroads was negotiated, seasonal student and migrant fruitpickers walking back from the fields along the roads after a hard day's work. There is a communications mast at the summit of Craigowl Hill, served by a pockmarked, private tarred road which provides a carefree easy walk for a while before pulling steeply uphill. The very top is almost four-points-of-contact steep as I left the road and went direct – and then I was there, the locked and deserted plant building at the communications mast humming to itself.

Although of modest height, this is the highest hill in the area and an excellent vantage point. To the southeast, the city of Dundee was laid out bright in evening sunshine, sandy shores bulging out past Carnoustie to the glistening North Sea. West, shading my eyes, the Tay, and north a view of the arable fields of Strathmore backed by the steep heathery Angus glens in the Highlands. A different aspect to that of the west coast: no islands in the sea, but a light dryness in the evening air and on the fertile ground.

Sheared sheep roamed free around the steep top of Craigowl Hill, shitting on the track and baa-ing at my approach.

Thacla *(hek-la)* – *homes, not hovels*
606m OS 22 NF 825345

Thacla, Beinn Corodale, and Beinn Mhor are three rough, interesting hills on the rocky east coast of South Uist. In a mirror image of Scotland, South Uist is rocky and roadless on the east coast, but flat and fertile on the west coast. The west coast contains the roads and only population. Visiting the Uists one summer holiday, I approached these hills from this direction.

Away from the sandy coast, the centre of the island is neither machair meadow nor rocky hillside. It is bog, and I splashed through it for a few kilometres, listening to the moorland birds. Eventually I reached steeper and dryer slopes, where the fun could begin. Thacla has a steepish, rocky west ridge, and halfway up it I glimpsed the east coast, impressively indented and island-studded, rough and unfrequented looking. There is a bothy on this coast, but it must be hard to reach and little visited. Then cloud descended, and I saw little except the rocks beneath my feet, the wind-blown mist, and my map and compass, until I descended from Beinn Mhor.

In Howmore Youth Hostel, a rough-hewn basic shelter, two Englishmen, a southerner and a northerner, argued over the relative merits of blackhouses *vs* modern houses. It was a battle between conservatism and social justice: the urge to preserve *vs* an appreciation of the reality of living in a hovel. I sat back and spectated. The southerner wished the islanders would preserve their quaint cottages, just like the thatched cottages in his Home Counties village. Irritated by the locals' neglect of ruined blackhouses, he could not understand why people would want to live instead in 'ugly box houses'. The man from Derbyshire railed against his countryman's wilful ignorance, contrasting the dirtiness and darkness of the traditional blackhouse with the cosier, brighter, more convenient but plainer modern home. I privately sided with the Derbyshire man, but wondered perhaps if people should care more than they do about their local environments. If the southern chap moved here, he would have formed a committee for blackhouse preservation and secured a government grant for it before he had stepped off the pierhead.

Sheabhal *(hay-val) – the perfect island*
383m OS 31 NL 678994

Barra is arguably the most perfect island in the British Isles. It is just big enough and just small enough; the coast and beaches and offshore islands are gorgeous; the movie *Whisky Galore* was filmed here based on true events; and the plane from Glasgow lands on the beach every low tide. Gaelic is spoken, Catholicism is practised, and rain seems to be more attracted to the higher hills of other, less fortunate, more Presbyterian islands.

On arriving on Barra midweek for a short overnight stay from South Uist, I discovered my car keys were missing. The car was parked on South Uist, but perhaps the keys were in my rucksack, or had fallen out my pocket in the hostel in Castlebay. A cursory search yielded nothing. I retired to the local bar where a miserable punter (probably a Lewis man) was hogging the bartop, and the only other people were a couple of foreign tourists.

Next day dawned promisingly clear, and I dawdled at the hostel before wandering up Sheabhal. But by this time – only a couple of hours after dawn – the clouds had started to gather, and I had a premonition that the summit was about to be streamlined by an Atlantic whitecap. I raced up the surprisingly steep southern slopes of Sheabhal, and lost the race with the cloud to the summit by a matter of minutes. But the view south from just below the summit was an incredible vista of sea, sky, islands, beaches, and Kissimul Castle on its rock in the bay, probably the most picturesquely situated castle in the whole of Scotland.

Descent took me past the statue of the Virgin, Star of the Sea, to the road and the sunshine again. I took a paddle round the fantastic beach at Eoligarry, visited Compton Mackenzie's grave, greeted three men thatching a roof, and was greeted in turn by a child alighting from the school bus. I wandered to watch the plane land on the beach at Barra's tiny airport. An older couple were waiting for the plane, and these complete strangers knew that I was looking for my car keys! If I had had to return to South Uist without any way of getting into my car I would have been unhappy, but what's the point in worrying? The bus for the Sound of Barra ferry arrived and I alighted, inquiring about some keys . . .

"Are *these* what you are looking for . . .?" asked the driver, pulling my keys out of the glove box.

"Aye!"

It is true that the weather was fine and I was only there a day – but visit Barra and you will wonder why you ever bother holidaying abroad.

PART FIVE
The Corbetts

What do you do when you've saved some money doing a reasonably interesting and well-paid offshore job whose life-style doesn't suit your temperament? Buy a house or invest the money, whilst keeping going and looking for something onshore? No, leave it of course, to try something completely different and impractical! I was getting more and more into writing music, a teenage passion that I had dropped a little during university. I didn't like my job and wanted to do something, something real, with music. Why not set up a recording studio, record and sell my work, and see if I could record others? I sat down and worked out a business plan.

The plan indicated that I would lose a lot of money. Besides, discounting my favourite genres of classical and folk music, I had barely been to half a dozen live gigs. Did these two factors deter me? They didn't, and as a bonus I got into the Corbetts and a new mountaineering club at the same time.

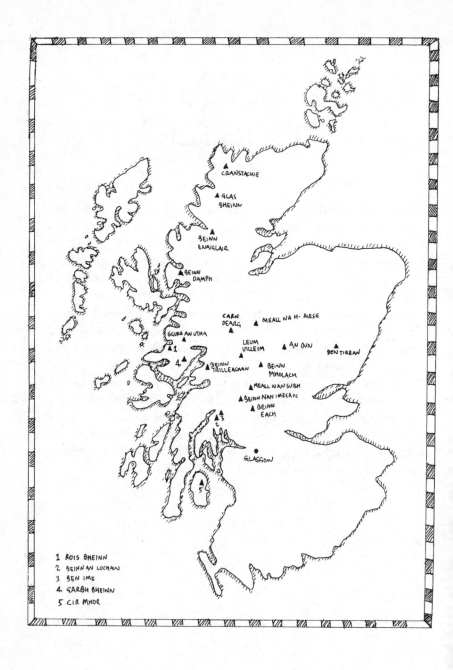

▲ CRANSTACKIE

▲ GLAS
  BHEINN

▲ BEINN
  ENAIGLAIR

▲ BEINN
  DAMPH

      CARN   ▲ MEALL NA H- AIRSE
      DEARG ▲
▲ SGURR AN UTHA
              LEUM
  ▲ 1   UILLEIM ▲   ▲ AN DUN
  ▲   ▲   ▲ BEN TIRRAN
  4 ▲   ▲ BEINN   ▲ BEINN
         TRILLEACHAN   MHOLACH
                   ▲ MEALL NAN SUBH
              ▲ BEINN NAN IMREAN
                   ▲ BEINN
                     EACH
         ▲
         3
         ▲
         2

              ● GLASGOW

         ▲
         5

1 ROIS BHEINN
2 BEINN AN LOCHAIN
3 BEN IME
4 GARBH BHEINN
5 CIR MHOR

Beinn Enaiglair *(beyn en-ayg-layr)* – hill, pub, bed
889m OS 20 NH 225805

On my way to Ullapool, I stopped by the Falls of Mesach car park, headed east past *'no entry'* signs leading to the local sporting lodge, located a stile further on, rounded the forestry land on a boggy trail, struck up past a wee loch, peched up the stony stalker's trail, entered the mist, bashed up to Beinn Enaiglair summit, and reversed my route. A shame it was cloudy on top, as I bet the westward view from here is very fine. On descent I decided it was worth expending the effort on a quick push – which rapidly degenerated into a slow slog – up misty Meall Dore Fhad too. I had a wee look at the Falls of Mesach from the cantilevered viewpoint, hanging over the evil dank walls of the Corrieshalloch Gorge, an instant exposure moment that never fails to thrill. Who needs the Aonach Eagach when you can get virtually the same effect 30 seconds from your car?

At Ullapool Youth Hostel, the warden informed me finger-waggingly that it was better I did not go to the pub, but have an early night in. She would lock up at 11pm, whether I was back or not. Naturally I ignored her good advice, wandered into the kitchen, and sneakily left the window off its latch. By the time I staggered back from the pub it was well past curfew, but the kitchen window was still open, so I clambered inside and went to bed with a smug glow of satisfaction.

Five minutes later I needed the toilet, so slipped into my boxers and padded out to the WC. But disaster! This hostel has locks on the dormitory doors to discourage petty thieves, and I had locked myself out of my room. It would have been unacceptable behaviour to wake my dorm-mates in the middle of the night by banging on the door and yelling, so I wandered back down to the kitchen, unsure of what to do. There weren't any blankets lying around and I was shivering in my semi-naked state, so I did the only sensible thing: dismantled the kitchen curtains for bedding and retired to the lounge area, where I made myself as comfortable as I could (which was actually pretty comfortable) on a sofa until the morning came and I was woken by tittering hostellers preparing breakfast.

Cranstackie *(kran-stak-ee) – the aftermath*
800m OS 9 NC 351556

The day after Beinn Enaiglair, I rose from the Ullapool YH kitchen sofa with as much dignity as I could muster, rehung the curtains, and returned to my dorm for an hour's snooze, feeling a little worse for wear. It was well into the afternoon before I got going, after reading the Sunday papers and enjoying a leisurely breakfast at a cafe. A good thing, I thought, to be alone, as my other friends would dislike this directionless lounging around. I had no clear plan beyond another Corbett.

I decided to head up to Canisp, but on arriving at its base, just kept driving. I picked up two German carpenters – two Zimmerman apprentices in fact, wearing rustic costume – and gave them a lift to Durness, before going for a wander on Sango sands in limpid weather, the breakers rushing in, wishing my Antipodean sister Fiona was there to see it. As beautiful as any beach in New Zealand.

Finally, with only about another three hours of daylight left, I headed for Beinn Spionnaidh and Cranstackie. It was a bit hazy to see much, but Foinaven was visible to the south. Barking dogs at the farm at the bottom, steep grassy slopes, stony characterful summits.

In Ullapool the previous evening I had by chance bumped into ex-Club stalwart Andy, and told him I would head for Inchnadamph as I'd heard the Glenmore Club would be there, the club of Alan Dawson, chronicler of the Marilyns and author of my hillwalking bible, *The Relative Hills of Britain*.

At Inchnadamph the lodge was fully booked, so the owner put me in a caravan by myself and showed me a TV in a deserted side building. Unfortunately I didn't recognise anyone from the Glenmore Club in the lodge, and there was no sign of Andy. So I went to the pub. I was astonished to find only four people there given the lodge was full, so sat with two of the night's punters, a local stalker and a thick-armed stonemason from Edinburgh. The young stalker bemoaned the lack of women locally and asked if the bar owner would organise a dance. And I thought it was hard to find a woman in Glasgow!

After the pub, I headed for the TV room with toast and two mugs of tea, flicking through the channels until I fell asleep. When I woke I didn't bother getting up till lunchtime, feeling restless but not very energetic, and wondered how I had managed to pay for two nights' accommodation but not actually sleep in a bed all weekend.

Ben Tirran *(ben tir-ran) – keen bagger, solitary bagger*
896m OS 44 NO 373746

The Clova Inn is a fine hostelry. After a relaxing evening in the Inn, we came out of the pub to the sound of music. There was a ceilidh going on in a barn round the back, and we were invited to join in.

As we came out of the barn, the next day's objectives were finalised. I announced I wasn't climbing Mayar or Dreish, or even going up the Mounth towards Lochnagar. I was going up Ben Tirran. "Craig Weldon, Corbett bagging saddo!" chanted Billy, and a couple of others in our group joined in. "Corbett bagger! Corbett bagger!" they said, pointing at me in time to their chant. Was it my fault I'd already finished the Munros? They were as bad as me, just not as advanced!

Next day, as everyone else headed for their Munros, I was left a pariah to ascend the Corbett Ben Tirran to the east of the glen, Billy's jeers dismissed from my mind. For I'd been looking forward to Loch Brandy and Loch Wharral, two round, corrie-nestling lochs that looked symmetrical on the map. I headed up the path into the heather for the ridge of The Snub. These lochs are less striking than I'd imagined, if nice enough. Clouds had gathered as I had been climbing, and once onto the plateau the rain started, becoming heavier as the day wore on. I trudged and splashed through a mossy bog. By Ben Tirran the cloud had come right down to cover the plateau, and I only came out of it at the shore of Loch Wharral, its crags flirting with the mist, my feet soaking.

The previous night, after a few pints in the Inn, I had briefly considered walking all the way to Mount Keen and back. I was glad I had dropped that idea. The terrain is thick, jungly heather all the way, and I wouldn't have been back for weeks.

An Dun *(an doon)* – *the autumn Corbett*
827m OS 42 NN 716802

November in the Highlands is dark, but not depressing like February, when it feels that winter will never end. November is the darkness of Samhainn, of thrilling new crispness and turning leaves, of cold breath in night air, dooking for apples, of the party season and eldritch tales.

It was in this alive darkness Alastair and I arrived at the gates of the forest on the A9, with an 8km walk in to Sronphadruig Lodge. The track disappeared into the trees and we switched on our torches. They illuminated a puny field of vision, weak circles of light surrounded by hemispheres of rustling darkness. I nearly took a wrong turning, but Alastair was more alert and we avoided becoming lost. Quickly, however, we were out of the forest and on the long haul through treeless moorland, with a fine starry sky above. Halfway in we swapped burdens: I took the sack of wood, and Alastair pulled away towards the bothy, leaving me walking alone in the dark. There have been times when he would go on ahead, wait in a ditch, and ambush passers by, but not tonight. Sronphadruig Lodge is surrounded by a stand of old, knarled trees, bats flitting about. A discreet distance from the lodge we pitched our tent. I got a campfire going as

Alastair played some folk tunes on his penny whistle and we did not speak very much, staring into the flames.

Next day the huge rampart of An Dun surprised us, having snuck up the glen overnight to glower over Sronphadruig. At night there had been no sense of its presence, despite the stars. Alastair, suffering from a septic toe, had no great urgency to visit a steep Corbett in his slippery Doc Martens (his only shoes comfortable enough to wear) and decided to potter around the river, so I headed for An Dun by myself.

An Dun is an unusual hill for its individuality in standing out from the surrounding plateau. Its neighbouring hills are some of the most extensive high mosslands in Scotland, but they have been cut by a navvy of a glacier to form the deep trench of the Gaick pass. An Dun seems to have flaked off from the steep sides of this pass, standing proud and individual as a seastack, with a tiny plateau area for a summit.

An Dun is a simple hill, and the direct ascent up its nose was one that required neither consultation of the map nor any doubts about where to go. The summit can be quickly reached, and it was worth taking a look down the eastern side up and down spooky Gaick. Cama Choire is seen to good advantage to the west, its unfrequented streams and lonely waterfalls draining the large Drumochter plateau of Carn na Caim.

I descended north-northeast, a brutal heathery descent, and walked back along the side of Loch an Duin to Sronphadruig. All that was required was to walk the 8km back out to the road, the track utilitarian and unexceptional rather than mysteriously eldritch in the bleak light of day.

Beinn nam Imrean *(beyn nam im-a-ran) – venison burgers*
849m OS 51 NN 419309

On a washout of a weekend when my motivation was low, no one rang on Friday. All I had planned for Saturday were a couple of bottles of beer from the Inveralmond brewery and a preposterous DVD (*Swordfish*, a so-called thriller where half the action takes place at a computer screen). Just when I was set for a particularly low-key weekend, Alastair called. He wanted to go walking next day. Gratefully, I agreed.

I picked him up on Sunday morning. We hadn't definitely decided where to go. The weather was foul with low cloud, snow on the hills and squalls of rain. The only possible motivation on a day like this was to bag something new, so we headed for Beinn nam Imrean, a Corbett above Auchessan farm in Glen Dochart. I remembered a visit to the next door Munros, and looking over to Beinn nam Imrean, thinking 'can't be bothered', then wondering if I would repent that decision some day. Well, here we were, and despite the weather I wasn't repenting – at least there was a worthwhile but manageable target for us on a foul day.

We stopped for a venison burger from a van just east of Crianlarich and commented on the bleak seeming location – but these burger van guys know their business, and the owner said he had been quite busy: his customers the previous day included some hillwalkers who had tackled Ben More. We looked up at this steep hill, but didn't fancy it in the high wind, covered in slippy wet snow. As we set off the rain stopped for a few minutes. It returned as a light smirr, so in the end the day turned out more pleasant than expected.

Once off the lower slopes, Beinn nam Imrean turned out to be not a bad slog; and on the way back we threaded through steepish broken cliffs, whose slush-covered gaps provided some sport. Glowing cheeked, we had another burger at the van. The rubbish weekend had turned out OK in the end, especially as I learned once home again that local student radio had picked up one of my songs and was playing it that week.

Meall nan Subh *(myal nan soo)* – *halfday* 806m OS 51 NN 461397

When a full day's walk won't do? Head for Meall nan Subh. This walk is made short not by the hill's height, but by the convenient road that climbs to 550m, leaving a quick jaunt of a mile to the summit. The road is a private one, owned by the water authority, but it is well metalled and is sometimes left unlocked. Meall nan Subh also looked as if it had a good view, so one dreich winter Sunday when I was feeling particularly lazy after my first gig, I donned my boots, jumped in the car, and drove up Loch Lomondside to Breadalbane. The water road was unlocked, so I drove to the top of the pass, parking in a snowstorm. White streaks of snow funnelled through the pass, a blanket of cloud hanging in the greyness. It was dark enough to require headlamps at midday, but invigorating being outside in the bluff coldness.

There would be no views today. The walk goes steep and direct straight from the road. Compass out, I yomped up the hill, pulling myself up on big lumps of heather, calves aching, circumventing rocks to a more level area where the snow was lying. I hoped the compass work was accurate: the summit is a bumpy, flattish area, and I walked over several lumps before deciding upon one that seemed to be the top. Without the presence of a trig point however, it can be hard to be completely sure in foggy conditions.

As I came down to the car, breaking out of the cloud, another car passed, lights on, windscreen wipers going. It was the only vehicle since Killin. I jumped into my own car, glowing and refreshed, and headed happily for home.

The gig the night before had gone well. I'd been contacted by a promoter after I'd recorded one of his friends, and the singer of one of the other bands that night was a set designer for a theatre company. So my first gig was performed surrounded by their set's fairy lights, coloured drapes and props – a nice start to my performing career! As I reached the climax of my set, the enthusiastic punters at the front of the room started dancing, and I got carried away in the moment, feeding off their energy, singing the simple, joyful tune to *Ten to 2*, my song about nightclubs in Aberdeen:

> *It's ten to 2*
> *the last song's being played*
> *everybody's got the ten to 2s*
> *trying to get laid!*

Beinn Trilleachan *(beyn trill-ach-an)* – *Gordon's gone*
840m OS 50 NN 086439

"I need a piss," said Gordon, ten minutes out of our refreshment stop at Inveraran.

"I'm not stopping!" replied Brian, his knuckles whitening on the wheel. Gordon – a colleague of Brian's – had been annoying him all the way up the road, and this was the final straw.

"Brian, stop the car! I need a piss!" exclaimed Gordon.

"Gordon, imagine your bladder is a balloon full of warm water, about to burst," said Alastair. "Think about rushing waterfalls . . ."

"I will piss in your car!" threatened Gordon.

After listening to Alastair witter on about forceful streams of water and warm liquids in constrained containers for ten minutes, I was keen to stop myself. We wound our way up past Beinn Dorain, across the dark waste of Rannoch Moor to the Kingshouse, and turned left for the dead-end road down Glen Etive. Still Brian refused to stop the car. It was a relief to arrive at last, decant, and empty bladders in a satisfying cloud of steam.

"I know a shortcut," said Brian, as we rummaged through our rucksacks. We were heading for Kinlochetive bothy, and normally we would park at the bridge and walk 2km along a deteriorating path. "There's no need to walk in along the path, we can ford the river." 'In the dark . . .?' I wondered, but Brian had a plan, and has a habit of heading off impatiently two minutes before everyone else is ready, thus forcing the group to follow him.

This time the group consisted of me, Brian, Billy, Alastair and Gordon. It was Gordon's first ever bothy. He was raring to go, fuelled by our stories of the great craic you get in bothies, and tall tales of our adventures. Really, we were as excited as he was as we remembered them all, and eager to find out what the night held in store. Gordon had brought his bodhran in anticipation of a good session, and we followed Brian down a stony track at the end of the road, heading for the mouth of the River Etive.

For about twenty yards.

Then Brian veered off into the bracken . . . "Where are you going Brian?" I asked. "It's this way, I've been here before!" was the reply – and we had no choice but to follow.

Brian led us into an area of thick gorse, Gordon cursing, the sound of the river in the dark disorientatingly close. Sweating heavily despite the cold December air, scratched and harassed by gorse, we broke out into an area which soon revealed itself to be a deep bog, sinking up to our knees in glaur. I could see Gordon in the arc of my headtorch, and from the set of his shoulders, he had the air of a man who would like to kill Brian. It was a look I recognised.

Finally we reached the river, and the problem of how to cross it. Fortunately we had arrived, either by accident or by Brian's genius, at its shallowest part. It was still deep and potentially dangerous, and it was a relief to reach the far side, even if it was to more gorse. At least the bothy was close, and once we had cleared the forest of thorns, we could see the welcoming light of candles flickering in the window just a couple of hundred yards away. Not far now, we said, and cheered up, wondering who was in already, hoping they had a good roaring fire going and maybe even playing a few fiddle tunes.

Andy was by the door, drunk and belligerent, and greeted Gordon to his first ever bothy.

"Who the hell are you, ya bas?!"

Next day, Alastair and I decided to head up Beinn Trilleachan – crossing the Etive by the bridge this time! The weather was poor with low cloud, slushy snow and a strong wind, but Beinn Trilleachan is lower than other hills in the glen, and we felt it was the best bad weather option.

We nipped up past the house and farm in the glen, a dog barking, for a hard and quick pull up to the treeline and the ridge of the hill. The upward journey continued into increasingly ferocious winds, until we reached a gap in the ridge. The cloud was low and thick, and there seemed to be no easy way onwards. The wind was strong and, not carrying crampons, I did not fancy my chances of balancing on the slabs that appeared to be the only practical way forward. No doubt there is a laughably easy route, but in the disorientating mist and strong wind we decided to descend and try again another day. After all, the view on a clear day down Loch Etive and back to Glencoe must be excellent. Disappointed, we headed back down to Kinlochetive, where we learned there had been further drama.

Billy had decided to cut some firewood, and Brian and Gordon had headed back to the car to collect Brian's tools and help out. But the river was higher than the previous night, and Gordon had been swept off his feet. "Gordon!" Brian had yelled, and retreated back to the Kinlochetive side of the river. He ran downstream, but couldn't see Gordon. Billy reports that he had heard the sound of running feet, and looked up from sawing a log to see Brian, soaking. "Gordon's gone!" Brian said, before they raced for the bridge, arriving at the car side of the river in record time. There they found Gordon, who had reached the other bank safely and found a canoe club who were staying in a hut next to the road. They were combing the river for Brian.

"Brian, I thought you had been swept away!" said Gordon.

"No, *you* were swept away!" replied Brian.

Gordon had phoned the police to rescue Brian when he had been found by the canoe club, and so Brian had to wait to explain the situation to the local bobby. It was a reminder that the River Etive – indeed, any river – should be treated with great respect. A river can kill more easily than a mountain.

Leum Uilleim *(loym oy-lum) – the bunker*
906m OS 41 NN 331641

Duncan, Jan, Alastair and Helen were staying at Corrour Station bunkhouse deep in the middle of winter, when the daylight is short and the hills covered in snow and cloud. I arrived Saturday lunchtime, dropped off my sleeping bag, and headed across boggy, snow-covered ground for the northeast ridge of Beinn a' Bhric, a subsidiary of Leum Uilleim. This is the hill visible in the background in the famous 'Scotland's shite' scene from the film *Trainspotting*, but today all it was showing was a hundred metres or so of its skirts, the rest of the hill hidden deep in the cloud. On reaching the top of Beinn a' Bhric, I reversed my steps for a short while to find the route to Leum Uilleim. There was no reason to linger at the summit, so I followed my footprints all the way back down the hill.

I laid a table, poured some whisky into glasses in the lighthouse-like lookout post of the bunkhouse – a feature of the old railway – and waited for the others to arrive for dinner. Dark fell, and I waited some more, turning on the naked lightbulb, perusing the board games and old *Scots Magazines* in a box. The wooden and glass tower swayed a little in the battering breeze, snow on the steel of the railway line below, stretching into inky darkness. My companions eventually arrived well after dark, after an epic trip accompanying a French girl up the Munros west of Ben Alder and becoming lost. Alastair arrived singing.

"On the twelfth day of Christmas Mr Zachariah gave to me:

> *Twelve boiled eggs,*
> *eleven boiled eggs,*
> *ten boiled eggs,*
> *nine boiled eggs,*
> *eight boiled eggs,*
> *seven boiled eggs,*
> *six boiled eggs,*
> *FIVE BO-ILED EGGS!*
> *Four boiled eggs,*
> *three boiled eggs,*
> *two boiled eggs,*
> *And a bo-o-o-o-oiled egg."*

Next day Duncan climbed Leum Uilleim alone, and the rest of us watched his heroic figure disappear into the cloud and drank tea and played games until the train came.

Rois Bheinn *(ross ven)* – *it was one of those rare days*
882m OS 40 NM 756778

If you want to know what the finest viewpoint on the entire
west coast of Scotland is, then climb Rois Bheinn late on a fine
winter's afternoon and you will probably be able to work it
out for yourself.

It was an uncharacteristically icy night when Billy and I
camped at Glenfinnan; such sharp evenings are common
around Braemar, but rarer on the mild west coast. At the
time I did not believe in modern fripperies like warm sleeping
bags, when my ancient cheap one and thick jumpers, a
balaclava, second-hand ski mitts, extra socks and a couple
of plastic bin-bags would do just as well.

We were cold when we rose, but it was a fine morning.
Winter in Scotland can be gloomy and dark, so moments like
this of fine sunshine – especially when accompanied by sparkling snow – are to be treasured.

Rather than head straight for the hill, we headed first for
Arisaig and Morar, gasping at the beauty of the beaches with
mountainous island views to Skye, Eigg and Rum, painted
with snow above a ruler line of temperature. The fine pale
beaches of Morar were frozen hard. Then we drove round to
have a look at the romantic ruin of Castle Tioram on its tidal
island. Eventually, just an hour or so from sunset, we set off up
Rois Bheinn.

The panorama that unfolded became finer and more extensive with every upward step. Eventually the entire rough
western seaboard from Knoydart to Ardnamurchan and Mull
was clear before us. Behind rose a fat moon, with the snows
shocking pink on Lochaber and Ben Nevis. But best of all were
the islands, the ever aesthetic Rum and Eigg, and the snow-
lined prickles of the Cuillin and vast, winged Skye. Fiery ribs of
cloud caged the western sky as the sun set. The best of
weather, on one of Scotland's best viewpoints. I believe we
whooped a couple of times.

The descent was made in the dark, a small price to pay.

Garbh Bheinn (gar ven) – expeditioneering
885m OS 40 NM 904622

Although Garbh Bheinn sits temptingly close to Glencoe, the barrier of Loch Linnhe prevented us from visiting for quite a while. Island-like Ardgour is easily reached by ferry across the Corran narrows but psychologically, it is a greater expedition than the similar journey to Fort William. Garbh Bheinn is in fact one of the finest hills in the Highlands, and the short ferry ride shouldn't deter anyone.

However, it always seemed to be raining in Ardgour whenever we planned a visit, even though Garbh Bheinn always looked so good from Glencoe. Then one day Alastair and I arrived on the west coast with the intention of walking in Glencoe, and at the last minute, hopped on the ferry to Ardgour and caught Garbh Bheinn napping. It didn't have time to pull in the bad weather, and so we had an amazing day of snow on a rough and unfrequented hill.

We had a debate as we walked up Coire Iubhair. Straight up the corrie to Garbh Bheinn's summit? Or round the side? We couldn't see the very top of the corrie – which exits right at Garbh Bheinn's summit – due to a cloud flirting with the top. Without being able to see the top, we couldn't tell if it was corniced or not, so I refused to ascend that way. Round the side we went . . .

This north & northwest face of Garbh Bheinn is incredibly rough. Directly west of the snowy bowl which might have given us access to the summit are Garbh Bheinn's famous cliffs, huge shoulders and plates of rock thrusting out of the ground. Further west still, the severity of these cliffs relents and they become more broken, providing excellent scrambling ground.

Alastair and I headed past the main cliffs and up towards a snowy col, with broken rock, gorges and little cliff faces all about us. The cloudbase had started to drop – Garbh Bheinn must have noticed we were there – and navigation became uncertain. Should we continue up if we couldn't see where we were going? We decided that so long as we could reverse our steps, we would push on, and so enjoyed a wonderful scramble through and around ravines and rocky outcrops. Each upward step took us further into this magical world, until finally the angle relented, the terrain became less severe, and we realised with great anticipation that we were nearly at the top.

We'd made it, found ourselves a passage through this difficult landscape without having to turn back! Unfortunately the summit was in cloud – a shame as the view from here must be very fine.

We descended steeply down easier southern slopes into growing darkness well satisfied with the days work, Garbh Bheinn visited and – if not conquered – most certainly appreciated.

The People With Computers in Their Head

The hills had become more and more of an escape. My music career was going nowhere, my CDs unsold and my studio unbooked by anyone. I had quickly realised that the only way people were going to listen to my music was if I played live, and so I had reluctantly been gigging. I sang my new song *The People With Computers in Their Head* for the first time in Glasgow's 13th Note Cafe. As I reached the climax of the song – "the people with computers in their head want you to join them" – I started to dance in spasmic jerks, and the punters at the front started laughing. Laughing! This was a vision of a dystopian future, not comedy! I pour my soul into my music, and these callous punters laugh! After the show, one came up to me and tapped me repeatedly in the forehead. I was taken aback.

"What's in there? That was the most extraordinary thing I've ever seen! You must have one messed up mind," he said. "I mean that in a good way," he added, as if to reassure me.

I sold a couple of CDs, which paid for my dinner that night.

Beinn Each *(ben eich)* – *Brian's dog*
813m OS 57 NN 602158

"I don't know how he does it," said Billy, more in envy than admiration, as we watched Brian disappear up the heathery, snow-streaked hill ahead of us. We'd picked Brian up from home where he'd informed us he'd stayed up all night getting pissed, smoking cigarettes and playing a game on his computer, before downing a two litre bottle of Coca-Cola just before we came around. He hadn't had any breakfast. Hey, he hadn't had any sleep. This would incapacitate most folks, but Brian is made of rare stuff, and was springing up the steep, heathery hillside like a shepherd's dug.

Beinn Each was the hill for the day, an obscure Corbett in the Trossachs, easily reached from Glasgow but ill-frequented compared to the neighbouring peaks of Ben A'an, Ben Ledi, Ben Venue, or the Munros of Ben Vorlich'n'Stuc a' Chroin, onto whose backside Beinn Each is stuck.

"Stuc a' Chroin!" said, Brian, and launched into his anecdote of climbing Stuc a' Chroin the hard way up its broken northeast face. "We should go there too!"

"Ah yes," said Billy, "lets do it . . ." and gave his own entertaining account of climbing Stuc a' Chroin, and how this marvellous peak had coloured his interest in the Scottish Hills.

I had also had fun on this hill in the past, and it was generally agreed that Stuc a' Chroin was on the cards as well today.

We arrived at the summit of Beinn Each, where it was blowing a gale.

Brian, Billy and I looked through our wind-vibrating hoods across to the storm-battered top of Stuc a' Chroin, and our enthusiasm for continuing drained rapidly.

"Naah," we said in unison, and descended.

"Don't you remember the time I introduced my friend Charlie to Brian?" Billy asked, on the way down. "I said, 'Brian, this is Charlie,' and rather than saying, 'Hello, Charlie,' he said, 'woof woof! My dog's called Charlie!' Don't you remember?!" It all came flooding back, Brian saying this right in Charlie's face, and Charlie standing there; Charlie, our new climbing partner for the weekend, nonplussed before dawn at Partick station, and Billy and Brian raced down the steep upper sides of Beinn Each whilst I lay in the heather, laughing fit to burst.

Meall na h-Aisre *(myal na hash-reh)* – *a glimpse of the Arctic* 862m OS 35 NH 515000

Although we had ceased to be members of the university club, a few of us still hung around a couple of years for the annual dinner meet. There were no better sources of fun than a student mountaineering club, the mixture of hills, drink, foolish banter and youthful enthusiasm being hard to give up. Thus Alastair and I found ourselves making our way to Newtonmore for the dinner meet, though in deference towards our un-student status, we travelled separately from the club and made our own sleeping arrangements.

These arrangements turned out to be a rough bivvy in our sleeping bags in a draughty shelter at Newtonmore station on a wild night. We were woken in the morning by a woman tutting to her family:

"They shouldn't be sleeping there."

The weather was diabolical. I was afraid to climb a hill in it. The wind was blowing strongly and was bitterly cold, and I didn't think my gear would be adequate for the job. Alastair lent me a set of thermals and, happy again, we headed for the summit of this Monadhliath Corbett.

I'd like to be able to tell you that this hill was a dull slog up an uninspiring Monadhliath pudding bowl, but it wouldn't be true. The Allt Coire Iain Og is a river of pleasantly shaped stones; the walk up to the top and back down again an entertaining, rosy-cheeked, full-body workout battling against a screaming, knock-you-over wind. On the top, where we could barely stand due to the wind and slippery ice, the cloud lifted for a moment to reveal a horizon-wide glimpse of the bare and beautifully slipstreamed high country of the Monadhliath stretching off to infinity, vast streams of spindrift howling across the surface. It was as close a feeling of being in the Arctic as I have had in Britain.

Back down, Newtonmore village hall was full of the un-characteristic sights and smells of climbers washing, grooming, deodorising, perfuming, and dressing. Steam billowed from the severely overworked showerhead into the main hall.

Most of the mountaineers – given that they had been up a hill or climbing route in severe winter weather – scrubbed up remarkably well.

Looking back though, I don't remember much. The guest speaker had attended St Andrews University, founded fifty years before Glasgow, so made a joke about Glasgow being 'a bit red brick'; and I probably got drunk.

Cir Mhor *(keer vor)* – *the blind spot*
799m OS 62/69 NR 973432

Now answer this: Where are the nearest great hills to Glasgow? Hills the near equal of those on Skye? Glencoe perhaps? No. The nearest top-quality hills – if, err, for the sake of argument, we ignore Arrochar – are on Arran.

Funny, isn't it?

No one ever goes to Arran. Glencoe, Torridon, Cairngorms, Skye: these are obvious. But Arran lies south of the Clyde, a direction hillwalkers afflicted with latitude sickness prefer not to look. Arran is full of tourists with woolly jumpers perusing candle and cheese shops in summer, and a few walkers and climbers venture towards this jewel of the Firth of Clyde then. Off-season, when the ferry cuts back its sailings and thoughts turn to easily accessible daywalks, Arran, close as it is to the Central Belt, still seems strangely remote, a blind spot in the imagination. Administratively Arran lies in North Ayrshire; but jumping off the ferry from the Lowland town of Ardrossan for Arran and driving round the coast to the north takes you quickly past Lochranza into a completely different world, a Highland world of peace and silent stones.

All the more reason then, when it's just snowed and the forecast shows a saucer of high pressure coming in, to visit Arran.

I picked Billy up from his folks, and we arrived in Ardrossan in time for the second sailing of the morning to Brodick. The sun was rising, picking out Arran's golden brown lower slopes and snow-defined ridges and corries, clouds beginning to mass over its hills in otherwise clear skies. It was going to be an excellent day, and I felt the excitement of anticipation welling up inside. All we had to do was get to Sannox, and we were sorted for the rest of the day. One hard long walk through a – God willing – superlative landscape, and we would be back in Brodick for the last ferry home.

At the pierhead, buses waited to distribute passengers all round the island. We jumped on a northbound one, along the coast past the start of the Goatfell track, to jump off at Sannox. Now nothing could stop us!

The sun had disappeared completely by now, the short dawn window of sunshine swarmed by spreading cloud. Glen Sannox remained impressive however, the ridges and Cir Mhor itself still visible. Glen Sannox is a shorter, darker glen than Glen Rosa near Brodick, little visited and tucked away both mentally and geographically. But it is more Tolkein-esquely scenic than Glen Rosa, its perfect U-shaped glen floor swooping steeply upwards to a crown of excitingly irregular ridges. Suidhe Fhearghais and Cioch na h-Oighe provide suitably spectacular gate guardians to the glen. We walked upwards along the boggy track in silent delight.

Unfortunately the weather went against us, and the clouds clamped in completely by the head of Glen Sannox. There was no chance now of a view over to Goatfell or Caisteal Abhail; a shame after such a promising start to the day. We replenished waterbottles at the river, and scrambled up to The Saddle separating Cir Mhor from Goatfell. Suddenly we were in proper winter conditions: thick cloud, mixed snow and rock, whiteout. I'd guess Cir Mhor is normally fairly easy from The Saddle, but today was extremely disorientating. Somehow though, Billy in front, we managed to reach the summit; and without lingering at the cold, windy, anonymous top, set a course for the Fionn Choire in Glen Rosa.

Once in the corrie, we came out of the cloud, and the rest of the way was a fast march down Glen Rosa's long miles. Billy went painfully over his ankle, and we slowed to hopping speed. But fortunately we managed to cadge a lift on reaching the road, just making the last ferry home from Arran.

Billy's ankle was knackered for a while, but we had other-wise shown that there was no impediment to visiting Arran for a daytrip, even in winter. On some of the finest hills in Scotland, just a couple of hours from Glasgow and with a good forecast, we hadn't met a single walker all day.

Beinn Damph *(beyn damff)* – *a new club*
902m OS 24 NG 893502

I joined the Lomond Mountaineering Club in Glasgow, a small friendly club who met in Wintersgills, a pub owned by a former Celtic player. I liked the Lomond because of the good mix of ages, sexes and interests. Other clubs I'd investigated, welcoming as they were, seemed to be mainly middle-aged male rock climbers. This was too much of a shock after Glasgow University Mountaineering Club, previously the source of so much of my social life. I wanted to go up the hills yes, but I still wanted to talk to people in their twenties and thirties and even the occasional female.

The day before my first trip away with the Lomond, my cousin and his wife visited, so I took them into town for a late lunch. After lunch, we met a drunk in the Scotia Bar. He had a guitar, but when I asked if he was playing later with a band, he said with a cackle and a dead-eyed stare:

"Aye, but I'm too pished noo."

He played a bit of Oasis. I played one of my songs on piano, and he took an instant dislike to me. The feeling was mutual, so I thought I'd get rid of him by moving to another pub. He followed us and demanded a fight. My cousin calmed him down, and we left him dialling up reinforcements on his mobile. There is no doubt the bampot quotient is higher amongst afternoon drinkers than amongst those who keep more sociable hours, and the kind of people I was meeting in my increasingly frequent afternoon wanders round Glasgow depressed me. I had long since finished my first album, and my studio was bringing in no other work. My future was unclear, a blank nothingness filled with uncer-tainty and debt. I needed to get a regular job.

When I had been working offshore, my trips to the hills were relaxed and enjoyable. But doing music, hills became necessary therapy. A blast of fresh air, hard exercise and physical beauty held my feelings of helplessness at bay. I had recorded barely half a dozen bands, and had performed only a few gigs. Anyway, the next day was my first trip away with the Lomond Mountaineering Club. I had been looking forward to it.

Torridon was my first official trip with the Lomond, and a quiet but friendly home help called Alex drove us up the road Friday lunchtime, nipping up Meall a' Bhuachaille near Cairngorm en route. The Ling hut was subdued when we arrived, with just three climbers who'd arrived the night before. An early night then, but we were woken by folks arriving late at night, doors banging, whispering, bags rustling, torches shining in faces, the cold coming off the jackets of the new arrivals as their senses adjusted to the environment of a dark dormitory.

Next morning brought unpleasant weather. It had warmed up with high winds and gloomy low cloud – but at least not rain. Whilst everyone else headed for easy Coire Mhic Fhearchair or the challenging traverse of misty, snowy Liathach, Alex and I chose the middle course of Beinn Damph.

We decided to head for the corrie directly east of the hill's summit to minimise contact with the day's strong westerly gale. A nice bit of pine-scented native forestry and a foaming river on the way up, then bog hopping over tough heather and moraine debris. I was wondering about the stability of the snow in the corrie as it was thawing so fast, but reckoned eventually that it was probably OK as it hadn't snowed for a while, and it would be soft at the worst.

We got to the corrie quickly, Alex a fast walker, me out of breath. Fortunately the cloud had lifted enough to illustrate the one feasible ascent line. It was still fairly steep, and I forced myself not to worry on looking down from near the top. The very top was slightly corniced, so we breasted the ridge via some rocks at the side. An excellent ascent, although I didn't fancy descending that way! Amazingly, the cloud was lifting at the same rate as we were climbing, and now we could see over to Skye, Kintail, and Glen Affric.

We waited at the top and the cloud cleared totally, providing a grandstand view all round: to Liathach, its arrowhead summit plastered with snow and sunshine; to Applecross, Skye, Torrridon and Kintail. Maol Chean Dearg and An Ruadh Stac looked magnificent, which made me think that Beinn Damph is surely the best viewpoint for south Torridon. I was really pleased we'd come up a hill that had such an excellent view. But of course, every hill around Torridon does!

We lingered at the top for a good twenty minutes or longer, drinking it all in. This was far more than we could have expected given the forecast, and I said "if we do nothing else this weekend, we've already got value for money."

We headed down and walked around the Shieldaig peninsula. This offers a good low level panorama, but it is not nearly as good as the view from Beinn Damph. It had also dulled over again, and we were happy just to head back to the hut. We were the last people back and everyone else had also had a cracking time. Someone wanted to play games and I introduced them to the table traverse, then Claire suggested limbo dancing and everyone had a roaring time at that. It was a good thing those games happened. The climbers were just embarking on a four-hour technical climbing conversation, which would have bored me to death.

Beinn Mholach *(beyn mo-lach)* – *a guidebook curiosity* 841m OS 42 NN 587655

After reading in the SMC guide to the Corbetts that Beinn Mholach 'must be one of the least visited summits in Scotland', my curiosity and itch to visit grew to intolerable levels, and I persuaded Alastair to come with me one March for an overnight trek, stopping off in Duinish bothy. We approached the bothy from the south, passing some Italians staying at the lochside hunting lodge before heading along a good landrover track into the back-country. Dark came quickly, and I cursed the weight of coal on my back on this 8km walk-in. Eventually the bothy was reached, and a fine one it is. The bothy book was full of entries from the nearby Rannoch School, and I was pleased that the bothy was so well used and maintained, although also glad that they weren't in attendance tonight.

Next day I felt unmotivated, with the hill in cloud, a chill wind blowing, and deep snow all around.

"I can't be bothered going up the hill," I told Alastair.

"I'm going to go up it myself," he replied, "then I'll have done it and you won't."

We both went. The hill was better than I deserved with my lack of enthusiasm, a huge gherkin of a cairn on top and unaccustomed views west, east and northwards as the cloud burned off and warm sunshine turned the snow to sludge. By now we were sinking into the melting snow, and the return route to Loch Rannoch contained deep banks of heather and a river crossing, by which we sat and marvelled at the warmth and sudden change in the weather. Scotland is infamous for changeable weather and clouds quickly rushing in and raining on previously happy scenes; it was good to have it the other way around for a change. I'm not so sure about the 'great atmosphere of space' the SMC guide goes on to talk about, but it is a good hill nonetheless.

Carn Dearg, Glen Roy *(karn jerrig) – the deluge*
834m OS 34/41 NN 345887

The weather was dreadful. Rain was streaming from the sky, the sort of rain Noah probably saw after building his Ark and said to himself "here we go!" Billy and I had arrived in Glen Roy via a wild camp the night before, after being tipped off about a fantastic site by a punter in the Commando Bar. However, after a clear and moonlit night, the morning had proved a washout; and only the thought of a new hill had provided enough motivation to get us up and going in the morning.

Thus we arrived at the roadend in Glen Roy, looking for an easy walk and a quick drive home.

We were barely twelve yards from the car when suddenly a people-carrier full of Israelis pulled up and stopped to ask us if it was possible to drive any further. We discussed the dreadful weather we were having.

"The rain in Scotland is terrible!" they said, looking at our already glistening waterproofs in disbelief. "How can you possibly go walking in this weather today!"

We were in philosophical mood, despite the rain dripping from our noses. "Ach well, everywhere has its downside," I replied. "Aye, if we only waited for nice days, we'd never get out on the hills," and they seemed to nod in, if not agreement, at least acknowledgement.

"Hey, we only have to put up with the rain, but you have to deal with the Arabs!"

Billy looked horrified, and I realised my unthinking comments had probably caused serious offence.

But the people-carrier folk laughed like drains. Just as well they weren't Arab-Israelis, I suppose.

We walked past Brae Roy Lodge into the teeth of a storm the nearby North Atlantic would have been proud of, heading for the Roads of Glen Roy and their unusual geological thrills on the other side of the river. There's not much to see, but once you realise the thin, landrover-track-like bands contouring perfectly round the hills are actually ice-age shorelines, the novelty value is pretty high. As the Burn of Agie falls past one of the Roads, a waterfall is created, the ancient shoreline sitting on a chockstone above. We looked down over this impressive tunnel, and headed northeast towards the River Roy, all thoughts of climbing a hill in this weather abandoned. The river was very high and the bracing weather wasn't improving. There was no way we could ford this seriously engorged river anywhere, and so on spying a bridge we crossed it and headed back.

Back at the car, standing in the shrieking gale force rain miles from anywhere, we discovered all the tyres had been let down. Hmm. Perhaps they had been Arab-Israelis after all.

Sgurr an Utha *(skoor an oo-tha)* – *cigarettes*
796m OS 40 NM 885839

Look at the map, OS Landranger 40. See that hill Sgurr an Utha? Doesn't look like much, eh? It is surrounded by other, higher, more interesting looking hills. It was with this mindset Brian and I set off up Sgurr an Utha late one spring day en route to a wild camp at Morar for a Corbett-ticking excercise, and nothing more.

In common with many of the hills in this area, Sgurr an Utha has lots of naked outcrops bursting forth from the soil, green green grass, and a rough, high-kurtosis outline. The initial slopes are a bit of a slog, but higher up it opens out to a wonderland of knobbles and crags, making for interesting rather than frustrating going, at least on a May day of good visibility. We found a miniature ravine with a waterfall, the deep pool at its base hoaching with frogs. On the summit the view was remarkably good for such an unassuming hill, with an amazing aspect into Knoydart, Loch Beoraid, Rum & Skye, Lochaber; and I knew that I would not stand to hear Sgurr an Utha dismissed in future.

Once down, we retired to our campsite. The area between Arisaig and Mallaig is littered with small, beautiful bays, each with a breathtaking situation looking over the sands towards the Inner Hebrides, with the triangular peak of Sgurr na Ciche behind inland. We cooked a leisurely dinner on daisy and buttercup strewn meadow grass, then had a paddle at the beach. The shore was teeming with life – the sand pale and near white, thousands of tiny, inch-long white-camouflaged flatfish scooting away underfoot as we approached, hermit crabs in the clear water, and streams of bubbles rising from footprints – evidence of ragworms underfoot.

After watching the sunset and being attacked by midges, we walked in to Mallaig for some drink. Later, coming back from the pub, Brian ran out of cigarettes. Back to the pub! But all the pubs were shut. Brian was agitated. "I need a fag!" he said. Yet – what was that noise of music and conversation coming from the village hall? We walked in, and found ourselves at a

40th birthday party. In the general confusion over who we were, Brian cadged some cigarettes, and a handsome, thirty-something woman gave me her car keys with the instructions to retrieve some cans of Stella from the boot. My mind boggled that a complete stranger had given me her keys, but I found the car, opened the boot, and there they were!

Back in the village hall the party was pretty much over, the music finished, but someone was up singing a Gaelic air. After they sat down to applause, Brian tried to get me up to sing *The Clashgour Ban*. I refused so he stood up himself, singing through his hand with a mad glint in his eye, a gatecrashing stranger drinking someone else's beer, smoking someone else' cigarettes, with a captive audience for his favourite song. The man who had organised the party (for his wife) introduced himself, and took us out to show us the car he had bought her for her 40th birthday – a beautiful, perfectly restored original VW Beetle. "She's a beauty, eh boys?" he asked. "Shall we go for a drive? Eh love," he shouted in to his wife, "can I take the car for a drive with the boys?" His wife was clearing up, stuck her head round the door and shouted affectionately "No, of course not! You're drunk!"

"Ah, whit a woman," he said. "Fine woman, beautiful woman, don't you agree boys?" and we could only agree, taking the opportunity to move on. We walked back to the tent, consuming the Stellas on the way.

Ceann na Baintighearna *(kan na vayn-tee-er-na) – competition on the hill*
771m OS 57 NN 474163

Although Billy liked to take the moral high ground over the issue of Corbett bagging, he had actually been up a number of them with me, his totals – if he were honest – probably not much lower than mine. "Ah, but I'm going away for the experience of the hills," he said, "not to get a tick on some sad list." But, being a Munro bagger, he was already a sad list-ticker. I was just converting him to the Corbetts by stealth.

Thus, after a drive up an unclassified road that turned into a mere track, Billy, Duncan and I clambered out and donned boots and rucksacks at the bottom of Ceann na Baintighearna – another Corbett.

Quickly, we were in amongst the hills, and the track disappeared. A herd of red deer congregated on boggy ground on the other side of the river. We crossed the river and they moved on only slightly, as cattle would. The grassy eastern ridge of this hill rose above us, so we ascended steeply to its long, undulating back, a subsidiary ridge connecting with the main ridge of this hill just before the summit. We soon passed two slower walkers. Ahead of all of us was the figure of a keen man.

It was fairly easy to construct what was happening. Mr Keen, fitter than his companions, frustrated at their slowness; had said "I'll see you at the top," and had shot off in front at his own preferred pace. He probably had the only map. It was clear what we had to do. It was our duty to burn him off.

Thus we continued along this ridge with renewed velocity and purpose, our target no longer the summit, but the quick figure ahead of us. We jogged when he was out of view. He looked back occasionally, perhaps to check up on his companions. They were well out of sight by now, but the important thing, we felt, wasn't them; we could almost feel his physical desire to reach the summit before us, and nuts to his companions. He disappeared beneath a steep dip in the ridge, and we ran for all we were worth. We would be almost on top of him!

But then he appeared below and in front of us, well ahead of where we expected, climbing as rapidly as he could. He had decided to race us and had jogged down the hillside whilst he was out of sight. This confirmed it: he was doing his level best to avoid being overtaken. The race was on!

We powered up the steep slope before the main ridge and the summit, overtaking him near the top. As soon as we had gained the advantage he stopped, sat on his rucksack, and looked contemplatively back towards the ridge we had come up as if this were his intention all along. Eventually his companions would appear. At least he could boast of his achievements to them.

Billy, Duncan and I laughed at all this. Hadn't we grown out of such behaviour years ago? Yet here we were racing a stranger on the hill! However, it was a good feeling to still be capable of burning someone off; and we had reached the summit far more quickly than we would have done otherwise.

Beinn Ime *(ben eem)* – *the ideal hill*
1011m OS 56 NN 255085

Beinn Ime always seemed to me to be an ideal hill. Its triangular aspect towers over everything else above Butterbridge, a memorable and awe-inspiring sight for a small boy whose grandmother lived south of Dunoon, and under which profound heights the family car had to pass to get to her house. One day, recounted by my sister, the car actually *drove through a cloud* at the top of the Rest and Be Thankful, and I was jealous that I hadn't gone with them that time. To an eight-year old boy, driving through a cloud must be the experience of a lifetime! Looking back, I realise that walking the hills has afforded me the benefit of the inside of plenty of clouds.

So Beinn Ime was always there from the very beginning: a mountain that lurked in the consciousness as much as on any map.

One glorious Saturday I headed up Beinn Ime with Claire from the Lomond, my last full weekend in Glasgow before heading to Birmingham to start a new job. It was a bittersweet occasion as I was happy to be going south, excited at the prospect of new horizons, and jaded with the Glasgow of failure I had come to know too well for comfort. This was tempered by the knowledge that I liked being near the hills, and Birmingham could not offer the same range and quality. But a year after launching my career in music, I was penniless, disillusioned, and desperate to leave Glasgow, even if this meant saying goodbye to the hills.

We ascended via an unfashionable route from Glen Croe, little frequented yet the shortest route to the summit. I tried some scrambling and dislodged a couple-of-hundred-kilo sized rock. Fortunately I didn't fall too far, managing to grab hold of something with my hands, and scrabbled frantically with my feet to stay above the falling rock. Chastened, I caught up with Claire on the summit.

We couldn't believe how good it was up here, the light feeling, a couple of speckled remains of snow, the immense visibility, including Arran, Rum, Mull, Cruachan, Bidean, Ben Nevis, Ben Lui, Breadalbane, Ben More, the Trossachs, the whole wonderful, green-flanked, cloud-dappled Southern Highlands. I had no idea the view from Ben Ime could be so good. It was just one of those amazing days.

A middle-aged man arrived at the summit, and we exchanged greetings. He lived in Lochgilphead.

"I've just come back from visiting my daughter in Winchester," he said, exulting: "What a day! I've driven all night, but when I saw the weather, I couldn't resist coming up here. Would you look at that view!"

"It's great to see my daughter, but I'm glad to be back," he added. I wouldn't want to live down there . . ." and we both shivered. For that one moment, I had forgotten I too was heading south very soon.

Beinn an Lochain *(ben an loch-an)* – *Arrochar no more* *901m OS 56 NN 218079*

There was a girl, about sixteen years old, chatty and self-confident, whom I met when I graduated and started work doing data entry for a credit reference company. I was twenty-one, and we seemed to have nothing at all in common. As I spent the dreary winter days of soulless labour dreaming up a scheme to walk the coast of the West Highlands from Ardnamurchan to Cape Wrath, she would be out partying at a rave with her friends, coming in to work and showing us her new tattoo.

Thus imagine my surprise years later on joining the Lomond Mountaineering Club, to discover she had also just joined.

Hers was a face I had never expected to see again, but it was a welcome one. Her name was Lynne, and after my last ever Lomond club meet in Wintersgills pub and just before I left for good, she wanted a hill.

Early Saturday, zen-like Paul picked Lynne and me up in his battered old car, and we headed for the Rest and Be Thankful past Arrochar, heading for Beinn an Lochain. The day was beautiful, cool in the morning but warming up as the sun climbed.

We headed up the sharp northwest ridge, the best route on this hill. We tried a bit of scrambling on dank turf crags higher up. There was a man at the top. "What did you do to deserve that?" he asked, when I told him I was moving to Brum. This was a popular sentiment amongst friends, and I was to find it hard to persuade them (the majority being hillwalkers) to visit once I had moved to the English Lowlands.

On the way down we sunbathed and stroked the grass. A quality hill, enjoyed by me as the condemned man might enjoy his last cigarette. Arrochar no more; Glencoe no more; Skye no more; Lochaber no more; Lomond and Paul and Lynne no more. The point though, was it meant unemployment, unhappiness and poverty no more.

Shortly after arriving in Birmingham, a couple of my songs were played on Radio 1 – The People With Computers in Their Head, and one I'd recorded for another band. It was to be my nearest brush with fame.

PART SIX

Furth of Scotland

From the Central Belt of Scotland where I was based, my hillwalking eye naturally looked north. My occasional forays south were made more for the sake of 'something different this weekend' than through a genuine interest in the Southern Uplands. And as for England or Wales? The Lakes and Snowdonia were all right, but with better hills – lots of them – closer to hand, they weren't worth the effort.

But then I got a job in Birmingham.

I'd completed the Munros a couple of years earlier, and had spent the weekends since wandering up other hills. I couldn't imagine life without hillwalking. But I was unemployed, skint, and had no partner. Perhaps Birmingham would bring the things Glasgow lacked? I might learn to enjoy chilling out, socialising, spending weekends in town, and mixing with people who weren't hillwalkers.

I managed all of that. I even found a few hills to climb, in the end. And I finally understood the mentality of the glossy outdoor magazine buyer, people who spend more time dreaming of the hills than just getting out there and up them. When you've been living in a big city, miles from bumpy countryside, and eventually walk up a hill for the first time in a month, it doesn't matter how unassuming that hill is – you enjoy it, appreciate it, and savour it like a rare malt.

Clent Hills – *what have I let myself in for?*
315m OS 139 SO 942798

I had been working in my new job in Birmingham for a week. When I asked my boss what there was to do in Brum over the weekend, she pointed me to various bars and shops. As I had no money and knew no one to socialise with, I worked that Saturday.

Back in my room, trying to sleep in the hottest weather I'd ever known, the air in inland Birmingham stifling, I opened my travel bag and reached deep inside for an emergency book, a source of inspiration and salvation, and one that was to save my sanity in Birmingham – my well-thumbed copy of *The Relative Hills of Britain*.

The closest Marilyn to Birmingham is Walton Hill in the Clent Hills. It is accessible by public transport, so that's where I headed.

On Sunday I took a train to Hagley, and crossed a roundabout at a dual carriageway to wander though fat fields shimmering in the heat, seeking shelter under big leafy trees, following rights of way. It was too hot and I was suffering; it was weather for watersports, not walking. My clothing was all wrong for the continental heat of Central England. Heavy jeans, waterproof shoes, waterproof jacket and a thick-weave t-shirt are ideal for a West Highland summer, but everyone else was gadding about in shades and open-topped sports cars, wearing three-quarters length trousers and sandals, drinking in beer gardens, flying St George's Crosses, and displaying other disorientating behaviour.

I found a definite track through some trees, and followed it uphill until before I knew it, I was at a summit viewpoint. All around were milling crowds, mountainbikes, *rrramblers*. I sat and contemplated the urban-industrial sprawl of the West Midlands laid out before me. The Birmingham conurbation, Black Mountain, Malvern Hills, Bredon Hill, Costwolds, even Chilterns, but mostly haze and fields and car-choked lanes under a thick hot grey sky. A couple came up behind me. "Oh, now look!" said the man. "Isn't that spectacular!"

'Dear Lord,' I thought. 'If this is spectacular, what have I let myself in for?'

Cadair Idris – *escape!*
893m OS 124 SH 711130

I had been lodging in Birmingham for six weeks and not seen a proper hill in all that time. Cabin fever! I went downstairs on Saturday morning for breakfast and my hosts tittered. "Do you not remember what happened last night?" asked the landlady. Apparently, looking for the toilet, I had walked into their bedroom drunk, mumbled "D'oh," then stumbled outside to pee on their lawn. I was mortified. I had to get out of town and get some air . . .

So I took my bike on the train to Machynlleth, and went up the road to spend Saturday night in Corris Youth Hostel. It was full of hippies. There was a lock-in at the local pub but, mindful of the previous night's excesses, I retired early for a good night's sleep.

The next morning I cycled in drizzle to Cadair Idris, and was so surprised to be charged for chaining my bike to some railings at the campsite at the bottom of the hill, that I forgot my usual financial rectitude and paid without complaint. It was a grey, drizzly, overcast day, but I entered the clouds and sniffed the scent of the hills, the scree, the rocks, the lochan, the wet grass . . . My legs pumped enthusiastically for the summit like a sperm swimming for an egg. I felt exultant, happy in a way I hadn't felt for a long time. I had been missing the hills!

Two mountain-bikers arrived at the summit and were ticked-off by a ranger – who appeared from nowhere – about cycling on the tops. I was back down at the bike in under two and a half hours, and rode out west to the coast at Tywyn and Aberdyfi. I feared my heart would melt. The sea! A beach! Oh, I hadn't realised until now how much I had been missing the coast! The sun was out and I wanted to stay. But the last train back to Birmingham would not wait for me, and I turned regretfully inland.

As I waited at the station, a couple alighted from the coast-bound train and the woman stole a glance at me. *Going back to the city?* the look seemed to say. A look of sympathy, I felt.

Worcestershire Beacon – *Malvern bag*
425m OS 150 SO 768452

It was a summer's weekend in Birmingham, a city where I knew nobody. There was nothing for it but to get out of the airless city and cycle the English countryside, basking under heat-hazy grey skies. The roads around Worcester and Broms-grove were busy, but I was inured to them thanks to my daily bicycle commute. Malvern came eventually and I was relieved, as the final pull up through the town is long and steep. The Malverns form a grassy spine of land plumped right in the middle of Worcestershire in the heart of the English country-side, and they were the butt of my jokes as a teenager climbing in the Scottish Highlands. They seemed then to form a large part of the outdoor Briton's consciousness. Was it just coin-cidence that half the outdoor magazines in my tiny collection mentioned the Malverns? Probably. It had seemed impossible when I was sixteen to open an outdoor magazine without an article raving about this miniature hill range. Here I was a decade later, finally about to climb them.

I chained my bike to a railing in the shadow of Worcester-shire Beacon, and powered up a hill path, reaching the top in a few minutes. Warm, hazy and populated, the Malverns are countryside, not wilderness. A better walk by far would be to traverse the entire length of the hill, but I had no interest in this, performing a mere smash-and-grab raid before returning to the city. I cycled to Malvern station to get the train back, giving some kids who were swearing at the ticket collector a quick double-barrel of threatening language. Unexpectedly, they quailed and backed off. You can take the boy out of Glasgow . . .

Bredon Hill – *this pleasant seat*
299m OS 150 SO 958402

I'd been past the prominent lump of Bredon Hill a couple of times on my bike, rising out of the Heart of England flatlands like a stranded whale, and never bothered to visit. On a bike trip into Gloucestershire, I decided on the spur of the moment that it was about time I popped up.

I wasn't sure where to start as I didn't have a relevant OS map and unusually, walked the hill blind. My start point, Ashton-Under-Hill, turned out to be the most distant possible point from the summit. But this was no hardship, with a bit of exercise on a pleasant hill the result of the day's endeavours.

I walked quickly up past some horse riders, then didn't see a soul until later descent. The path is a flat meander across an elevated ridged plateau, but not dull, since it has views around Worcestershire. It was sunny and surprisingly warm, with happy birds in the trees.

At the far end of the plateau ridge sit the ramparts of an iron-age hillfort, topped by what seems to be a Victorian folly. This is a nice place to be, king of the surrounding farmlands. However, so flat-topped is this escarpment that I was confused as to where the actual summit was. It seemed to be further east, back along the way I came and off the path a bit. I meandered aimlessly around a few seeming highpoints, unsure if I had visited the actual, official, very topmost point on this hill.

I rode back to Birmingham for a Sunday pub dinner with new friends. My employers were a computer company, and soon after arriving I was put in charge of their website content.

Most of the employees were twenty-something graduates, and there was a buzz and sociability about the open-plan office that was welcoming to a stranger in town. I made friends with Matt, a fellow Glaswegian, and Greg, who had interviewed me for the job. Alice and Chris were mellow rockers, and through them I got to know the Birmingham music scene. Charlotte and Soheb worked with me on the website, and I hung around with Dave the South African and party-lover Whisky Jim.

Meall nam Maigheach *(myal nam my-ich)* – *Caledonia calling*
780m OS 51 NN 586436

In the summer of the year that I moved to Birmingham, I arranged to meet friends from the Lomond Mountaineering Club and returned north. I had arranged to go to Ardgour with Lynne and Paul for a walk up Garbh Bheinn on Saturday, but the forecast wasn't good, and they'd decided to go to Northumberland instead. I certainly wasn't going to head south again on a rare foray north, so hung around my parents in Helensburgh instead, playing piano and working in the garden. Not really what I'd expected of the weekend.

For Sunday I'd arranged to go walking with Alan from the Lomond. We hadn't decided on a destination, but I was determined that if I was going walking in bad weather, I wanted it to be worth a Corbett or two. Alan felt exactly the same way, except that he wanted a Munro, not a Corbett, and we swithered between Tyndrum and Glen Lyon. I argued for Glen Lyon as the further east we were, the better the weather would be, and we would also – though I didn't say this out loud – be further away from the Munro Alan wanted to do. A few months away from the hills and spending more time around people, and my persuasive powers were already more sophisticated! Thus we eventually climbed a Corbett.

Despite a bad forecast, the weather was all right. But what

surprised me was that I didn't feel a misty-eyed sense of homecoming. I was expecting it, looking forward to it, to some kind of Local Hero moment, the heart-stirring breasting of a ridge with a familiar and achingly beautiful scene laid out before me, and a feeling that I was home. But no. The best bit in this area was the tree-lined glen looking over the river to the ridges leading up to Ben Lawers. The hills themselves were bleak and featureless. Meall nam Maigheach gave a perfunctory ascent of misty, dew-speckled heather brae from the highest part of the road, with a cairn on the top. Beinn Dearg in Glen Lyon was a bit more interesting – a steep grassy corrie above a soft fertile glen, a top, and a descent. But I still didn't feel like burning my return ticket.

Thanks to flexitime, I didn't have to start work till Monday lunchtime, so I stayed in Scotland on Sunday night and took the earliest train to Birmingham. Somewhere about Lancaster, the sun came out. It had been sunny here all weekend. I walked out onto Birmingham New St, and it was good to see all the girls with their flattering clothes and people looking happy in the sunshine, instead of Monday morning rain and Glaswegian commuters with their faces tripping themselves.

Titterstone Clee Hill – *a Shropshire yomp*
533m OS 137/138 SO 592779

Another car-free weekend in Birmingham. I took an early train to Shrewsbury and Ludlow, the unfriendly ticket office staff telling me I would have a problem with my bike. It annoys me that you can't take bikes on so many of Britain's trains. Fortunately it was OK in the morning getting to Ludlow. I would worry later about getting back.

I discussed the quickest way out of town with a horsey country woman, and followed the steep road she indicated until I was at the hill. It was a hard ride, more knackering than expected. Could I be unfit, or could the lack of quality of the bike be showing? Let's blame the bike! I schlopped across a muddy field to an unmetalled track, then strode quickly to the top. The summit area is littered with disused quarries, abandoned torched cars, and a radar station on the very top. An unsightly hill. Not much view either, on a dull and windy day. Back down, it took a long time cycling along steep, muddy – and shitty – country roads to Brown Clee Hill, though this was a slightly better top. I felt light-headed through dehydration on the way up but, with the smell of manure all around, was afraid to drink water from the burns.

I was getting through the Marilyns though, and having a good workout into the bargain. The next hill for the day was Callow Hill which I slithered up, unable to avoid falling over in mud, covering myself in it, sweating and cursing. The summit itself was hard to find on the flat-topped, tree-lined ridge. Back down at Craven Arms railway station it was decision time: should I attempt the next hill on my list, View Edge? There was only an hour of daylight left. However, this final Marilyn looked the least inspiring of the lot and might involve some frustrating beating through forestry, so I decided to call it quits for the day and get an earlier train. I bought some heartily enjoyed fish & chips while I waited. It had been good to get some exercise, even if I found myself wondering what the point of this Marilyn bagging was.

Ingleborough – *fresh air*
724m OS 98 SD 740745

A pent-up frustration was building in me – I needed to get out of Birmingham. I had worked three of the previous four weekends, and was getting cabin fever. However, with the trains in the state they were in after the Hatfield crash, there were no guarantees about getting anywhere, or of getting back again. Fortunately my colleague Ben came to the rescue. He arranged to take me and another colleague, Gareth, to the Three Peaks of Yorkshire, a trek I'd heard was a good long walk. We were really looking forward to it.

I was wakened late by Ben phoning. I was annoyed with myself, but he was only calling to say he was just setting off, and also late. Unfortunately Gareth wasn't, and had been standing on a cold street corner for 45 minutes waiting for us.

Dawn was just breaking as we left Brum. North Yorkshire is a long way up the winter motorway, and it was over three hours later when we arrived at Whernside. We stepped out to a cold bluff breeze, invigorating and unpolluted. I hadn't noticed the bad air in the city until now, and we breathed in lungfuls of fresh air. Ben parked near the Settle-Carlisle railway viaduct, and we headed up the path.

"Straight up?" I queried.

"No, dogleg along the path," insisted Ben, laughing, "look how steep it is!"

'I've been steeper,' I thought to myself, but it was a nice walk, the view from the top being of empty moors stretching as far as the eye could see east and northeast, with the Howgills to the north and the Lakes just visible through the mist. No sea though. The other Yorkshire Peaks were to the south, Ingleborough the most shapely of the trio, with Pen-y-ghent being little more than a pimple on the moorside. Down Whernside, we headed for the sculpted flank of Ingleborough, going fast over limestone escarpments, dry moor grass, and buckboards that had been laid across a boggy section of moor. On the top of Ingleborough it started to sleet, the cloud closing in. We headed north back to the car, deciding to leave Pen-y-ghent for another day, and Gareth and I drank a couple of pints in a local pub. This beer was amazing! I could finally understand why a couple of beer-loving climbers in the Lomond Mountaineering Club were always banging on about having a trip to Yorkshire. Why couldn't places like the Kingshouse in Glencoe serve a decent pint? It was a fantastic day out in Yorkshire, and just what the doctor ordered.

Note: since first writing this, the Kingshouse has begun selling ales from Kinlochleven's Atlas Brewery – a commendable development.

Hutton Roof Crags – *the hill of mirrors*
274m OS 97 SD 556775

Once I got hold of a car, I didn't take the train between Birmingham and Glasgow so much. And once I had wheels, I was on the lookout for Marilyns lying between Scotland and the Midlands. Hutton Roof Crags, just off the M6 opposite where the Lake District starts, was the most obvious candidate. I had my eye on it for a while before eventually visiting.

Once off the M6 motorway, the roads are narrow country lanes, bordered by high hedges. It is impossible to see what's round the corner, to know if there's a car, bicycle, pedestrian, or horse looming. And round here the roads are a thicket, splitting like branching veins at every opportunity. I could only find the start for Hutton Roof Crags, just a mile or two from the M6, with the greatest of concentration.

Normally in the Lowlands, the hardest part of a hill is finding the start, and I presumed Hutton Roof Crags would be no different. The story of climbing it seemed simple. A climb, a swift denouement, and home in time for tea, barely sweating, the mud of Hutton Roof Crags shaken from my boots. I set off obviously uphill, and entered a densely vegetated area. No matter – there appeared to be a path leading upwards, which even ran like a tunnel through dense hedge-like trees. But when it exited, I was confused to find myself on a plateau of grey limestone escarpment and trees.

I wandered all over the escarpment for a while, which seemed to be split by a mild dip into two equally high areas of chaotic rock. It was impossible to tell if any point was higher than any other. Eventually, convinced I must have surely wandered over the highest point, I headed down. But, over in the trees – could I be sure the highest point wasn't over in the trees? It was impossible to know, even if I went over to find out. I didn't fancy aimlessly pushing through the trees, branches in my face, deep in the forest, no horizon, sweating, for no result. Perplexed and disarmed, I headed down.

To this day I have no idea if I have been to the top of Hutton Roof Crags or not.

Bishop Wilton Wold – *the easiest Marilyn*
246m OS 106 SE 821569

It was the last week of work before Christmas, and I was looking forward to heading home for a couple of weeks holiday. I was driving Matt home to Glasgow, and his girlfriend, from East Yorkshire, wondered if she could get a lift home too. "Sure," I said – then looked at the map, and realised that East Yorkshire is quite a large detour between Birmingham and Helensburgh. But then I looked more closely – she lived near Bishop Wilton Wold! Bishop Wilton Wold is the easiest Marilyn by a fair margin. I would make the most of this detour. Thus we arrived late on the last Friday before Christmas in Driffield, the local police flagging me down on the outskirts of town and sniffing for alcohol.

Next morning Matt and I set off for Bishop Wilton Wold. In deep, picture-postcard snows, I parked the car. We crossed a fence, and in a few yards were touching the trig point. This Marilyn (I hesitate to call it a hill) is next to the village with the rudest-sounding name in England, Wetwang. Wetwang's mayor at the time was Richard Whiteley, of the TV programme Countdown. This area of the country is well worth a visit, if for a couple of odd, trainspotterish reasons. Here are two of the most singular things in Britain – the easiest Marilyn, and the rudest placename – despite there being nothing spectacular of note to see. I felt as a historian might feel standing in a housing estate that used to be a great battlefield, feeling the greatness of the place despite any visual evidence to the contrary.

Shining Tor – *the rambler's peak*
559m OS 118 SJ 994737

Everyone knows someone like Norman. The annoying windbag, the party bore, a person you couldn't call offensive, but your heart sinks at the thought of spending time in their company. Because you know they will make it feel like a lot of time.

Norman's speciality was complaining. He could win the lottery and still find something lacking in the experience – perhaps the colour of the decor in the lottery company's offices – something that had to be expounded upon loudly and at length. He wanted to go cycling with me, but wouldn't ride round the West Midlands generally because it was too hilly. He was from East Anglia. This should have been a warning to me to restrict my contacts with Norman to the pub table, but in a post-nightclub hangover one Saturday morning, Norman called and, in my weakened and confused state, I agreed to go hillwalking with him on Sunday.

Next day it was snowing, but Norman was still up for it. I had planned Kinder Scout, but it didn't look promising. There are tales that the top is so flat yet ridden with peat hags that it is hard enough to find the summit even on a clear day. It wasn't a great day weatherwise, with salt from gritted roads spraying the car windows. The passenger footwell was full of water too, because someone I'd lent the car to had left the window open on a rainy night. Norman knocked over the chemical dehumidifier I'd installed to fix this, spilling calcium chloride everywhere, which didn't lighten my mood.

It took a couple of hours from Birmingham to reach the walking-off point for the first hill, Black Hill, and as the road rises to a good height it was ridiculously easy in effort, if a test of navigational skills in thick mist. Norman seemed to find it rough and let me know about it but, unsympathetic in my waterproofs and proper boots, I didn't care. He is a rambler. Hillwalking has a different meaning to ramblers. In more adventurous company I might have attempted Kinder Scout, but quartering the plateau for something resembling a summit in this mist didn't seem appealing, and Norman's presence tipped the balance. We drove instead to Shining Tor, one of the easiest and most inconsequential hills I've ever done. It was an odd feeling to drive for so long for such a short walk, but Marilyn bagging in the south will always be like this. All the effort is in the road navigation, driving one-armed, the other hand wrestling with a map. The walking itself is the work of moments. This may, of course, be a blessing in disguise if it persuades Marilyn-baggers to create devious and tortuous routes round places of local interest just to bump up the mileage, and to take an interest in the local history and wildlife, thus gaining a more rounded experience as a result!

Back home we had a good chat and Norman lent me a CD-ROM with some useful programs that I wanted, and I had to acknowledge that our friendship was not all bad. Who else, after all, would come with me for a day of Marilyn bagging in poor weather?

Cleeve Hill – *a Cotswold ramble*
330m OS 163 SO 997246

I plugged my drum machine into its wall-wart transformer, and smelt smoke. Damn! I'd plugged it into the wrong transformer, the one for the reverb unit. The drum machine was knackered, so I had to find a new one. A man in Cheltenham was selling a second hand drum machine at a decent price in the local Exchange & Mart, so I decided to make a day of it and wander up a Marilyn into the bargain.

After picking up the replacement drum machine, I drove around Gloucestershire for a while, getting lost, before finally finding the road to Cleeve Hill. This is the highest point in the Cotswolds and is surrounded by surprisingly steep sides. It might be a small hill, but as it sits on an escarpment, it has a nice feeling of elevation, making the most of its modest height. There is a road to within a couple of hundred metres of the summit however, and it only takes a couple of minutes to bag. On touching the trig point I experienced that familiar anti-climactic feeling that Marilyn bagging in Lowland areas provides – drive for hours, walk for minutes. Finding the start is the hardest part for a great deal of lower Marilyns; that, and dealing with access difficulties.

It was such an effortless top that I walked a bit further across Cleeve Common to another trig point, indicated on the map as a viewpoint. It was a little lower, but right on the escarpment edge. The summit itself had been neglected by other visitors, but Cleeve Common was busier, with horse-riders and walkers, and I found a discreet bush of gorse for a quick leak, looking northeast down a green, chalky gully.

The Cotswolds in general are nice, but not in a couthy People's Friend kind of way. Even if they aren't ostentatious, there are too many wealthy people in the Cotswolds for it to have the same feeling as Galloway or the Campsies. Porsches and Mercedes are parked up driveways of small but ancient houses in mellow, honey-coloured, picture-postcard villages.

Esgair Ddu – *a blast of fresh air*
464m OS 125 SH 873107

At a party at Dave's the night before, Whisky Jim was riding on the shoulders of a burly work colleague, yelling "Yehhah! Giddyup!" and banging his head off the ceiling. In the kitchen, a drinking game called 'Five's Alive' was being played. I remembered lying face down on the stairs, absolutely buckled, thinking 'if I can just get home without being sick, everything will be all right.' Two work colleagues carried me into a cab, but afterwards I could only remember who one of them was.

Jim and I were feeling the worse for wear next day, and wanted to get out of Birmingham to recuperate. I suggested the Youth Hostel at Corris that had served me well as a base for Cadair Idris. So, late in the afternoon, we set off along the M54 to Shrewsbury, then wound along the Welsh back roads to Corris.

We stopped off en route for a quick jaunt up a hill. The weather was dreadful. Howling wind, lashing rain, cold and murky with cloud down to the road. Excellent! This was just what we needed to clear the cobwebs. We set off up a steep hillside, views of nothing except mud, grass and bog, and continued to the top. The wind was strong enough to knock us over, and we crawled at some points. There was nothing on top to detain us, so we reversed our route, holding our arms open for a thrill, battered by the strong wind and driving rain.

Back at the car, rosy-cheeked, I was looking forward to

removing my waterproofs and being dry. "Wait a minute," said Jim. He removed his boots, tipped them upside down, and sighed as water poured out of each boot. Our Saturday night was quieter than Friday had been.

At work on Monday, I recounted the story of the weekend, wondering who Friday night's second Good Samaritan was, the unknown colleague in the cab who had made sure I'd arrived home OK. It had been quite a mystery.

"Ah," said my boss's boss. "That was me."

Bardon Hill – *a Leicestershire quarry* *278m OS 129 SK 460132*

Bardon Hill is probably the dullest and most inconsequential Marilyn I've visited. Still, it provided a half-day out from Birmingham, so in a flat county like Leicestershire was worth a look.

In the event, it wasn't even worth that!

I drove to Bardon Drive Farm, had a look, then decided not to attempt walking up the private track past the farmhouse to Bardon Hill, but stick instead to the right of way which takes an awkward and roundabout route. It was crazy to go this way instead of straight up the private track, but the trespass laws in intensely farmed areas like the East Midlands are strictly enforced.

So I parked where I could on an unclassified road between Copt Oak and Greenhill, and walked along the roadside to the right of way. It doubled back following the line of the road, but after passing under some huge electricity pylons, the track took a ninety-degree turn towards Bardon Hill. It then disappeared, so I guesstimated the route, threading around deep clumps of thistles over a heavy, uneven field. I recrossed under the pylons through an ugly dug-up field, then the path became distinct again for a few metres, before crossing through the back yard of another farm, full of machinery and a farmer in a tractor unloading stuff from a lorry. So far, so very different to most hillwalking experiences.

Finally, after this farm, the right-of-way rejoined the vehicle track from Bardon Drive Farm and became plain sailing – and even pleasant for a short time in the trees. The summit was underwhelming: a view north of a quarry, as one side of Bardon Hill is cut away completely. Trees obscured any view to the other side.

I didn't spend long at the top, and descended the way I had come up. Dave and his flatmates were hosting another party that night. At the party, Charlotte and I were catching up on the office gossip, when Chris came through with an incredulous look on his face. "Whisky Jim just ate my dinner!" he said. "I left for two minutes to wash my hands, came back and it was practically gone!" When it came to food and drink, publicly schooled Jim was an out-and-out communist.

Billinge Hill – *the zen of bagging*
179m OS 108 SD 525014

If you have ever driven between Birmingham and Scotland, you have probably noticed Billinge Hill sitting between the two somewhere near Liverpool, begging to be climbed. Oh, perhaps you haven't noticed? Perhaps it is only Marilyn-baggers who notice places like Billinge Hill, a good twenty mile drive out of the way along knotty wee roads, roads whose navigation is the hardest part of Billinge Hill.

Perhaps you are driving between Birmingham and Glasgow and have decided to take the awkward detour to Billinge Hill, a place which seems merely unprepossessing on the map but which, on investigation, genuinely questions your motivation, your commitment to a certain bagging ideal, and your philosophy of life. Frankly if you can get all this quality psychology from an elevated piece of field, I would definitely recommend it.

Billinge Hill itself consists of suburban housing battening down against the grey storm, a track and green field beyond, leading to a short wander in some refreshing wet air to a top of sorts with a communication mast, and an overwhelming sense of anti-climax.

What was the point of visiting this hill?

Only those who have been to Billinge Hill can truly know the answer.

Hoove – *British mud*
554m OS 92 NZ 003071

Before driving south again from the West of Scotland to Birmingham, I decided to visit a Marilyn on the way. Map-browsing the internet, Hoove seemed a nice easy one, so I printed and pocketed a mini-map of the hill, ready for use on my way back down the road.

I took the fast road between Penrith and Scotch Corner, turning off for an insignificant backroad over the moors. I was soon at the county boundary at the top, a place with a sense of space after a steep road climb through some trees.

The top of Hoove was barely a mile away, and little higher than the road.

I parked, and wandered over the moor. It was boggy and full of drainage ditches. Birds sang. The side of a peatbank obstructed my way, and I jumped into the clart. Is there any mud in the world like mud on British uplands, oozing, black, glutinous and waterlogged? As I pulled my boot out with a satisfying 'scchhlllloooopp,' I thought there was not mud to match this anywhere. There was more of it, then a short, drier pull up to the summit plateau. Nowhere on this plateau seemed the obvious high point, and there was a view all round only of moor upon moor, villages hidden in dale bottoms. Once I had made a circuit of the likely tops of this flat hill, I descended the way I'd come.

In all my time in Birmingham, I climbed very few Marilyns in company. I sometimes missed my regular hillwalking companions. But they would not visit Birmingham – 'a waste of a weekend' they would say. 'Come back up north instead.' This annoyed me; Birmingham was not as bad as its detractors painted it.

Lleyn Peninsula – *the spout of Wales*
564m OS 123 SH 365447

Another weekend had arrived in Birmingham, and I had nothing planned. I hated this. After breezing through the week in a social whirl of quick pints after work, the weekend would come and, unless I had already made arrangements, I could be quite lonely. Although I had made a lot of friends, most weren't that close, and I never got round to joining a mountaineering club. Hanging around a city by yourself is rubbish, so I decided to get out of town for Snowdonia to bag a few peaks. It was a fine, sunny Friday evening as I left Birmingham, jealous of the people abroad on their nights out: but the Carnedds, Tryfan, and Glyders would make a good big walk in compensation.

Eventually I reached Capel Curig after dark, but by now it was windy and raining heavily, a foul Friday night. It looked unpromising, and I had dressed for good weather in shorts. I slept in the wind-buffeted car, waking in the Bethesda valley to ominous notices telling me my car would be wheel-clamped if it was parked here. The cloud was down to 500m. The rain had stopped, but might return. Cold, lethargic and unmotivated in this unforecasted bad weather, I couldn't be bothered heading for the high hills and decided instead to go to the Lleyn Peninsula – hopefully, there would be some clear views from its lower hills, and a couple of Marilyns could be bagged.

At Lleyn the cloud was even lower. I headed up the first Marilyn of the day, Gurn Ddu, half expecting to be shouted at by farmers, but there were no humans about. A mangy farm dog barked, sheep baaed, and ravens hovered in the wind. I strode over slippery rock to the mist-clad summit, and saw a fox on the way down. Wales is good for wildlife – it may not be known for eagles or stags, but there is plenty of everything else.

For the next hill, Yr Eifl, I drove part way up a lumpy unsurfaced road, before parking due to concerns over the state of my car's exhaust and suspension. I completed the rest of the way on foot, scratchy heather against bare legs. The day's first moment of beauty: a view was revealed, looking past a small seacliff to the beach and village of Morfa Nefyn, before disappearing into the mist again.

I hadn't brought a map of this area, so stopped at Nefyn to consult one in a local shop. The next Marilyn was Garn Boduan, and by now I was harbouring ambitions of bagging every hill in the Lleyn peninsula, a good feat at seven Marilyns. Garn Boduan was a quick and unremarkable tick. I drove across country to Garn Fadrun, the fourth Marilyn, a rapid romp up steep screes to the summit. These hills were just too easy! There was an air of unreality about bagging here as you could drive halfway up a hill, and each summit took less than half an hour of walking to reach. At the base of Garn Fadrun I stopped in a small local shop for some ice cream. An old lady appeared from the house next door.

"Ice cream?" she said. "You can have strawberry colour or vanilla colour."

The character of the peninsula was increasing nearer its end: Welsh flags; patterned fields broken by low steep hills; narrow hedgerowed lanes. It was more like Western Ireland than anywhere else in Britain. Mynydd Rhiw was another easy Marilyn, and my favourite of the day, an excellent viewpoint for the rest of Lleyn and Snowdonia, and an immense coastal panorama from Holyhead to St David's Head – the length of Wales.

Another two Marilyns to go. The next had nowhere to park. Halfway up, I had to run back down to move my car so a working vehicle with trailer could get past. Back off the road, I hid from a farmer in his tractor whilst crossing his fields to the hill. Once on it, it took only a few minutes. Back down and driving out on the single-track country lanes, a car approached in the opposite direction. I reversed into a passing place, and as the driver went by she wound down her window to pass on a greeting in Welsh I couldn't understand. She probably assumed I was a local – a nice touch to the day however!

There was one more Marilyn – Moel-y-Gest, but this one was a little more involved, and the last two super-easy ones had made me lazy. It was also raining heavily by this point.

Now that the rain was back on I couldn't be bothered, so left my bag for the day at six Marilyns, driving back home for a quiet night in.

Long Mynd – 'What are you doing in Shropshire?'
516m OS 1370 SO 415944

I spent part of one Saturday in Birmingham looking round the shops, and it was later than I intended before setting off for my hills. It would be a race to do them before dark. Perhaps I would just do them in the dark anyway. The hills? Caer Caradoc, Long Mynd, Stiperstones and Heath Mynd.

Some time earlier, on my way to a job interview in Cardiff, the train had stopped in Church Stretton in Shropshire. Ramblers with rucksacks, stout boots, and breeches tucked into their socks disembarked to climb the hill above town. "Is that the Malverns?" I'd inquired of a tweedy woman, as the Malverns were the only hills I had heard of round here. "No," she replied: "Long Mynd and Caer Caradoc – they are higher than the Malverns." I'd looked up at these tiny lumps and was appalled. Was this what there was to climb in the southern half of the country? What was I letting myself in for? In the end I turned down the Cardiff job, taking a more exciting one in Birmingham instead.

And now I had returned. After a drive along seemingly endless country roads to the Welsh borderlands, the sun was setting and I was at the base of Caer Caradoc. By the time I had raced across the field to the top it was sunset, and would be dark in half-an-hour. As I ran downhill on the farm track, a Land Rover full of young teenagers gave a guilty start and cigarette butts were flung out of the windows. They must have thought me the farmer, catching them smoking!

I drove to Long Mynd. It was easy-peasy, but interesting. A remarkable road climbs the side of a steep, narrow glen right up across the hilltop, quite a curiosity. A level walk of a few hundred yards from the top of the road took me to the summit itself. It was dark now and lovely with the moon up, but not peaceful. There were a lot of youngsters roaring along this hill

road in their compact cars, lights blazing, and I didn't fancy
my parked car being crashed into by a teenage driver racing
about the Long Mynd. So instead I headed back to my car,
wondering if I should drive to the Stiperstones carpark, and
sleep there. But what should I see on the way to Stiperstones –
a pub, still open at 11pm! Surprised, as Birmingham pubs all
closed by 11pm, I went in for a couple of pints, and was soon
talking to a man from Devon.

"Devon! What are you doing in Shropshire?!" I asked.

"What are *you* doing in Shropshire!" he replied.

The barman indicated that he would keep the bar open as
long as people continued to imbibe, but the other patrons
drank up and left by 11:30pm, so conditioned were they to the
eleven o'clock curfew in force in most of the rest of England. I
slept in the pub car park, and woke late to a glorious hot day.

Once I had parked, the ascent of Stiperstones was the work
of a couple of minutes, but it was the best hill in England I had
visited since moving south, with some scrambling on one of its
tors. There was a good view too over the hilly-ish Welsh
border country of Shropshire, and I spent more time on it than
expected, having to abandon plans for one more Marilyn –
Heath Mynd – to head instead back to Brum for the annual
works summer party. Held in a country house, with fair-
ground stalls, crazy golf, free food and drink, and the US staff
flown over at company expense, the party was a lavish
statement of prosperity by the owner. After it ended, we
returned to Birmingham for a pub crawl. Jim and I found
ourselves in the lobby of the Americans' hotel, drinking after
hours as their unwanted guests. They yawned and looked at
their watches, but were too polite to tell us to leave. We
ignored them, and sat there brazenly until the last went to bed
and the hotel owner threw us out onto the quiet, dark street.

"Kebab?" said Jim. "There's a bottle of vodka in the
house . . ."

Shortly after, Jim left for a new job in Oxford. We still met
on the occasional weekend, but gone were the days of a quick
post-work pint turning into a 2am stagger into our favourite
kebab shop.

Pen-y-Fan – *leeches and beaches*
886m OS 160 SO 012216

My cousin was visiting for the weekend, and we decided that the best course of action would be to get out of Birmingham. The Brecon Beacons? South Wales was virgin territory for us both, so off we went.

We arrived on Saturday lunchtime in Brecon without a map. I dislike walking the hills without one, but we found one pinned to a board outside the tourist information station, and memorised that. After that, the hardest part of Pen-y-Fan was finding the car park. It took less than an hour's walking to reach the summit of this green-tiered pyramid, but we did stop a rugged-looking couple at the top to confirm that we really were there. We looked over to the wild wastes of the Black Mountain, and the most striking hill in the area, the small pimple of Sugar Loaf. The couple mentioned a lochan with newts and leeches in it, two creatures I had never seen. When we visited the lochan, we found both creatures. I was chuffed to see these two new species, the most fascinating thing I'd seen for ages. The cool wee newts were swimming about by the shoreline of the lochan, and so were the leeches. I really liked the newts. One leech had fastened its obscene mouth to a newt, which would die with such a large blood-sucker attached to it. I found the corpulent leeches repulsive. My cousin inexplicably preferred the leeches to the newts. 'Mon the newts!

There were a group of lads drinking and camping at the lochan. One of them jumped out of the tent naked to run round it as we approached. There were a couple of soldiers too, preparing to bed down for the night. My knee-jerk reaction was: aren't the Brecon Beacons a bit *soft* for learning soldiering? I'd camped and hiked over much tougher terrain. It all depends, of course, what the army does with the Brecon Beacons.

After the hill we still had some daylight to spend, so visited the Gower Peninsula. This was a revelation: bright green, fertile fields fall in sharply defined, shapely cliffs to gorgeous beaches. Why hadn't I been informed before that South Wales was so lovely? We wandered out to a tidal island called Worms Head, and returned for an evening in Mumbles, a picturesque seaside suburb where the sun-tanned youth of Swansea conduct their mating rituals.

The Wrekin – *falling in love*
407m OS 127 SJ 628081

One golden summer evening after work, I drove out of Birmingham to climb The Wrekin. I reached the top just before sunset and was taken aback by the panoramic view. In the distance before the sun lay the Welsh border hills, and rising up from the low, fertile English countryside were the beacons of Long Mountain, Long Mynd and Caer Caradoc. I could see Wenlock Edge, the whaleback of the Malverns, the Cotswolds, Bredon Hill, and in the far distance, the Chiltern Hills moating North-West London. It was not the large distances I could see that caught my breath though, but the beauty of the view. This is not a harsh Highland beauty; it is a welcoming, modest beauty, the England of 'mists and mellow fruitfulness', a land that speaks of home comforts and the possibility of a good life. Finally, I had fallen in love with England. I ran my fingers through the sun-bathed grass.

The next day, Dave had decided to have a braai, the South African version of a barbeque. But as this was England rather than South Africa, the weather had turned overnight. "Come round anyway!" said Dave. I turned up in my hillwalking jacket with some meat from Tesco. Dave was standing over the braai, a tarpaulin rigged over it so the rain would not put it out. The other guests were huddled indoors. The bucket of ice Dave had placed outside for the beer seemed superfluous. Yet he would not give up, and when he had become so saturated that it did not matter any more, he stripped to the waist. Most of the guests left early, but a couple of us joined Dave outside in the garden with our shirts off, shivering, soaking, drinking beer from the ice bucket, eating the cooked meat, cold rain bouncing off our shoulders in the gathering darkness, and remarking on what a lovely day we were having.

Longridge Fell – *foot and mouth frustration*
350m OS 102/103 SD 658410

It was during my time in Birmingham that the foot and mouth crisis erupted, putting paid to weekend walking for several months.

Eventually, with summer well advanced and the epidemic officially over, at least as far as access to the hills was concerned, I gladly returned to the countryside for a long-overdue wander over some Marilyns. I'd spent the summer cycling instead of walking, and had missed the hills. Thus maps for Longridge Fell, Pendle Hill, and Boulsworth Hill were printed from the internet, and I set off one Saturday eager to bag.

Off the motorway, steering wheel in one hand and road atlas in the other, I followed the road as it branched, till breasting the shoulder of the hill I found the start of Longridge Fell. The summit was a short distance away, it was a beautiful sunny day, and I broke into a jog as I followed the path up to the top. It was great to be out and about in the outdoors, and I ran back the way I'd come, eager for more.

I drove through Clitheroe and the small village of Down-ham, with elderly gentlemen passing the time leaning on the bridge over a sparkling brook. Pendle Hill lay above, and I took the rising road for my walk start point. But Disaster! Here there were still big 'KEEP OUT' signs, warning of foot and mouth. Although most of the countryside was open, there remained occasional pockets like this. As I believed that walkers did not spread foot and mouth I would have happily ignored the signs, but it was all in good view of the farmhouse. I had an allergy to walking past farmhouses, and I didn't want the Sod's Law luck of being the first walker in history to be proved to have spread foot and mouth . . . Pendle Hill lay above, steep and short, tempting me out – dammit! I thumped the steering wheel in frustration, and drove on to my next hill. I couldn't believe Pendle Hill was still shut. What a load of rubbish.

Boulsworth Hill, in the moors above the post-industrial town of Colne, was my final destination. At the top of the moor road a Land Rover track heads towards the top, and I parked next to some vehicle debris and walked along the track. This eventually peters out in a shallow corrie, and I headed up heather – steep for a short while with a fragment of cliff – for the very summit, and sat down on a rocky ridge.

All around were views of flat-topped moors, hiding human habitation in their valley bottoms and appearing deceptively wild. Only to the north were there signs of humanity, where walled green fields led to the populated Ribble Valley and the prominent landmark of Pendle Hill, taunting me. A local couple arrived at the top and we had a pleasant chat. There is no doubt that hillwalkers in the Pennines are friendlier than those in Wales or the Lakes. I don't know why this is, but I was often struck by it.

After a while soaking up the sunshine, I headed back down via a small outcrop called Dove Stones to the car, and a long drive through heavily populated areas to the nearest motor-way and the road back to Birmingham, a city to which my attachment was weakening.

It had never been strong, and had lasted only as long as the good times. The company had overstretched itself financially, and recently announced forty job losses – one fifth of the entire staff. "I've a family and a mortgage," said Norman. "They can't make me redundant!" But they did. The heady atmo-sphere of fun disappeared, to be replaced by dropping sales, vanished bonuses, and increasing stress levels. Jim was in Oxford, Dave planning to return home to South Africa, and Matt was training the company's new staff in Mumbai. I was getting itchy feet again.

High Raise – *click clack, knick knacks*
762m OS 89/90 NY 280095

When David, an old, Lancashire-based school friend, invited me to the Lake District for a weekend, I didn't hesitate. With Dave's no-nonsense Lancastrian friend Alan, and another of my old school friends Cameron in attendance, I knew I'd enjoy the company. That the Lakes were about the closest real hills I could get was an added bonus.

I arrived at the campsite late Friday. It was 1am, and everyone was just leaving the pub. Impressed at the late opening hours, I resolved to take full advantage next evening.

In the morning Alan took us up Coniston Old Man. The weather was fresh and misty, but we didn't waste time, walking past some mines, then up onto a ridge. It was just like being in the Highlands except for a feeling of smallness and fine detail, with grass of a marginally richer hue and a wee signpost indicating the route. Alan told us tales of this beck and that tarn, top dog through his familiarity with this compact area. We walked up onto the Old Man, and straight back down. Coniston is a wasteland of gear and gift shops, full of immaculately clad, humourless walkers with their rucksack belts tightly fastened and twin poles clack-clacking their way round the displays of Beatrix Potter knick-knacks and other tourist-targeted produce. People were everywhere, including a bewildering number of for-eigners. And yet somehow this seemed preferable on a dreich day to an echoing empty Highland glen with only the oozing peat, harsh rain, and shy deer for company! I must be going soft.

Later, we drank locally brewed Bluebird Ale in a low-beamed pub and talked nonsense.

On Sunday, Alan had a treat for us – High Raise via a scrambling ledge called Lord's Rake. It was an excellent route. After a short, well-made path we reached Stickle Tarn, rounded it, and Alan led us up a gully that turned into a ledge, high above the lochan of Stickle Tarn with a cliff face above and cliff face below. The ledge turned inwards for the crux – happily devoid of exposure – with two impatient army types descending and turning us on the far more exposed outside edge of the ledge. Above were slabby blocks to climb, and great satisfaction to be had in the all-limb exertion, our senses heightened by the easy but absorbing exposure. We walked over the plateau towards High Raise, enjoying the contrast to the ledge of this free-limbed striding. We were alive and happy. At the top a couple asked Alan to confirm their map reading. "This is Langdale Pikes?" the woman asked.

And then something happened I'd not heard in all my time hillwalking.

"No, High Raise," replied Alan. "You don't know what you are doing – go down. Follow *this* path," (he pointed) "follow it down to your car."

"But . . ." she began to argue.

"Go down!" Alan is a large fellow and, intimidated, the couple didn't argue. I began to laugh. As we left the top heading for Sergeant Man, we saw them – clearly at a complete loss as to where they were despite their brand new map – discreetly follow us . . .

It is disturbing to discover people on the hills who can't tell one end of a map from the other.

Kinder Scout – *the hag*
636m OS 110 SK 086875

The tales of Kinder Scout's summit are legend.

Flat-topped and peaty, it is supposedly impossible to find the actual top with any degree of certainty – for each time you climb out of the peaty trenches criss-crossing the summit plateau, another part of the plateau appears to be slightly higher. When the fog comes down, any foolish attempt to locate the summit should be abandoned entirely, and the walker should content themselves with a wander along the Pennine Way, followed by a pint of real ale in a local pub. Today however was clear and sunny, so I parked at an incredibly busy Edale, leaving the village as quickly as I could for the relative sanity of the hillside. Powering past Grindslow, I was up on the plateau in twenty minutes, where the fun of the day could begin. Operation: Locate the Top!

The southeast corner of the plateau already felt quite high, but a marginal swelling seemed to be occurring north and westwards. I headed in that direction, slipping down the side of a canyon-like trench in the peat, cut by one of the many plateau streams. This quickly became disorientating, twisting this way and that, so I climbed back out to get a bearing, walking as straight as I could, up and down several more streambeds. Eventually I was on – or near – the high point. However, there were more high-looking points both north and south-west. I went north, enjoying the view ahead past Black Hill over further upland moors. There was a little cairn. Could this be the summit? No, the point I came from originally now looked higher. I backtracked, and headed for the western edge of the plateau. This wasn't the high point either.

I wandered back in to the interior of the plateau, the south-western sector this time, an area where every little lump of heather seems to be the highest point, sporting its own cairn. This would be completely impossible in mist or fog.

I ended up above the Crowden Tower and sat around Pyms chair, enjoying the view back down into the dale, deciding I'd done enough to claim this summit as mine. There was a path here, and crowds. My final high point of the day was Kinder Low. This boasts a trig point and feels like it should be the highest point on this perplexing plateau, but the map says it isn't.

I stumbled across the Pennine Way and felt an imperceptible tug north. Just turn around, and start walking for the border . . . Instead I turned south for Edale, with the impressive, wedge-shaped Mam Tor dominating the southward aspect, and descended the hard stony path back to the glen, where I watched trout in the river for a while before immersing myself back in the noise and bustle of Edale.

Burrow and Heath Mynd – *get off my land!*
452m OS 137 SO 336941

My employers had opened an office in Scotland!

I applied for a transfer and was accepted. The Scottish office was tiny, but staffed by older, steadier, and wiser heads than the hothouse of head office. However, this meant I didn't have much time left in Birmingham. It would be nice to finish the Shropshire Marilyns before heading up the road, as I doubted I'd return much once I moved back north.

There were three remaining – View Edge, Burrow, and Heath Mynd (which I'd already planned to visit twice, and failed to climb, twice).

Thus on a winter's day with dirty grey clouds in the sky threatening snow, I drove out of the city for the countryside along clear roads. I reached Stokesay Castle beneath Craven Arms and drove over the hill road that doubles round on itself past the forested slope of Stoke Wood, before parking at a cottage on the very summit of the road. Louping over a fence, I spent about five minutes bashing through a lumpy field, snow falling, to reach the top. The summit lay over another fence at the top of Stoke Wood, so I jumped it and stood in trees with an underwhelming sense of completion. Back at the car I pulled out the roadmap, most essential of bagging equipment out here. Burrow was not far away.

After a couple of miles and a few turns in the road I was in the hamlet of Hopesay, the hilltop just 1km from the road. After looking for a place to park, I walked past the kirk, past a sign saying 'Shropshire Way', and followed the muddy track for a while before striking on directly uphill to the trees that moat this hill. The sun was coming out.

The other side of the fence has a track, and I followed it for a short distance to a rampart in a clearing, an old hillfort. This was an entertaining summit, wide and spacious, but unfortunately viewless as enclosed by forest. I circumnavigated the entire hillfort rampart before descending. It covers a wide area, and must have been an impressive fortification once.

There was just one Marilyn left – Heath Mynd. At last I

would bag it! However, there was nowhere to park on the narrow country roads round here: so I started driving up a private road, only to be faced by half-a-dozen country types with shotguns, two of them carrying dead rabbits by the ears.

"Where are you going?" one asked.

"Heath Mynd," I replied.

"Not up this way," he replied; and I had little option except to double back. Damn landowners. Beaten by Heath Mynd!

Back in Scotland, I was faced with an array of Munros, Corbetts and Marilyns in winter raiment, and soon forgot about Heath Mynd.

PART SEVEN
Return of a Bagger

After Birmingham had taught me how to relax, I was ready to return home. I'd got the car, I'd got friends, I'd got the comfortable lifestyle, but Scotland still called. One spring weekend I visited my parents, and cycled round the Rosneath peninsula. The beauty of the landscape hit me. I had taken it for granted before. I left my bike unchained outside a local shop, and inside a young farmer was showing a girl a lamb. It seemed a gentler place, less crime-ridden than Birmingham. I was glad when I got the chance to head back north.

Many of my friends were still in the Central Belt, and we resumed where we had left off: just older, fatter, and more confident.

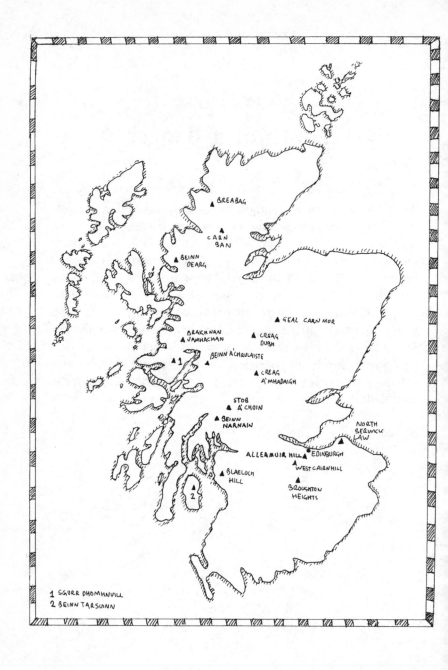

BREABAG

CARN
BAN

BEINN
DEARG

GEAL CARN MOR

BRAIGH NAN
IAMHACHAN

CREAG
DUBH

1

BEINN A'CHRULAISTE

CREAG
A' MHADAIGH

STOB
A' CHOIN

BEINN
NARNAIN

NORTH
BERWICK
LAW

ALLERMUIR HILL

EDINBURGH

WEST CAIRNHILL

BLAELOCH
HILL

2

BROUGHTON
HEIGHTS

1 SGURR DHOMHNUILL
2 BEINN TARSUINN

Stob a' Choin *(stob a con)* – *shortcut*
869m OS 56 NN 416160

It was an exceptionally fine winter morning when I drove Brian in my elderly car past Balquidder for the road end at Loch Voil. Stob a' Choin presents an impressively steep-sided, bold aspect when seen from the Crianlarich hills, and I had been hoping for a while to visit it. Like many things in life, it had to wait for the right moment.

Now that moment had arrived, and we set off in crisp January air along the track to the hill. A rising traverse along the lower northern slopes brought us to steeper ground and the snow. Halfway up, Brian decided to head not for the enticing northern ridge that we had agreed upon, but for the lower northern corrie, and hared off in this direction. I was about to follow when I remembered one of life's harder won lessons: 'Brian's shortcuts always take longer.' I decided to continue for the northern ridge, which provided a superb, steep but easy mixed rock/snow scramble that ended abruptly at the summit. It was a clear, snowy day and the views of the surrounding hills were fantastic. I called for Brian, but there were no footprints. He was a further twenty minutes in arriving, breathless. "The snow's really deep in the corrie!" he said.

We descended via the corrie, the deep snow cushioning our descent. We had had a fine day on the hill, with the forecast promising more to come. I had the whole first week in January off work, and it was going to be an exciting and memorable return to proper hillwalking.

The weather was fine, but I was unable to enjoy the rest of

the New Year holiday. The alternator on my car burned out, and we didn't get back down the road until very late that night.

I spent the next couple of days retrieving my car, and it spent the rest of the holiday being repaired. One day, I promised myself, I would buy a reliable car.

Allermuir Hill – *Edinburgh's hill*
493m OS 66 NT 227662

When I was a teenager, my contemporaries in the West of Scotland spent their days trying to impress girls, but not me. I liked maps. While my peers were having sectarian rammies and playing on railway tracks, I was looking at maps.

One day, I had a look at an atlas of Britain to work out which city was closest to hills. I felt confident it would be Leeds or perhaps Glasgow; so imagine my surprise to discover it is actually Edinburgh. The Pentlands start literally on Edinburgh's doorstep – you can get a city bus to their base at Hillend. Many years later when I moved to Edinburgh and had a free afternoon, I remembered my teenage astonishment and headed for the closest of the Pentlands, Allermuir Hill.

Instead of taking the bus I parked at Boghall, where Volvo-driving couples in fleecy jumpers walk their dogs. They all disappeared very quickly, and soon I had only sheep for company. The crown of the Pentlands ridge surrounds Boghall Glen, cradling the burn in its modest, horizon-limiting bosom. Vegetation is short-cropped thanks to the sheep, and you have the sense of being in a well-managed country park rather than wild moorland. I felt unfit as I peched up the short steep section towards the dome of Allermuir Hill's summit.

I found the view from here a revelation. South – the mass of the Pentlands, tempting me to abandon my initial plans and instead wander far. North – all of Edinburgh. I thought the view from Arthur's Seat was elevated! Arthur's Seat appears tiny from here, and the entirety of Edinburgh and its setting on the shores of the Firth of Forth, with Fife and the Ochils behind, can be appreciated. West – what's that sharp lump? Arran? No, Loudon Hill, scene of one of Robert the Bruce's famous battles. I was amazed to see it from this angle. And yet – did my eyes deceive me – could that be Arran hazily appearing in the very far distance? I hurt my eyes staring into the sun, and couldn't quite decide. Livingston and the rest of the West Lothian Lowlands lay directly below, between Edinburgh and the Southern Highlands.

Enjoying this panorama immensely, I decided to prolong the view as long as possible by wandering in the sunshine and bracing air over the modestly defined ridge to Caerketton Hill, and a short but very steep descent to the dry ski slope at Hillend. Finally, a bash through dead bracken back to Boghall farm and a complicated jouk round outfield fences and farm buildings brought me back to the car.

Some people in Edinburgh never climb Arthur's Seat, and many more never visit Allermuir Hill. But climbing these local hills should be a compulsory part of every young Edinburgher's general education.

Geal Charn Mor *(jeel karn mor)* – *a Monadhliath morning* *824m OS 35 NH 837124*

"Are you a Presbyterian?" asked Miles, stirring his latte.

"That is my background," I replied.

"Ah," he deduced. "A climber should only ever be seen sleeping in bus shelters, drinking Irn Bru and eating fish suppers, is that it?"

Perhaps I had been growling too much about what massive gaylords we were, taking coffee and cake in Aviemore's Mountain Cafe on a sunny day.

It had all started the previous January night on descending an icy Cairngorm by torchlight, when Miles, a musician of rare interests as he also liked hillwalking, hatched the plan of sleeping in the woods that night. It was cold, but once in the Bridge Inn, Miles began to talk me round. "It will be fun! There will be no deprivation!" he argued. I disagreed. If we left the pub at closing time, a forest bivvy would give us at least eight hours of uncontrollable shivering in our thin sleeping bags between midnight and the pre-dawn, rising sleepless and exhausted. Fantastic! Recently I had taken to staying in B&Bs, so a good night of deprivation and misery would help me rediscover my roots, that kind of thing.

We left the pub looking for something to eat, and the picnic tables outside, clear just an hour earlier, were now covered in hoar frost. It was going to be bloody cold. Miles' expression changed. "Perhaps we should find a hostel . . .?" I suggested. It would be a miserython otherwise. "OK," Miles conceded. God help the wild animals and the rough sleepers.

Waking before dawn in the Aviemore Youth Hostel, we set off for Geal Charn Mor, breath turning to frost in the mysterious pre-dawn of sodium lit, pine-lined streets. It became light at the Scripture Union centre near Lynwilg, unseen buzzards mewing in the trees.

We bashed quickly up the well-made track, rising with the sun, which eventually broke above the barrier of the Cairngorms as we crossed the Monadhliath summit plateau to the top, flooded with new light, a cold wind coming on like a knife. No wildlife up here; but short tundra, gravel, low rocks, frost, and long shadows cast by every hummock, rock and tuft of vegetation in the reddy-golden light. Our dawn shadows strode across the land like giants, heading away towards distant snow-capped Ben Wyvis, already bathed in the sun.

Other distant Northwest Highland peaks became visible – and then the top, and a western look over the flat expanses of the Monadhliath, the distant Drumochter hills, Ben Alder forest, and Creag Meagaidh rising snow-capped far away. "The Magnificent Monadhliath!" I exclaimed, and Miles, a Munroist to the core, viewed me askance. "Magnificent? *Magnificent?!*" he scoffed, and I made sure to photograph him at the summit cairn. A piece of Corbett-related blackmail against the ideologue Munroist.

Not much snow up here, but extensive frost. Above all, a bone-chilling slipstream of wind. It was tolerable thanks to the bright sunshine, but we had no doubt about how dangerously cold we would become should we spend too long up here on this bright but freezing place.

The wind dropped as we reluctantly left the plateau, and as the sun continued its rapid winter climb we were even able to look at and admire the Cairngorms, lying directly into the sun. It was markedly colder than the previous day. Before heading back down the road for home, a stop in a cafe seemed in order.

No woods the night before. And now, here we were, eating expensive cake and drinking expensive coffee late on a fine sunny morning in winter, surrounded by loud, gear-obsessed skiers.

Gaylords indeed.

Creag a' Mhadaigh (crayg a vad-ee) – the walk in 612m OS 42 NN 634650

Elena was up for anything. Over from Spain, via year-long stays in each of Italy, Denmark and France, she was the consummate European, fluent in three languages, competent in two others, working as a dictionary translator and eager to see and do as much as possible in her time in Scotland before she headed off somewhere else on her European adventures. So when Elena heard about bothies one night in an Edinburgh pub with other music friends, she was all ears. Bothies, eh? This was something new, and novelty was what Elena liked.

I waxed lyrical on the wonders of bothies: a short but entitling walk along a pleasant path, a fire, whisky, folk music. She was, of course, hooked. Her friend Celine was visiting from France, so the pair of them came away with Alastair, Helen and me for Duinish. It was October, no snow yet, but the hill grass was dead and brown and the hilltops black. I'd chosen Duinish for its ease of access, and because I had already visited. I wasn't going to take them to what might turn out to be a roofless doss. A small bunch of Glasgow folk Alastair, Helen and I knew from university days was coming in from the south, so a good crowd was guaranteed. The route from the north is a couple of kilometres shorter, so from the map this seemed the obvious approach, especially as it is more easily reached from Edinburgh.

It was raining hard, but everyone had waterproofs. It would be OK. With an hour-and-a-half of daylight left on a dirty winter evening, we walked in along the stony trail, heads down, rain pockmarking Loch Garry. Not the best of days, but there was over one and a half hours until sunset – plenty of time surely to reach the bothy, only 6km away. Helen, Elena and Celine played 'I-Spy' in French. We stopped to take stock at a two-storey concrete hydro housing. Only 3km in and we had taken an hour! Well, we were carrying coal, and the path was rough. Never mind, another hour at most, and we would be at the bothy, and surely there would be half an hour of gloaming after sundown?

Shortly after this point, we received our answer. The path disappeared entirely, to be replaced with acres of quivering bog. Snowshoes would have been welcome as legs sank into the glaur. – Darkness came rapidly, no gloaming at all on a dismal night. It was disorientating without a path, heading in the general direction only. "I'm sorry," I started to apologise, fretting. But Elena and Celine were enjoying themselves. Frankly, I was bemused. If someone had led *me* into a bog in the dark, in the rain, without knowing where they were going, it would cheese me off. It seemed that Elena and Celine, however, were made of the Right Stuff.

By now it was pitch dark. Alastair had forged on ahead, but we could see his torch again and hear the roar of the river. I hoped he had found a place to cross, but the reason he waited was the opposite. There was nowhere. "Perhaps we could ford here?" he said hopefully. First, we headed upstream, to confirm whether or not there would be somewhere better to cross.

At this point, having lost any path, and unsure whether or not there was a bridge (having never come this way before), the possibility we would have to retrace every step of the last three hours back to the car gnawed at my mind. Alastair was all for stopping and attempting to ford further downstream. "A little more, just a few more hundred yards," I insisted. A bridge appeared in Alastair's headtorch. Relief and elation –

for me at least. The bothy was just a few hundred yards further past the bridge, on an excellent landrover track. "Yeah, I knew there was a bridge all the time, honestly!"

Inside we were soon warm, with the fire going. Andy, Niall and other friends from Glasgow greeted us, and we had a good chat as we dried out. Niall bantered, Alastair played his whistle, I sang. Socks hung on a string above the fire, steaming. Andy recounted a true spooky tale of the time he had got a job house sitting a repossessed mansion on his own. We sat in silence, listening. The flames in the grate flickered.

On Sunday, everyone who was doing a walk went for Beinn Mholach. I had already climbed this with Alastair and was feeling lazy, so went for a wander up Creag a' Mhadaigh, the sort of low, nondescript Highland hill that only a Marilyn bagger would visit. The approach was boggy, but nothing compared to the previous night, and the view from the top was new. I lay at the top a while, hood up, wind blowing, taking it in.

Back at the bothy we walked out. The bog was less disorientating in daylight, but the river was intimidating, roaring in power, impassable. "We would never have forded this," said Alastair with a shudder, standing on the bridge.

Beinn Narnain *(ben nar-nayn)* – *Billy's last Munro* *926m OS 56 NN 272067*

Beinn Narnain is one of my favourite hills, though it is hard to say why. The Cobbler preens next to it, lower perhaps – but shouting "look at me!" like an attention-seeking child. Nearby Beinn Ime is higher and more classically shaped; and every Glaswegian's favourite hill, Ben Lomond, lies just across the water from Beinn Narnain. So I'm not sure why I like Beinn Narnain so much. I just do. Its couthily knarled outline *is* the Arrochar hills to me, hills I spent my hillwalking apprenticeship exploring. Beinn Narnain distils everything that is the Arrochar hills into one shape. It may not grace calendars of Scottish scenery, but to know its wavy schistose is to know the essentials of this area.

Today was Billy's last Munro. I was astonished that he had never been up my stalwart friend Beinn Narnain – and we were standing in the freezing winter rain in the car park at the bottom of the hill, swapping banter, shaking ourselves to keep warm, waiting for Simon to arrive.

Apart from Simon and me, and today's main man, Billy, there were also a grinning Dave, on a weekend pass from his young family; Brian; robust Christian guy Tony, and Graham from the same church as Tony. Once Simon arrived we didn't hang around, but headed up the old Cobbler track, the steep remains of concrete blocks from the foundations of a ratchet & pinion railway acting like giant steps.

Higher up, we stopped at the Narnain boulders. In good weather this is a fine place to linger, but today there was no view of the Cobbler, the bouldering was slippery, and the rain raw and freezing. Rather than take my favourite route north-east up this hill, we continued on up the increasingly boggy and waterlogged path to the pass between Beinn Narnain and The Cobbler, swapping banter all the way.

Beyond the flattening of the pass, the wind came screaming at us. We doubled back to head up Beinn Narnain's backslope, the easiest and safest route to the summit. We were nearly bent double, conversation impossible in the screaming wind as freezing rain slashed at our wet clothing, the wind snatching our words and tearing them to shreds as soon as they left our mouths. "Nearly as bad as my last Munro!" I yelled. "Nah, worse!" signalled Brian.

The slopes seemed to narrow, and there was a cairn. But thanks to previous visits, I knew this wasn't the summit. Taking out the map and compass, we allowed ourselves to be blown across the small plateau of this hill to the summit cairn – a difficult top for first-timers to find in thick mist. Billy touched it first.

Billy had always specified that his last Munro should include a piper. He should be piped to the summit through a processional avenue of fellow baggers, then handed a ceremonial claymore, which he would then symbolically thrust Excalibur-like into the cairn, leaving it vibrating as he walked away, never to set foot on the mountains again. In the imagination, this took place on a warm, lazy summer day. However, this wild day was not one for hanging about. Dave reached into his jacket and handed Billy a bottle of malt whisky, Simon gave him a mug and a toy bear, and I took a photo. Brian had no gloves and had started shivering, so we headed back down eastwards. Again, previous experience helps, as there appears to be a number of possible gullies to descend. The correct one however is fairly close to the summit cairn and goes just north of Spearhead Arête.

Back down we warmed ourselves up with a meal in the Cobbler Hotel, toasting Billy's achievement and looking forward to a night of carousing and reminisces in Clashgour.

"When I was younger, thinner, and fitter," said Dave, still grinning, "I was a real miserable git. But now I'm married, I'm a cheery fat soul!"

Beinn a' Chrulaiste *(beyn ach-roo-last-ee) – the viewpoint 857m OS 41 NN 246567*

'Cruel & Nasty', Brian, Alastair and others liked to call this hill, but I never worked out why, unless they just liked distorting the name. It had always been a fine hill from my point of view.

And what a point of view! My first ascent was up a pink granite rib halfway between the summit and Lagangarbh, easy rock, hardly a scramble at all. I deliberately kept my head down, to be all the more impressed by the summit view. It is probably the finest viewpoint for the Buachaille Etive Mor – especially pointy from here – contrasting with the expansive wastes of Rannoch Moor, the lone sail of Shiehallion rising in the distance. Blackwater Dam is forlorn and mighty to the north.

Such an unassuming looking hill on first impression, is Beinn a' Chrulaiste, but such a mighty view. Boswell to the Buachaille's Johnson. Enthused for all time about this hill, I didn't hesitate to recommend it to Billy on a Sunday of unexpectedly heavy snows. We walked up the West Highland Way in good spirits, with me looking for the pink rib of easy-scrambling granite. Then a snow storm clamped in, reducing visibility dramatically. Oh well, so much for the view! Upwards we climbed, ever steeper, on slippy wet snow, unstable heather and iced-over rock. It was getting a bit serious. I looked down. It wouldn't do to fall! A woman had been found dead the previous day on the hills . . . Billy didn't look happy, and I started to wonder what we were doing in this unexpectedly serious situation . . . 'Keep the heid' I kept repeating to myself. Maybe this was 'cruel & nasty' after all . . .

At the top of the line of broken cliffs we had been ascending, I refused to go any further, some moves on uncertain holds requiring to be made. Billy traversed and yelled a 'hallelujah!' from round the corner. I followed his footprints to find us on easy ground, Billy grinning.

"I'm happy now!" he said. The sun had just come back out. We had been so engrossed in the difficult terrain, we hadn't noticed the snow had stopped falling.

"Look – look behind you!" I said, awed.

The Buachaille was shrugging off the mists, its majestic peak thrusting up through the clouds, spindrift trailing off its pointed summit. We sat in astonishment as the weather cleared, the Buachailles and Glencoe peaks appearing fresh-snowed and achingly beautiful, mountain butterflies shedding their cloud chrysalises. We laughed and grinned. What a contrast to the scares of just a few minutes ago. What a hill! What a day!

Back down, we saw Jimmy Saville walking along the road.

Sgurr Dhomhnuill *(skoor don-ill) – dark shapes of deer*
888m OS 40 NM 889679

Billy and Dave were in the Kingshouse, waiting, as we were to rendezvous there. By the time I arrived they were a few pints happier, and we camped by the infant Etive, waking to a gorgeous, winter day.

"Did you guys bring a spare axe?" I asked hopefully. They hadn't. I'd forgotten mine in my rush to head off on Friday night. Hopefully Glencoe Mountain Sports had one to hire. When we got there, all they had left was an ice hammer at £3.50 for the day's hire – not ideal as it lacked an adze for cutting steps, but hopefully it would stop me in the case of a fall. They might be shut by the time we got back on Sunday, but it was no bother – "Just drop it off at the Ice Factor in Kinlochleven, and I'll get it from there."

It was good to see Dave again. He was nearing the end of the Munros, but had never visited Ardgour or Moidart before, so we crossed the Corran narrows and headed for Sgurr Dhomhnuill. Garbh Bheinn was pencilled in for Sunday as the others hadn't been there yet. I didn't mind visiting it again so long as I got Sgurr Dhomhnuill.

This is the highest hill in the whole island-like area south of the A830 Fort William to Mallaig road. Several times near the start of my hillwalking career, I'd looked across the West Highlands from some Munro or other and wondered what that prominent peak was in the distance. It took me a while before I twigged that the reason I couldn't place it was because it wasn't another Munro, but a Corbett: though at 888m, it is not far off Munro height, and it has to be approached virtually from sealevel.

We parked on a glorious spring-like morning, gaining distance quickly and easily thanks to the old mining track through the moss-heavy forest. There are some old mines at the lip of the corrie, but there is little to see except small spoil heaps and a couple of walls, blending in well with the surrounding scenery. When we exited the trees, the north wind hit us hard. It was our constant companion until we regained the trees at the end of the day. It was a fantastic late winter day of sunshine and wind, crocuses and primroses by the roadside and snow on the tops. As we climbed higher, the views improved – Garbh Bheinn, Beinn Resipol, Ben More on Mull; and east, Glencoe, Cruachan and Lochaber – an unaccustomed aspect for Dave, and he voiced his approval. "I'm coming back to this area again!"

Full of high spirits, we continued onwards for the final pull to the summit, taking photos of the fine scenery, our heads down against the occasional band of stinging hail. We took a southerly line to avoid the buffeting wind, and there was a bit of mixed snow/rock scrambling. All good healthy fun, but we decided it was best not to descend this way. The summit was uncomfortably windy. The wind made it hard to stand, and it cut through our clothes like a stiletto shower. Only a Corbett! But we were glad not to be higher with this wind. "Let's go down the other way," I shouted, "then head down the glen." "That's what I was thinking," said Dave, and so we headed northwest from the summit.

Dave was leading. The way seemed to end at a cliff face. "No way down this side," he indicated, and I tried the other side. It looked steep, a snow slope leading who knows where? I hesitated, suddenly nervous, and Dave took the lead again. The snow was disturbed, so presumably someone had already come down this way. This was of some comfort. Dave descended, then the wind caught us again. I crouched and grasped my hired axe as tightly as possible. The slope we were on ended in nothing.

I *really* didn't want to be blown over it or slip. Dave took a side way down, sending up clouds of stinging spindrift. Crouching, head turned, I waited it out until the spindrift passed, then followed him over the lip of the snow bank. Below was nothing but a further snow slope, even steeper now, ending in nothing. I wasn't happy. Descent seemed slippy. It was hard to tell with a face full of spindrift where I was putting my feet in all this sugary snow, so I turned again until it cleared a bit.

Billy was above, having had to wait for me to finish moving before being able to continue. When I turned back, Dave had disappeared. I dropped a little further, getting closer to the edge. There didn't seem to be any safe way. Surely he hadn't . . . my heart hammered hard and senses became super-alert as I considered the serious risk I might be taking if I went on. I looked across, and realised a large block of snow had carved a path of sorts away to our right before disappearing over the precipice. Suddenly it hit me. The disturbed snow we were following was not old footprints – it was avalanche debris! I stopped, and waited until Billy reached me.

"I'm shitting myself," I told him. "I'm going back to the top." But where was Dave? We had to contact him. The horrible thought came to me that he might have slipped to his doom, and we were helpless to act. Then –

"Dave!" shouted Billy. He had spotted him. A second later I saw his axe battering at the edge of the precipice, and he hove slowly into view. 'Back up?' I pointed. 'Back to the top,' Dave signed.

Billy led the way, slowly making sure of each step, slipping occasionally. I tried cutting steps with the ice hammer. Some of the snow was hard, but much of it was sugary, and would provide no purchase for arrest in the event of a fall. Back into the screaming wind, legs tensed for all they were worth, we made a slow ascent. Billy waited for us on higher, safer ground, lying down holding his axe. We laughed in relief. Dave appeared. He had cramp, and didn't feel like laughing.

"It was icy, sheer rock. Terraced cliffs. I was slipping . . . too far round to the north for the col . . . not a good descent route."

There was only one thing for it: descend the way we had come up. Dave hurried us along despite the gorgeous sunset over Beinn Resipol, despite Garbh Bheinn turning a deep blue. We reached the 'ascent's steep bit' and laughed. We could descend this facing forward! It was nothing compared to what we had just foolishly attempted.

"I forgot the rule," said Billy; "NEVER follow old footprints." Especially when they aren't footprints at all.

As darkness gathered, the constant wind started to get to us. But once back on the mine track our spirits were restored, though we were humbled by the lesson a mere Corbett had taught us, amazed that despite our experience, we could still have such a close scrape.

"Well Craig," said Billy, "at least we know what your life is worth!"

"What?"

"Three pounds fifty!" he said, remembering my hired ice axe. Dark shapes of deer flitted silently through the trees.

Blaeloch Hill – *Brian's book*
407m OS 63 NS 243553

Is there something about hillwalkers that makes them less eager to settle down than the general population at large? Or was it just me and my friends? Most of us remained single for a long time, and haven't rushed to start families. Could it be the sense of self-reliance and independence that heading into the hills brings, the realisation that pregnancy and the appearance of small children will take priority over even the weather forecast in the quest to climb icy mountains? One doesn't have to be a particularly self-reliant type to realise that freedoms will be curtailed.

Apart from Dave, who had settled down early, few of my friends looked likely to start a family as we entered our thirties. The next after Dave was Brian, who met a good woman whilst at the Kingshouse, and brought her back to Glasgow to live and work. I saw less of Brian after the birth of his daughter, but was pleased for him, knowing he was much more content than before. He no longer travelled far, but I'd wanted to climb Blaeloch Hill near Glasgow for a while, thinking it might have a good view down the Clyde. So one day, Brian and I took a Sunday afternoon trip for Ayrshire.

Driving through Glengarnock and Kilbirnie's narrow streets, we arrived at a pair of reservoirs, crossed the dam of the highest one, and made the short, wet ascent to Blaeloch's top. There wasn't a particularly great view down the Clyde, but the weather made Irish Law look impressive from this lower hill, sunshine on its cloud-capped slopes. Brian told me about the second print run of his book, *Guardian of the Blackmount*, a history of the Kingshouse Hotel in Glencoe. You can still buy copies of Brian's book behind the bar at the Kingshouse.

Creag Dubh *(crayg doo)* – *history stones*
756m OS 35 NN 677972

'Creag Dubh!' The slogan of the Macpherson clan. When the chief put the fiery cross round the glens to prepare for battle, the fit clansmen were duty bound to gather at the base of Creag Dubh. Before setting off for battle, each man placed a rock on a cairn. When he came home, each man took a rock away with him from the cairn. Every stone on that cairn represents a dead Macpherson, fallen in battle.

Those days are far distant from us weekenders, comfortable in our Kingussie hostel with boxes full of supermarket food. But a faint echo of them can be found by wandering the same sods, and on Sunday I set off alone for Creag Dubh.

On a blustery day, sun breaking through occasionally then turning instead to short flurries of rain, I parked amongst a stand of trees, taking to a hillside that steepened dramatically to dangerous cliffs. With this blustery wind, I took care to keep well clear of the edge of these cliffs when above them. After Culloden, a cave in the cliffs was used as a hiding place by Cluny of Macpherson, the local clan chief who had supported the Jacobite cause, but I couldn't spot it. Probably a good reason why the cave was used as a hiding place! It would have a superb situation looking down Strathspey, the movements of government troops easily spotted.

Once above this line of cliffs, the walk turned into a slog, battling high winds and heavy underfoot conditions. The views weren't great, with cloud covering many of the surrounding higher tops, but it was easy to appreciate what a pivotal spot this is in Strathspey. Behind, the Black Craig split the Spey and Laggan straths, the iron age ruins of Dun-da-lamh (*fort of the two hands*) somewhere in a thicket, silent places filling the air with whispers of history past.

Beinn Dearg, Torridon (*beyn jerrig*) – *the neglected hill* 914m OS 19/24 NG 895608

'The Torridonian Triptych': A well-known phrase, and a Munrocentric view of this area, as there are really four fine hills accessible directly north of Torridon village. Of course the fourth in height, Beinn Dearg, is a Corbett: and therefore a second-class hill to many. I pondered over this as I climbed this hill, devoid of crowds or paths in a popular area, the irony being that my first three hills in Torridon were, of course, the three famous Munros.

I slept under a full moon to the eldritch mewing of wildcats in the Coire Mhic Nobuill carpark, waking to a bright morning. The first walker had already arrived for the day. I was happy to be in the fresh air and hills, stopping by the river just above the pine forest to soak in the atmosphere. Beinn Dearg was the ultimate aim, and a path leads most of the way to the bealach between Beinn Dearg and Beinn Alligan. I was surprised how many other walkers there were in the glen. However, once I started on Beinn Dearg, I saw no one else.

Beinn Dearg is a tricky hill. No Munro, so no boot-worn path, and no obvious route up or down the banded lines of cliffs that circle the hill. It is certainly possible to find a way both up and down, but I would not like to attempt it in winter or bad visibility. Fortunately the visibility was good, and I revelled in the views of Torridon and further north. Beinn Eighe, Liathach, Coire Na Caime, Slioch, and Baos-bheinn all rose out of the Torridon moorland; but above all for beauty stood Beinn Alligan, with its graceful curve and horns.

East of Beinn Dearg's summit, the ridge narrows and a tricky downclimb had to be undertaken. According to the guidebook this is bypassable to the south, but I saw no path. Although lower, this hill is trickier than Beinn Alligan or Beinn Eighe, if not as hard as the traverse of Liathach. I cursed the effort and concentration required for the descent of the south face, threading through bands of cliffs via steep heather terraces, and was glad to reach a stand of birch and the path in the glen. Suddenly, I was amongst people. A good day on the hill. I had seen buzzards, ptarmigan, a lizard, frogs, deer, some late snow, heard a wildcat, sat by the river, climbed a summit, and was content.

West Cairn Hill – *the revelation*
562m OS 65/72 NT 107584

I had just arrived back in Edinburgh and was shocked to the core. Edinburgh, beautiful Edinburgh – what had happened to it? It's nothing but a dark, dirty, grey town of rough surfaces and a biting raw wind. Yet only a couple of weeks earlier, I had believed Edinburgh to be one of the most beautiful cities in Europe.

What had happened? I had spent a holiday in Central Europe, being bewitched by sunny Bohemia, by stylish people and excellent beer, a place where the sun bouncing off pastel-painted buildings necessitated shades. I had thought Edinburgh was one of the loveliest cities anywhere, but now I realised, compared to somewhere like Prague, it is a dreary, chilly place of lumpen people. What the hell was I doing here instead of Central Europe? Everything depressed me. Why aren't Edinburgh buildings painted bright pastel colours? Let's start a campaign!

This feeling lasted a good few spring days. Then, the Sunday before returning to work, a brisk southwesterly sent clouds scudding across the freshly scrubbed, pale blue sky, and I went for a walk in the Pentlands. West Cairn Hill was the day's target, and here, on the moorland track surrounded by space and larksong, the wind tousling my hair in the soft gaps of sunlight, it hit me.

Scotland *is* a dark place, restless, a place of strife, but also a place with a spirit of creativity born of necessity. True, there might not be much of the Good Life, the beautiful streetscapes of Prague, the cafe culture of Paris, or the people-watching of Milan, but there is a merit here. Of a stricter form perhaps, but merit all the same.

Breabag *(brae-bayg) – the underestimated hill*
814m OS 15 NC 287158

A cursory glance at Breabag from the road gives the impression that this hill is a dull slog up quartzite screes. The truth could not be more different.

After a long discussion over what to do one day when camping in Coigach, Andy, Helen, Duncan, Jan and I plumped for Breabag as Andy and I had yet to climb it, but Helen's insistence that Cul Mor was a better hill rang in our ears. However, only half a kilometre up the glen towards Breabag, a strange sight greeted us: the Allt Fuaran nam Uamh, a river bursting fully formed from the base of a cliff. It does not come out of a cave: it just appears fully formed from the ground, and in a few feet becomes a torrent. Upstream, the main river is dry, and it is possible to walk up the riverbed. It is not often one can do this in such a consistently rainy place as Scotland! The reason is that this is a limestone area, with caves and subterranean rivers and other unusual geological features.

Higher up are the Bone Caves, and we took our torches to investigate. They are dusty, and the cave with the largest entrance has a very narrow passageway some distance in the interior. I would not want to get stuck in there! Above the Bone Caves was the only dull part of the walk, a medium-angled slope of boggy moorland, but even here we spotted and caught a tiny lizard, which was content to sit gaining heat from Andy's hand. "I am glad you saw it had legs," joked Andy. "I was worried it might be a snake . . ."

Just before the summit of Breabag lies a line of quartzite slabs. Not steep enough to be called a cliff face, they make an excellent summer-conditions scramble. Their difficulties are bypassable, and the consequences of a slip are grazed hands rather than death. At the top we enjoyed a panorama of the whole Assynt-Coigach area, from Ben Mor Coigach to Quinag; also to An Teallach and the dark brooding corrie on Ben More Assynt that holds the Dubh Loch. The convex northeast cliffs of Breabag are also worth a (careful) look, with a tiny heart-shaped lochan at their base.

On the descent it is possible to go past an impressive waterfall (unmarked on the map) on the main river with a cave behind it, a secret area that would give excellent summer swimming. Andy shot off ahead to swim in a limestone sinkhole further down by the main path. Not as interesting as Cul Mor? On the contrary: this hill, it turned out, offers even more than Cul Mor, and we were well satisfied with the day's walk.

Carn Ban, Freevater *(karn ban)* – *a miniature expedition* 845m OS 20 NH 339876

It was Saturday morning. Duncan was doing his last Munro – the awkwardly inaccessible Seana Bhraigh. Everyone else – Duncan & Jan, Andy, Stuart & Rebecca – had arrived at the bothy from the north on Friday, but I had a gig on Friday evening. I nearly didn't go due to the cost of petrol in driving up to Sutherland by myself. But I was glad I did, as it was a fine weekend, and I got to visit the Seana Bhraigh area at midsummer – a big contrast to a previous time in midwinter, when Billy and I didn't even summit until two hours after dark.

I arrived at Glencalvie Lodge at 3pm, and headed directly up Glen Alladale. There is a nice riverside start and, from a certain angle, Carn Alladale looks for all the world like the Boar of Badenoch above the A9. Once on the large plateau of Carn Ban heading for the subsidiary top of Bodach Mor, the sun disappeared and the weather cooled, helped by a chilling north-westerly wind. Ideal walking weather for these long Scotch kilometres. This long hillside must be virtually unfrequented, and subsequently hosts a great deal of wildlife and nesting birds. I nearly walked over a ptarmigan nest, but the hen squawked and flapped straight at me, startling me, whilst her chicks scattered outwith my peripheral vision. Then she pretended to have a broken wing, weaving about the rocks and moss with one wing stuck out at an uncomfortable looking angle, goading me to follow her away from the nest and ignore her chicks. After I'd watched her a while, she flew off. Her brood was nowhere to be seen. A remarkable display. There were also plovers, dunlin, frogs, and deer.

The Carn Ban plateau is covered with grey stones, but

ironically the one part that isn't a 'carn ban' is the summit itself, a squelchy dome of moss, grass, and peat. From here I could see the remote eastern flank of Seana Bhraigh, and a simultaneous view of both the North Sea and the Summer Isles in the Minch, as this is the narrowest part of the UK mainland. The Macgillicuddy's Reeks-like side of Seana Bhraigh that was revealed further on descent was very impressive, with the fine Luchd Coire and a large, scrambly-ridged peak dominant in the view. Yet how well known is the long northern or eastern approach to Seana Bhraigh? Not well known at all.

I felt a surge of happiness on catching sight of the bothy, realising it would be full of my friends. Smoke rose from the chimney, and there was a good welcome inside. It was still light enough to walk outside without a torch at midnight.

I considered walking back to Glencalvie on Sunday via Seana Bhraigh, but the compleationist and companions, who had cycled in from Oykel Bridge, wanted to climb Carn Ban. Thus I ascended this hill for the second time in two days, this time in company. Today the weather was better, and a snow-clad Beinn Dearg, An Teallach, the Assynt-Coigach foreland, Ben Hope, Ben Loyal, and Ben Klibreck were all visible, as were the unexpected hills of Morven and Scaraben in Caithness and something – possibly Ben Rinnes – on the other side of the Moray Firth. Scottish Western territory.

I removed my boots and walked the last 2km to the summit barefoot, revelling in the oozy mud, sharp grass, and painful stones. Duncan found a plover nest of four camouflaged eggs in a tiny grassy hollow, the parent bird calling anxiously from a distance. Jan pointed out some plants with leaves like wild strawberry.

After a summit stop, I bade my companions farewell as they turned back to the bothy and the cycle to Oykel Bridge. I knew they would be at the road before me, as I had a fair walk to go. I turned up the hood on my jacket and turned mentally inwards. This time my route was different to the walk in, tackling the long, gradual slopes of An Socach, a subsidiary top that seemed to take an age in coming.

The summit area of Carn Ban is surprisingly large. I found a fragile, broken plover egg, as thin as discarded snakeskin, and wondered if it was hatched or plundered. The wind that had risen after I'd left my companions gave way to warm afternoon sunshine, and the finest landscape of the whole day came on descent towards Gleann Mor, with the most beautiful river and hill and forest scenery at the confluence of the Alladale River and the Abhainn a' Ghlinne Mhoir, bathed in late afternoon sunshine. It was a Chinese landscape painting come to life, and I reflected on the three very different landscapes this walk had brought: this forest and river; the large monotonous plateau of Carn Ban; and the sharp, exciting thrust of Seana Bhraigh. A miniature expedition.

The river was tempting, and I stripped off at a pool under an alder tree to enjoy an invigorating skinny dip. The final walk out along the forest track was hot, dry, and satisfying. I was glad that I had come, and this walk had reminded me how beautiful the Kyle of Sutherland & Strath Oykel area is. There are no prominent Munros or hordes of tourists, but wild handsome rivers, large forests, and the charming coastal towns, links and beaches of Easter Ross & Sutherland.

Beinn Tarsuinn *(ben tar-swin) – did I tell you the one about Glen Rosa?*
826m OS 62/69 NR 959412

I had made some new friends from Billy's church, and now that summer had keeked its head above the parapet, we were planning a walk in Arran.

"A'Chir is a good route," I'd said, and that, it seemed, was the route we were doing. I was too excited about finally doing A'Chir – a tough scramble that I'd had to abort twice previously – to worry about the seriousness of the planned route. I just assumed that everyone else knew what they were getting themselves into.

This notion was soon disabused.

Eagerly bashing up Glen Rosa next morning from our base

at the campsite – where geology students with tape measures waded in the river – and then up the Garbh Allt, it became apparent all was not well. The path disappeared, and then reappeared on the other side. There was nothing for it – we had to drop deep into the gorge of the Garbh Allt, ford the burn, and climb back out again on the other side. Routine stuff. But my companions had assumed previously I knew what I was doing in leading them up this hill. Now that they saw me in action, however, the consensus was clear that I didn't have a clue. Their protestations were loud, though not especially serious. Loudest of all was Quentin, who had recently started a stand-up comedy act, so I had better take care. Keep this kind of ascent up and I might become *material*.

Eventually we all crossed the Garbh Allt safely. The track turned a corner and the angle relented as we entered a corrie that rose all the way past Beinn Nuis to Beinn Tarsuinn. My companions uncomplainingly shouldered their calf-burning burden, with the reward of a box of squashed cakes to share on the summit.

We walked on over increasingly slabby terrain, and by Beinn Tarsuinn, it was pretty clear that we wouldn't be visiting A'Chir today. The descent from Beinn Tarsuinn on light-grey sculptured slabs was quite complicated. Best to turn back. Fortunately at the Bealach an Fhir-Bhogha – one of my favourite placenames in Scotland – there is an option to head down Beinn a' Chliabhain and pick up the Garbh Allt path again. We took this route back to Glen Rosa (this time from the easy, northern side of the Garbh Allt). It had been a long walk for beginners, and we all deserved a pat on the back.

Except me, obviously: I'd brought a bunch of first-time walkers up A'Chir and failed, once again, to even reach this tantalising, ridge.

Billy left the church later. He had been enthusiastically faithful for a time, then had some bad experiences. After weighing up the evidence, he concluded that he must have been crazy, and promptly became an atheist.

Braigh nan Uamhachan *(bray nan oo-vach-an) – the inflatable guide*
765m OS 40 NM 975867

The night before Braigh nan Uamhachan, Billy and I couldn't be bothered camping. As a B&B was so cheap, why not splash out? And so we spent an evening of sybaritic comfort in a B&B in Fort William. "Just think," I said to Billy. "Ten years ago, I would have asked you to kill me on the spot if I knew I was going to be spending nights in B&Bs, rather than bothies or tents. We've gone soft!" But I didn't mind. Not hard and hungry any more – soft and happy.

Next morning, we took the track up Glen Dubhlighe, all rough grass, rocky outcrops and baby Sitka spruce, then headed up the hill itself, opposite Streap. There wasn't much to report – certainly no caves, despite the name (*cavey hillside*) – and reached the ridge and the long pull to the summit somewhere near Na h-Uamhachan. It was a sunny landscape of grass, grey rock and glinting bog. "What we need is an inflatable Brian," said Billy.

"What?" I said.

"Something that will show us the correct direction," Billy explained. We had been discussing Brian's talent for taking terrible shortcuts. "An inflatable Brian," he explained. "Just add water, the Brian inflates" – he did the actions – "and says, 'it's this way! A shortcut!' – and all you have to do is go in a *different* direction."

Now, there is no doubt Brian is a good navigator. He can navigate in whiteouts, in gales, at night, over any terrain. Yet equally, when it comes to shortcuts, something in his brain seems to short circuit. We knew by now that following Brian on a last-minute detour would lead inevitably to unwanted adventures. So it was a fair plan. Every climber should carry an inflatable Brian.

We headed over the misty top of Sron Liath, reached the summit itself entirely unaided, and decided to descend from the col between these two tops to the highest point in Glen Dubhlighe, a different way down to our ascent route. The sun shone on a silvery strand of river at the unfrequented head of this glen, and we started down on a shortcut.

It was a nightmare. Instead of an easy col, this was a route of steep, clumpy grass between chunks of dark cliff, our only aid being the natural steps created by each lump of peat-oozing grass, which at least remained solid underfoot whilst we tried to work out how we could have been so stupid to have descended this way. Finally we reached the river – which had to be forded – and breathed a sigh of relief.

Looking back up, it was clear we had descended the hairiest possible part of this hillside. 'Who needs an inflatable Brian,' was the sheepish consensus, 'when we can so easily mess things up ourselves.'

Broughton Heights – *an urbanite's adventure* 571m OS 72 NT 122411

Alastair woke me around 11am with a phone call, wondering what I was up to this Saturday morning. I had arrived home at 3am the previous night from playing a gig and was feeling pretty slow. Fortunately so was Alastair, so we left at 1pm on a warm Edinburgh day, crowds playing and sunbathing in the city parks. I had wanted to climb Broughton Heights for a long time, partly because of a Colin Baxter photo I had seen many years ago. And very quickly after leaving Edinburgh and Penicuik behind it is easy to feel deep in the countryside. Yet despite the pleasantness of the landscape, hillier and hillier the further into the Borders we drove, there was very little traffic. In shorts and t-shirt weather like this, everyone else heads for the Highlands or coastal districts.

After parking, we took a modest line from Broughtonknowe over Clover Law to Broughton Heights, and back via a very obscure enclosure (marked on the map as settlements). Broad Law and Culter Fell blocked the view south, but we could see over the Pentlands to Fife and the Forth (Edinburgh entirely hidden), and over solitary Tinto past Eaglesham Muir to the Campsies and the distant Highland peaks of Ben Vorlich, Stuc a' Chroin, Ben More and Stob Binnein. I had no idea such a view was possible from Broughton Heights. Despite the lack of any visible built-up areas, it felt not deep in the Borders but on the very brink of the Central Belt. We talked about mutual friends, work, football, and went for a curry back in Edinburgh. A dead fox lay on the road home.

A little while later, I was round at Helen and Alastair's for dinner with my girlfriend Katherine.

"How many Corbetts have you done?" Helen asked me.

"I don't know, I'm not counting." I had no intention of revealing my hand.

I was sure I had done more than Alastair, but had been cultivating the opposite impression, intending to lull him into a false lack of urgency over our race to completion.

"He's done 112 – he told me last night," said Katherine, giving the game away.

Alastair, on his mere 109 Corbetts, narrowed his eyes. "Really?!" Katherine and Helen rolled their eyes at each other.

Alastair put on a sprint over the next few months, pulling decisively ahead. With my increasingly tortoise-like pace in Corbett bagging, our mutual friend Andy had already overtaken both of us. Alastair knew he was on winning ground competing instead with me!

North Berwick Law – *the ceaseless sea*
187m OS 66 NT 556842

Get on your bike, cycle from Edinburgh, climb small but characterful Berwick Law, and try telling me that Scotland isn't brilliant for the outdoor life: even in an arable part of the Lowlands like East Lothian.

You start in Edinburgh, a remarkably situated city with a medieval spine, running down from a castle on a naked rock towards a 21st century parliament, past the lopped-off Highland peak of Arthur's Seat, windy views glimpsed down towards the Firth of Forth and the North Sea. As you head towards the sea and leave Edinburgh behind, the landscape gradually becomes more rural and traffic-free: a posh school, a racecourse, a disused mine, a power station, a fishing village, and then suddenly golf links country. It was once reported that the Danish consul was driven through East Lothian and noted:

"I see that all the land not fit for golf in Scotland is used for agriculture!"

After a few golf courses, pretty villages, and a ruined medieval castle, Berwick Law is approached, rising above the low arable landscape like a prowling shark fin. This remarkable protuberance is the remains of a volcanic plug, just like Arthur's Seat, or Bass Rock, or Trapain Law, or Largo Law across the water. All these abrupt volcanic lumps can be seen from the top of Berwick Law.

After the fine approach, the hill itself does not take long. Following the road past a primary school to the base of Berwick Law, I locked my bike at a car park and headed uphill. The hill's striated, rabbit-infested sides are steep but short, and ten or fifteen minutes later I was on top: looking south towards the Lammermuirs and the cliff-girt Berwickshire coast; east to Tantallon and the gannetry of Bass Rock; north to Fife and the other islands lying lazily in the Firth of Forth, ships weaving their way in and out to the ports of Leith and Rosyth; west to Edinburgh, Arthur's Seat, the Forth Bridges, and the Highlands beyond Stirling. A view halfway across Scotland.

The strangest thing about Berwick Law however is the large decorative arch right at the very summit: this was the jawbone of a whale, caught in the 19th century when this and other coastal towns in Scotland were whaling ports. From the depths of the ocean, filtering krill, the jawbone had been transported to the chill winds blowing over Berwick Law, eroded like the stones of Callanish. The whales are rare and endangered now, and North Berwick long ago reinvented itself as a doucely upmarket commuter town for Edinburgh, with a good school and grey Victorian villas surrounded by golf courses. The whale's jaw reminds us of one of Berwick's much older, more essential relationships, if we stop and look and listen awhile:

not with Edinburgh's white collar job market, but with the ceaseless sea.

The Clashgour Ban

Autumn. The air smelt of damp leaves, kindling anticipation for my imminent journey. I checked the water levels of the car, and headed off alone towards the greying western sky.

Alastair had told me about the old guard meeting at Beinn Glas farm in Glen Falloch. I really wanted to go but couldn't, as I was playing a gig on Saturday night. Then the gig was cancelled, and I could go after all.

It was dark well before Helensburgh, and the rain in the Highlands was torrential. I pulled into Beinn Glas farm, expecting very little. Were they all in their tents? But what was this? A pub sign. It was several years since my last visit, and there had been changes, including this new bar. Unsure of what to expect, I pushed open the door of the bar and walked in.

The light was subdued and relaxed, and as I adjusted to the faces it seemed that I knew everyone here: with a sweet swelling of joy I recognised many people I hadn't seen in years. On the left, Pete was playing the Lowland pipes, with Stevie on guitar and Bill on bodhran behind. On the right, Susan had her accordion and Alan was on the tin whistle. Children – who were still in nappies last time I saw them – were running about joyfully. Pam and Dave waved a greeting. At the bar, Alastair and Brian were talking.

"Hello," I said. It was as if I had died and gone to heaven, and my friends were here waiting for me. I told them so.

Brian showed me his car windscreen that was smashed when some youths threw a rock through it as he was travelling at 60mph on the A82 near Balloch. "I nearly was in heaven," he said, shattering my warm feeling. The rock had missed him by about a foot, landing in the passenger seat. He'd failed to persuade his girlfriend along, but she would have been in the passenger seat if she had come.

"I'd like to go back and catch them at it, just to talk to them," he said. "They could have killed me, did they think of that?"

Later, as the drink flowed, Bill recounted an old story of leaving the Scotia Bar with Brian to get the late bus home to the Southside of Glasgow. Brian had stood up at the back of the bus to sing *The Clashgour Ban*, a song about the GUM Club hut (to the tune of *The Black Velvet Band*) he had made his own. Normally this would constitute a nuisance, but by sheer chance a complete stranger recognised him from a photograph on the back of his book, *The Guardian of Black-mount*, and shouted, "listen to him sing! That's the man who wrote the book about the Kingshouse!" resulting in the rest of the passengers enthusiastically dinging the 'stop, please' buttons in time to the song, to the frustration of the driver. The image of the bus winding its way through the streets of Glasgow with an irate driver, dingers ringing like church bells, passengers unable to get on or off in the chaos and Brian, on top of the world, orchestrating it all; will live for a long time in my imagination.

SELECT BIBLIOGRAPHY

Borthwick, Alastair, *Always a Little Further*, Faber and Faber, London, 1939

Brown, Hamish, *Hamish's Mountain Walk*, Gollancz, London 1978

Brown, Hamish, *Climbing the Corbetts*, Gollancz, London, 1988

Butterfield, Irvine, *The High Mountains of Britain and Ireland*, Diadem, London, 1986

Dawson, Alan, *The Relative Hills of Britain*, Cicerone, Milnthorpe, 1992

Doogan, Brian, *Guardian of the Blackmount*, Glasgow, 1998

Drummond, Peter, *Scottish Hill Names*, Scottish Mountaineering Trust, Glasgow, 1991

Dutton, GJF, *The Ridiculous Mountains*, Diadem, London, 1984

Gray, Muriel, *The First Fifty: Munro-bagging without a Beard*, Corgi, London, 1991

Hewitt, Dave, *Walking the Watershed*, TACit, Glasgow, 1994

Kemp, Peter, *Of Big Hills and Wee Men*, Luath, Edinburgh, 2004

Milne, Rob & Brown, Hamish, *The Corbetts and Other Scottish Hills: Scottish Mountaineering Club Hillwalkers' Guide*, Scottish Mountaineering Trust, Glasgow, 1990

Mitchell, Ian R and Brown, Dave, *Mountain Days and Bothy Nights*, Luath, Edinburgh, 1987

Munro, Hugh, *Tables giving all the Scottish mountains exceeding 3,000 feet in height*, Scottish Mountaineering Trust, Glasgow, 1891

Murray WH, *Mountaineering in Scotland*, J M Dent & Sons, London, 1947

Murray, WH, *Undiscovered Scotland,* J M Dent & Sons, London, 1951

Scott, Alastair, *Native Stranger*, Little, Brown and Company, London, 1995

Steven, Campbell, *Enjoying Scotland*, Robert Hale, London, 1973

Weir, Tom, *Weir's World: An Autobiography of Sorts*, Canongate, Edinburgh, 1994

USEFUL WEB SITES

The Angry Corrie: http://bubl.ac.uk/org/tacit/TAC
Ann Bowker's homepage: http://www.keswick.u-net.com
The Great Outdoors magazine: http://www.tgomagazine.co.uk
Love of Scotland: http://www.loveofscotland.com
Marilyn News Centre: http://www.rhb.org.uk
Met Office: http://www.metoffice.gov.uk/weather/uk/uk_forecast_
   weather.html
Mountain Bothies Association: http://www.mountainbothies.org.uk
Munro Magic: http://www.munromagic.com
Ordnance Survey: http://www.ordnancesurvey.co.uk
Scottish Hills forum: http://www.scottishhills.com
Scottish Mountaineering Council: http://www.smc.org.uk
Streetmap: http://www.streetmap.co.uk
UK Climbing forums: http://www.ukclimbing.com/forums
Walk Highlands: http://www.walkhighlands.co.uk
Richard Webb's bagging diary: http://www.sub3000.com
Who owns Scotland: http://www.whoownsscotland.org.uk